Mat
625

D0425906

REPUBLICAN POLITICS

Republican Politics

THE 1964 CAMPAIGN AND ITS
AFTERMATH FOR THE PARTY

EDITED BY

BERNARD COSMAN

AND

ROBERT J. HUCKSHORN

FREDERICK A. PRAEGER, *Publishers*

New York • Washington • London

FREDERICK A. PRAEGER, PUBLISHERS
111 Fourth Avenue, New York, N.Y. 10003, U.S.A.
77–79 Charlotte Street, London W.1, England

Published in the United States of America in 1968
by Frederick A. Praeger, Inc., Publishers

© 1968 on Edited and Original Materials by
Frederick A. Praeger, Inc.

Library of Congress Catalog Card Number: 68-16082

Printed in the United States of America

To the memory of
PAUL TILLETT
(1923–66)

■

PREFACE

■

"No America without democracy, no democracy without politics, no politics without parties, no parties without compromise and moderation." In this way, Clinton Rossiter begins his discussion of *Parties and Politics in America*.* Most Americans would agree with the spirit if not the detail of Rossiter's view. To be sure, the American two-party system is not without its critics. These abound. Some political scientists, and not a few active participants, have bemoaned the fact that our two national political parties are loosely structured, heterogeneous groupings, lacking in ideological purity and fervor. But, despite what some regard as weaknesses, parties and the party system are thought of by many Americans as indispensable to the workings of their democracy. For, in the broadest outline, it is the political party that aggregates interests and seeks to convert these into public policy by winning control of public office. It is the political party that supports the democratic system by providing a peaceful means of conflict resolution and of power shifts. And, in a democratic system, the minority party plays a special role: It is charged with the responsibility of offering the electorate alternatives to the majority party. In short, even a cursory listing of party functions

* Ithaca, N.Y.: Cornell University Press, 1960, p. 1.

underscores the critically important role of the party in the American democratic system. If, indeed, democracy provides a peaceful answer to the age-old question of who shall rule, then it is the political party that makes popular sovereignty a reality, an elemental point not to be lost on a nation of 200 million people.

Because it is an indispensable component of democracy, the party system is a subject of continuing concern. When, as in 1964, one of the two major parties suffers a staggering defeat, critics and supporters alike join in dialogue to ascertain what can be done to restore the disadvantaged party. The Goldwater outcome caused many Republican politicians to engage in careful and sometimes painful reappraisal. Their Democratic counterparts were also caught up in the wave of concern for the future of the GOP, though often, one suspects, with something less than sincerity. The magnitude of the Goldwater defeat also gave pause to those academicians who had advocated tightly organized, well-disciplined, and ideologically differentiated parties. Goldwater had set out to build just such a party, as his adoption of the slogan "A choice not an echo" makes clear.

Surprisingly, there has been no outpouring of books about the Goldwater phenomenon. Those published have, for the most part, been addressed either to the question of what led the Republican Party to nominate the Senator or to the reforms that must be instituted if a repetition of 1964 is to be prevented. REPUBLICAN POLITICS is primarily concerned with what happened to the Republican Party during the Goldwater campaign and, afterward, during the rebuilding period. Accordingly, the book is divided into two parts. The first, "Party and Electorate: The 1964 Campaign," is devoted to various aspects of the campaign—from the interaction between Goldwater forces and the party's professionals, through party finance, southern support, and electorate performance. The second, "The Party in Defeat: The Rebuilding," covers the years since 1964 and, in particular, the in-fighting, retrenchment, and maneuvering that has occurred as the GOP has sought to recover its position in the American party system.

Though the various contributors to this book have consciously refrained from inserting their own value judgments as to what direction the party should take in future, it is their collective hope that readers of this book will gain a greater understanding not only of the Goldwater outcome and aftermath but, more importantly, of the role and place of a minority party within the American system of government.

In assembling this volume, the editors have accumulated more than the usual debts of gratitude. We are, of course, grateful to the publishers of works reproduced here for permission to reprint. To all of the authors go our thanks for their patience and their promptness in meeting a rather demanding schedule. We are particularly grateful to Mrs. Marian Wood of Praeger whose editorial skills, encouragement, and gentle prompting were invaluable. Thanks also are due to Mrs. Minerva Phillips, Mrs. Clara Baskin, and Miss Shirley Brashear, secretaries of the Department of Political Science at the University of Alabama, and to Mrs. Myrtle Cassel, secretary of the Department of Political Science at Florida Atlantic University, all of whom typed and retyped the manuscript. It is part of the conventional wisdom to thank wives and children, without whose tolerance and understanding little is accomplished. We are not exceptions in this regard. Finally, there is our debt of gratitude to Paul Tillett. He provided the idea and the inspiration for this book and, until his death, continuing encouragement. We have dedicated the volume to him as a measure of our gratitude. We hope he would not have been disappointed with the outcome.

Bernard Cosman
Robert J. Huckshorn

CONTENTS

xi

I.

Party
and
Electorate:
The
1964
Campaign

■

EDITORS' INTRODUCTION

■

Before the electorate can play its role of determining who shall rule, political parties must structure the electoral situation by selecting candidates and offering alternative programs. At the national level, in the quadrennial struggle for the presidency, each political party must agree on a presidential and vice-presidential candidate and adopt a platform. The national convention is the mechanism through which national parties perform these functions. In the most basic sense, the national convention is an integrative mechanism; its purpose is to unite state and local party leaders and their resources in support of the party's nominees for president and vice-president. The degree to which the national convention is successful in this regard varies. More often than not, the critical factor upon which unity hinges is whether or not the party's nominees have a chance to win. The expectation of victory breeds party unity. The expectation of defeat not infrequently moves state and local party leaders to play down the national ticket in the hope of winning—or, at worst, minimizing losses—at the state and local levels.

As an integrative mechanism, the Republican National Convention of 1964 was patently unsuccessful—a not unanticipated consequence. It seemed to many observers at San Francisco that

3

Senator Goldwater purposefully intended to bring unity to the party by the simple process of excluding those Republican leaders uncongenial to his brand of conservatism. "Anyone who joins in all sincerity, we welcome," declared Senator Goldwater in accepting the nomination. "Those who do not care for our course we do not expect to enter our ranks in any case." In this context, Senator Goldwater was speaking less as a national party leader than as the leader and spokesman of a resurgent, militant conservatism that, in earlier editions, had been led by Senator Robert Taft of Ohio. Seemingly, he did not intend to build a consensus that would embrace the diverse elements of the Republican Party.

The 1964 Republican Convention ended more than twenty years of frustration for Republican conservatives. From 1940 to 1952, the conservative wing of the party had failed in its attempts to win the GOP presidential nomination for Taft. Defeat was especially bitter for conservatives in 1952, when Taft, who by then carried the title "Mr. Republican," was defeated for the nomination by a newcomer to Republican politics, General Dwight D. Eisenhower.

With President Eisenhower as an extremely popular incumbent seeking renomination, intraparty peace and harmony prevailed at the 1956 National Convention. After 1956, however, the conservative wing of the party began to grow restive. One cause for conservative concern was Eisenhower's apparent failure to build the party at the grass roots. In 1952, and again in 1956, he won the presidency with commanding majorities of both the popular vote and the electoral college, but his party had not fared so well at the grass roots. The GOP decline was especially severe in congressional races. Eisenhower carried the slimmest of congressional majorities into office with him in 1952, but the Republicans lost control of Congress two years later. The Democrats maintained their congressional majority in 1956, despite Eisenhower's landslide victory, and, in the off-year election of 1958, they scored their heaviest gains since 1934.

Added to conservative displeasure with Eisenhower's failure to strengthen the party at the grass roots were recurring policy differences between the conservative and moderate wings of the party; these differences nearly erupted into an open clash at the 1960

National Convention. Arizona's Governor Paul Fannin nominated Senator Goldwater for the presidency, but the Senator, to forestall this direct and obviously futile challenge to the leadership of Vice-President Richard M. Nixon, asked that his name be withdrawn. Then, in a moving and eloquent appeal, he called for party unity:

> This country is too important for anyone's feelings. This country, in its majesty, is too great for any man, be he conservative or liberal, to stay home and not work just because he doesn't agree. Let's grow up, conservatives.
>
> Let's, if we want to take this party back—and I think we can, someday—let's get to work.
>
> I'm a conservative, and I'm going to devote all my time from now until November to electing Republicans from the top of the ticket to the bottom of the ticket, and I call upon my fellow conservatives to do the same.[*]

Four years later, with Senator Goldwater as the GOP nominee, control of the Republican presidential party passed from its moderate wing to its conservative wing. In wresting control of the party from the moderates, Senator Goldwater not only rejected the national convention as an integrating mechanism but also repudiated the interpretation of the realities of American presidential politics that had been advanced by moderate Republicans and that had, from the time of Wendell Willkie, guided the choice of party candidates and shaped party strategy. Moderate Republicans—with their center of gravity in the East—had urged that, to win the presidency, the GOP nominee cast his net broadly, appealing to the great mass of voters at the center and left of center of the political spectrum, as well as to those of more conservative persuasion. To weld the moderate center to the conservative right required that GOP presidential standard-bearers profess some enthusiasm for major New Deal–Fair Deal social and economic programs. Former Governor Thomas E. Dewey was, in essence, arguing for moderate Republicanism when he criticized those who

> . . . want to drive all moderates and liberals out of the Republican party and then have the remainder join forces with the conservative

groups of the South. Then they would have everything neatly arranged, indeed. The Democratic party would be the liberal-to-radical party. The Republican party would be the conservative-to-reactionary party.

The results would be neatly arranged, too. The Republicans would lose every election and the Democrats would win every election.*

The crux of the problem for Republican strategists was their party's minority position. Less than half the electorate identified even casually with the GOP. To win, Republican presidential candidates needed the votes of Democrats, and Dewey, Eisenhower, and Nixon had broader appeal than did Taft or Goldwater. The latter two, it was argued, would be unable to construct the broadly based coalitions necessary to win the presidency—a political liability dramatized, in 1952, by the slogan "Taft can't win."

But Goldwater was convinced that he could win, and not by "playing Tweedledum to the Democratic Tweedledee." The Republican nominee cannot be a "little Sir Echo of Democratic ideology," Senator Goldwater said, "since this would deny the American people the clear-cut choice they want."† The choice to which Goldwater referred was obviously a conservative alternative; offering such an alternative was the most vital feature of Goldwater Republicanism. Goldwater supporters assumed that the electorate would respond favorably to conservative cues. As the Senator's campaign director, Denison Kitchel, put it, "A majority of voters in the United States favor conservative principles and philosophy but they have never had the opportunity—I shouldn't say never—in a long time to have [a] choice."‡

Central to the Goldwater-conservative interpretation of the realities of American presidential politics was the southern strategy. Although Eisenhower was the first GOP presidential candidate to break the southern campaign barrier, his strategy for victory did not include the South. Neither Willkie nor Dewey had troubled

---

* Quoted in V. O. Key, Jr., *Politics, Parties, and Pressure Groups* (5th rev. ed.; New York: Thomas Y. Crowell, 1964), p. 221.

† Speech to the Republican Men's Club, Bartlesville, Oklahoma, September 13, 1964.

‡ Interview with Dension Kitchel, NBC-Television, July 17, 1964.

to campaign in Dixie in the 1940's. Eisenhower did establish a precedent for the party's presidential candidates when he went into the South to campaign in 1952, and again in 1956. Both times, however, he focused his drive for votes, as had his predecessors, outside the South. Nixon, following Eisenhower's lead, carried the Republican message into the region in 1960. He made several appearances in Texas and Florida and at least one appearance in each of the five states of the Deep South. Nevertheless, Nixon, like Eisenhower, concentrated his major efforts on non-southern states.

Senator Goldwater was the only Republican nominee ever to make victory contingent upon winning southern electoral votes. The Senator stated repeatedly, both before and after his nomination, that no Republican could win the presidency in 1964 without the South. "I say that it would be foolhardy and unrealistic for the Republican party to adopt a strategy aimed at the Northern big cities to the exclusion of the South," Goldwater told the delegates to the Georgia State Republican Convention, in May, 1964. "The Republican party can win in 1964 only if it can win substantial support in the South."*

How Goldwater conservatives organized to implement this strategy and carry the conservative message to the electorate after the Republican National Convention is the subject of the first selection in this volume, Karl Lamb's analysis of the Goldwater campaign staff. The response of the electorate to conservative strategy is analyzed by Philip E. Converse, Aage Clausen, and Warren E. Miller in the selection that follows. Using national-survey data gathered by the Survey Research Center (SRC) of the University of Michigan, Converse, Clausen, and Miller examine both the assumption that significant numbers of voters would rally to Senator Goldwater's conservative appeal and the efficacy of the southern strategy. The SRC group then speaks to the questions of whether Senator Goldwater was—as his critics repeatedly charged —the minority candidate of a minority party and whether the electorate responded negatively to Goldwater the candidate, to his conservative philosophy, or to both. The authors conclude by discussing why Goldwater conservatives so miscalculated electoral

---

* *Atlanta Constitution*, May 3, 1964.

reality in 1964—a question with significance extending beyond the Goldwater outcome to embrace 1968 and after.

The Goldwater southern strategy was something less than a roaring success; only in the Deep South did it produce impressive results. In the third selection, Bernard Cosman is concerned with party leadership in "Goldwater's South"—the five Deep South states of Alabama, Georgia, Louisiana, Mississippi, and South Carolina. Not only did Goldwater carry this subregion, but Republicans made substantial advances at its grass roots. Seven of the ten new House seats won by Republicans in 1964 were captured in the Deep South. This third selection analyzes the personal, political, and attitudinal profiles of the Deep South Republican leaders and concludes with a discussion of their strategic dilemma, which, in its broader outline, reaches beyond the subregion to the nation and to the Republican Party's prospects for the future.

The Goldwater campaign may have had its greatest success in its fund-raising activities. Herbert Alexander, in his discussion of party finance in 1964, finds that the financing of the 1964 presidential campaign was in marked contrast to the voting patterns. The Johnson victory rested on a narrow financial but a broad electoral base; the Goldwater candidacy had a broad financial but a narrow electoral base. This fourth selection concludes with an analysis of party finance in the wake of the Goldwater outcome; as such, it serves as a departure point for the second part of this volume, which concerns the aftermath of the 1964 election.

1

■

UNDER ONE ROOF:
BARRY GOLDWATER'S
CAMPAIGN STAFF

■

Karl A. Lamb

The Republican and Democratic national committees consist of two persons—a man and a woman—from each state. In the Republican Party, state chairmen from states that, in the most recent elections, cast their electoral votes for the Republican presidential nominee, elected a Republican governor, or elected a Republican majority of their congressional delegation also serve as members of the National Committee. Committeemen and committeewomen are officially elected at the national conventions; in fact, the conventions merely ratify selections previously made according to the procedures of each state delegation.

The national committees serve ceremonial functions, meeting to legitimize decisions—the selection of a convention city, the replacement of a national chairman—that have been worked out in prior contacts between national and state party leaders. A few

One version of this piece was originally prepared for publication for the Eagleton Institute of Politics. Used by permission of the Eagleton Institute.

9

national committeemen wield great power in their respective states; others are generous contributors rewarded with an honorific title; some are party senior statesmen, such as candidates who, having campaigned hard in a hopeless year, are similarly rewarded. Many national committeemen and committeewomen serve as the principal liaison between the state party organization and the national party staff, including (in presidential years) the staff of the national campaign. But the committeeman is only one possible point of contact among many, including the state chairman, the governor, other state party officials, and the leaders of groups outside the formal party structure. Whatever influence a national committeeman wields within the state party does not result from his position as national committeeman. Rather, it explains why he was made a member of the national committee.

Work done in the name of the Republican National Committee is not, in fact, accomplished by the two or three committeemen from each state. It is done by the headquarters staff under the direction of the national party chairman. In common usage, this office and staff are referred to as "the National Committee." When Barry Goldwater announced that he would run his 1964 campaign through the National Committee, he was referring to this headquarters staff.

The officially constituted Republican National Committee plays no role, as a body, in presidential campaigns, nor did it do so in 1964. It met, at the conclusion of the San Francisco Convention, to ratify Senator Goldwater's choice of Dean Burch as national chairman. It did not meet again until January, 1965, when it convened to ratify the agreement through which Dean Burch would step aside for Ohio State Chairman Ray Bliss.

The story of Barry Goldwater's campaign headquarters, therefore, is the story of the merger of the existing party bureaucracy with the Goldwater preconvention campaign staff and of the expansion of the resulting organization. The problems that resulted from the merger were related to the very different natures of the two organizations. The story of each must be considered, if one is to understand why their juncture was imperfect.

The activities of the National Committee depend on the experience and convictions of its national chairman; the extent of these activities depends on the money he can raise. The two national committees have been aptly described as engaging in "politics without power."[1] The real work of organizational politics is carried out on the local level, and the national headquarters provides only a network of communication. One state party can learn what another is doing and what somebody in Washington thinks ought to be done, but no sanctions can be applied against local or state parties that refuse to cooperate. A national committee staff can cajole and persuade. It cannot command.

A national committee is not a national party organization. National parties barely exist in the United States, except, fleetingly, during a presidential campaign. A national committee staff serves as the substitute for a national party. But their influence is so transitory that both Democratic and Republican national committees rent office space in a city that blossoms with the shiny new buildings owned and occupied by interest groups as diverse as the AFL-CIO, the National Education Association, and the National Riflemen's Association.

Even the idea of a permanent headquarters staff for the Republican National Committee is of comparatively recent origin. The modern form of the Republican National Committee staff dates from the 1936–40 chairmanship of John Hamilton of Kansas, who was probably the first to hold the position on a full-time, salaried basis. As part of his program for rebuilding the party after the landslide defeat of Alfred M. Landon, Hamilton promised to create a permanent Republican headquarters staff of paid professional workers. To encourage the development of a cadre of party civil servants, Hamilton suggested a pension fund for the employees of the National Committee. It was not until 1956, however, that such a fund was established (in conjunction with that set up for the staffs of the Republican congressional and senatorial campaign committees).

Participation in the Republican pension fund is voluntary. Employees are eligible to join after serving the organization continuously for two years and suffering the anguish of one presidential and one congressional campaign. The fate of the fund provides a measure of the impact of the Goldwater management upon the established party professionals. The normal "off-year" staff of the

National Committee numbers between seventy and eighty people. At the time of the San Francisco Convention, thirty-eight National Committee employees participated in the fund. By December, 1964, eighteen had resigned their positions and withdrawn their contributions from the fund; only one of the eighteen had reached retirement age.

Despite the pension fund, there has been little assurance of continuity in either the personnel or the activities of the Republican National Committee staff. The notion of a full-time, professional chairman was abandoned when Wendell Willkie appointed Congressman Joseph Martin of Massachusetts as John Hamilton's successor. Nearly every subsequent shift in the party's fortunes has brought a new chairman.

One reason for the lack of continuity in the work of the Republican National Committee is its position vis-à-vis the two "Hill committees"—the Republican Congressional Campaign Committee and its counterpart for the Senate. The three organizations have overlapping functions, particularly in the stimulation of local organization and the generation of national publicity. A political scientist who observed the Republican scene in Washington during 1963 and 1964 remarked that the Congressional Campaign Committee, which then enjoyed a larger budget than the National Committee, performed with greater professional polish and with a more conservative orientation than did the National Committee.

In recent years, open conflict has been avoided by electing a member of Congress as national chairman; William E. Miller of New York was the latest in the series. An effective national chairman must enjoy the confidence of the most powerful elements of the party, and the most powerful national figures of a minority party are usually found in Congress. With one of their own number serving as its chairman, Republican congressmen had little reason to fear that the National Committee would usurp their policy-making prerogatives.

The goal of both the Democratic and the Republican national committees, beyond arranging the next national convention, is to pave the road to the White House for the presidential candidate. This must be done without knowing who he will be. Even if congressmen were not hostile to the assumption of a policy-making role by anyone else, the National Committee would be unable to develop policy positions very far removed from those of the leading potential candidates. The headquarters staff prepares statements for the national chairman, which answer the most partisan thrusts of the opposition, but the staff is preoccupied with encouraging the organization of local party activities. Committee employees remain officially neutral regarding prospective candidates, and the development of policy positions is left to Republican congressmen—or to the president, should he be a Republican.

The Lessons of 1960

The Republican Party experienced a painful defeat in 1960. When a candidate begins from a hopeless position, nobody can claim that changing a few details of his campaign would have achieved victory. Richard Nixon came so close to winning the White House that almost any aspect of his campaign could be regarded as the crucial mistake.

Republican analysts soon marked two facets as critical. The first was the lack of organization in the big cities, where little machinery existed to bring Republican support into the open and to the polls. In Chicago, there had not been even the skeletal organization needed to staff the voting places to ensure an honest ballot count. Yet, a slightly larger Republican share of the big-city vote would have elected Nixon. The second aspect was the internal direction of the Nixon campaign, which the National Committee professionals, in particular, felt had failed to make effective use of the resources of the Republican National Committee.

Ray Bliss, the most respected state organizational leader in the Republican Party, was appointed chairman of a committee to examine the problem of Republican weakness in the big cities. (See Chapter 6.) The committee's report was presented to a meeting of the full Republican National Committee on June 1, 1961. It did not discuss issues or offer new policy questions. As a political technician, Bliss left the definition of policies to candidates and officeholders. However, a section on survey research recommended the use of public opinion polls to bridge the "communications gap between party leaders and the general public."

The report diagnosed the Republican defeat in the big cities as resulting from a failure to organize support among identifiable groups: business, labor, Americans of foreign origin, and Negroes. The committee recommendations, Bliss pointed out, contained no miracle remedies. A model urban party organization—full-time and professional—was outlined and suggestions were made for increasing the effectiveness of the Republican National Committee staff.

In the two years following the presentation of the report, $250,000 were spent in implementing it. The Minorities Division of the National Committee, which had worked for years to organize Republican support among Negroes, was strengthened. The work of the Committee's Nationalities Division among Americans of foreign descent was expanded. Efforts on a smaller scale were undertaken in the fields of voter registration, labor, and veterans' organizations.

The organizational drive in the big cities, with its heavy emphasis on cutting into the Democratic allegiance of Negroes, was carried on at the same time as new resources were being poured into a second major enterprise of the National Committee—the Southern Division.

Known popularly as "Operation Dixie," the Southern Division invaded the states of the old Confederacy to establish party organization at the grass roots. The possibility of such an assault was suggested by the southern "presidential Republican" vote cast for Dwight Eisenhower in 1952 and 1956. From its inception in 1957, Operation Dixie was headed by I. Lee Potter, Republican national committeeman from Virginia. Potter was convinced that southern Republicanism had to be based on the separation of conservatism from racism by building organizational strength in the cities, where Negroes will vote in increasing numbers, and in the suburbs, where the new generation of voters may have fading memories of the racially conscious southern rural culture. Barry Goldwater agreed with this interpretation; Potter became one of Goldwater's earliest and most enthusiastic supporters. Indeed, Potter gives Goldwater a major share of the credit for the birth of the new Republicanism in the South. The party's growth in the South was, he believes, due to Goldwater's tireless campaigning, from 1958 onward, for the conservative cause in that region.

Potter found the South ripe for Republican organizational work. In most southern states, the Democratic Party was a formless collection of competing factions and leaders that left little room for an ambitious young man. Potter singled out capable young men and appointed them to positions of immediate influence. Having stimulated initial organization, however, Potter could not direct its growth or policies. Some state organizations became openly racist. (The Mississippi Republican State Central Committee displayed a Confederate flag on its letterhead.) The apparent contradiction between wooing Negroes in the North while simultaneously building an organizational framework in the South did not seem to bother Republican National Committee staff members. The Democratic Party had encompassed both regions and races for years. Moreover, the traditional function of American parties has been, in seeking to build a majority, to enlist many groups under their banners, even if those elements are hostile to each other. Many students have concluded that the most beneficial function of our parties has been this tendency to resolve, or at least obscure, certain conflicts within their ranks, rather than to make them issues upon which the two parties disagree.

The work undertaken to implement the Big City Report made political sense only if the candidate in 1964 would appeal to the same attitudes within the electorate as had Richard Nixon. Because Nixon's strategy was not theirs, some Goldwater supporters began to suspect that the National Committee's traditional neutrality had been abandoned. Other incidents seemed to confirm this suspicion. When, after the 1962 elections, Wirt Yerger, the Mississippi Republican chairman, attempted to hold a pro-Goldwater rally of southern chairmen in Dallas, National Chairman William Miller vetoed the idea. In retaliation, Yerger attempted to oust Miller from his post. At a tense meeting of the National Committee in Washington, Miller won a vote of confidence. But he had received a strong taste of the fervor of the Goldwater supporters.

The Miller Report

On February 5, 1964, William Miller rendered a report of his stewardship to his colleagues in the Republican Conference of the House of Representatives. He began by asserting that Richard Nixon had lost the election because of his failure to carry the nation's largest cities. He reported that the National Committee had done all in its power to implement the recommendations of the Bliss report. He recounted Republican gains in those cities in the 1962 elections, citing the contribution of increased Republican votes in the big cities to the victories of Scranton in Pennsylvania, Romney in Michigan, and Rockefeller in New York. In addition, Republican organizational effort among Negroes had been remarkably successful in the city of Baltimore and in the state of Kentucky. According to Miller, the National Committee had spent nearly $500,000 on Operation Dixie since its beginnings in 1957. As a result, said Miller, "whoever is our presidential candidate in 1964 will do as well in the south as Nixon did in 1960."

Miller next reported on the arrangements being made by the National Committee for the 1964 presidential campaign. He promised that the second presumed major mistake of the Nixon campaign would not be repeated in 1964. The campaign would be run under one roof, at Republican National Committee headquarters. Additional space had been leased to make this possible. "I have had assurances from the serious presidential candidates," he said, "that, if nominated, they would cooperate in accepting this set-up." Miller then affirmed his belief that the organizational structure of the party would be ready. Finally, he gave assurances that policy matters were outside the domain of the National Committee. He acknowledged that, between presidential elections, party policy is developed by Republican congressmen. "We need now to develop on Capitol Hill a climate which will be helpful in stimulating our troops on the field of battle," he concluded.[2] The Republicans in Congress, he implied, could foster a party image that would ease the task of the presidential candidate.

Miller's report carried no hint of the developing contest for the Republican nomination. It did not speculate on the political consequences of choosing a candidate who would oppose the majority of his own congressional party on such issues as the Nuclear Test Ban Treaty and the Civil Rights Act.

Staff and Strategy

Miller's report did not suggest that other Republicans might find different lessons in the 1960 election. There were, in fact, many who interpreted Nixon's defeat as yet another example of the Republican folly of nominating a candidate who accepted liberal Democratic positions. With no candidate to represent their views, conservative voters presumably stayed away from the polls.

In announcing his candidacy, on January 3, 1964, Senator Barry Goldwater of Arizona promised to offer the voters "a choice, not an echo," to seek out that conservative majority he and his close advisers believed to exist. The long road leading to this formal announcement had been prepared by a small group that had met, at the call of F. Clifton (Clif) White, in a Chicago motel on October 8, 1961. Under White—a former member of the New York Republican organization—the group began gathering convention delegates. This work progressed well, and, on April 8, 1963, a National Draft Goldwater Committee was established. From its inception, Goldwater's attitude toward White's draft movement had been ambivalent. He did little to encourage it; on the other hand, he never issued a denial of candidacy on the model made famous by General Sherman. Although the pressures were growing, Goldwater was determined to preserve his freedom of choice and he felt that he owed nothing to the White group, which began its operations without Goldwater's knowledge. In early 1963, Goldwater consented to the organization of a small personal staff in the Carroll Arms Hotel in Washington, but this office was strictly separate from the White organization.

This separation marked the early use of a principle recommended to Goldwater by Raymond Moley, once an associate of Franklin D. Roosevelt but, in 1964, a leading conservative journalist-scholar. The two men were friends of long standing, and Moley's public writings articulated many of Goldwater's attitudes toward American politics. Moley began from the premise that a latent conservative majority existed in America, which could be called forth by joining Republicans with conservative Democrats in a straightforwardly conservative campaign. Most campaigns, Moley argued, have no intellectual unity, because the candidates respond to local politicians, who are momentarily alarmed by the response of their constituents to this issue or that program, and because candidates spend too much energy attempting to follow public opinion when they should be leading it.[3] The consequences of these views for political organization were spelled out in a memorandum Moley addressed to Goldwater in October, 1963. A campaign staff, he said, should consist of two parts. One part should deal with the ideas, policies, and speeches of the candidate and provide the intellectual substance of the campaign. The other part should deal with the political mechanics of the campaign—political organization, precinct canvassing, and the scheduling of speeches. To ensure that the worries of the politicos will not distract the issue-oriented experts from their task, there should be little contact between the two halves of the campaign staff. "Political operators should not interfere with or attempt to dictate the nature of what the candidate says." Furthermore, the speeches of the candidate should be prepared by a single writer.[4]

Goldwater's Washington office was organized by Denison Kitchel, an attorney from Phoenix, Arizona, following the Moley guidelines. Kitchel, a graduate of Yale College and Harvard Law School, was a long-time friend of Barry Goldwater, but he had been little involved in party politics. He was to devote his full energies to Barry Goldwater, without pay, until the conclusion of the campaign. Kitchel felt he could not recruit the segment of a campaign staff housing political technicians before Goldwater announced his candidacy, but he could make tentative preparations for developing the intellectual context of a campaign. In September, 1963, he hired three staff members; they proceeded to set up the Recordak, an information-storage system intended to make available the twelve-year record of Goldwater's remarkable candor in discussing public issues. He also enlisted the volunteer services of Edward McCabe, a Washington attorney who had served President Eisenhower as associate counsel to the White House and who had taken part in several presidential campaigns. McCabe was given the title "director of research." During this period, he established a correspondence network of conservatively oriented academicians who prepared material for Goldwater's consideration. He would later serve as general campaign trouble shooter and consultant on both policy and organizational questions. He was also to be a valuable contact between Goldwater and former President Eisenhower. In late 1963, Kitchel was joined by Dean Burch, a thirty-six-year-old Tucson lawyer who had served as Senator Goldwater's administrative assistant from 1955 to 1959.

When the candidacy became official, an official organization—the Goldwater for President Committee—was formed, and Denison Kitchel was appointed to head it. Kitchel immediately began forming the political segment of a campaign staff. He selected the most effective of Clif White's associates, and the White staff was dismantled as a functioning organization. Goldwater and Kitchel felt no obligation to continue existing lines of authority, and the Moley memorandum forbade granting real authority to the "political technicians." White was asked to serve as codirector of field operations with Richard Kleindienst, who would unsuccessfully seek the governorship of Arizona in 1964.

Barry Goldwater surrounded himself with men whose judgment he trusted as a result of long acquaintance. Noteworthy among them was Tony Smith, Goldwater's press secretary for many years. Another member of Goldwater's inner circle was William J. Baroody, president of the American Enterprise Institute for Public Policy Research (AEI), of Washington, a nonprofit, nonpartisan organization. Although its orientation is officially favorable to the "free enterprise system," AEI's policy of supplementing meager congressional research staffs has won praise from all points of the political spectrum. Baroody worked with McCabe to bring the intellectual spokesmen of conservatism into a closer alliance with the movement's acknowledged political leader. Like McCabe, Baroody worked without pay; unlike McCabe, he concerned himself only with policy issues and took little interest in organizational details. One of Baroody's former employees at AEI, Karl Hess, who had worked with Goldwater in the past, became Goldwater's chief speech writer after the New Hampshire primary. He filled this role until the general election campaign, when he was assigned to travel on the campaign plane.

Kitchel, Smith, Baroody, McCabe, and Hess were the inner circle of advisers. Of these, only Smith and McCabe had extensive friendships in the world of American politics. A second group was at work gathering convention delegates. The success at this task of Dean Burch, in the California primary, Wayne Hood, in Wisconsin, and John Grenier, operating at state conventions in the

South, was to win for these men the highest organizational positions in the general campaign. Hood's national political contacts were a decade old; Burch and Grenier were newcomers.

Before the Convention, nobody was free to plan for, or even consider, what would be needed if Goldwater won the nomination. What happened in the campaign, therefore, may have been to a larger degree than usual influenced by what happened at the Convention.

The composition of the national convention changes substantially every four years, as the changes within state parties are reflected in their delegations. Both in 1952, when a massive battle took place for the nomination, and in 1956, when the incumbent, Eisenhower, was due for reanointment, 60 to 70 per cent of the delegates had not attended the previous convention. But the 1964 Republican Convention was dominated by amateurs—74 per cent of the delegates had attended neither the 1960 Convention nor the 1956 Convention.[5] These were the men and women who had fought for Goldwater in county, district, and state conventions. In San Francisco, Goldwater's opponents in the party were a distinct minority; most of the delegates were in no mood for shilly-shallying or compromise. They had not come to San Francisco to negotiate or to read public opinion surveys. They had come to nominate Barry Goldwater.

Goldwater did assure Republican organizational leaders that the "movement" would not monopolize his campaign; it would be run by the headquarters staff of the Republican National Committee and it would be conducted through the regular party structure. The point of contact between the national and local campaigns would be the regular state Republican headquarters. This decision followed naturally from Goldwater's long experience as a Republican regular and from his conviction that the national party organization should be retrieved from the Eisenhower doldrums. It also made good the promise that the 1964 campaign would be run from the National Committee office.

Barry Goldwater, singularly uninterested in seeking personal political power, inspired spontaneous enthusiasm which politically knowledgeable men had converted into a successful assault on the established structure of influence in the Republican Party.

After the Convention, hostile Republican factions were faced
with the problem of fighting the Democratic opposition, instead
of each other. The magnitude of that problem was not immediately clear. Some of Goldwater's closest advisers, assuming that
national conventions are the bodies which best represent the
mood and convictions of the entire party, claimed the massive
first ballot vote for Goldwater as proof of unified support for
Goldwater's candidacy. Few seemed to appreciate the fact that
the amateur delegates might have relatively minor positions in
their state parties. Indeed, Goldwater's close advisers seemed
unaware of the divisions created by the work of Clif White's
people within various state organizations. When the wounds of
the Convention were finally recognized, Edward McCabe succeeded in arranging a "summit conference" of Republican leaders, presided over by former President Eisenhower, in Hershey,
Pennsylvania. Nixon and Scranton found enough assurance in
these conversations to campaign for Goldwater. Other governors
went home to run separate campaigns. Goldwater made no public
concessions to the policy attitudes of the moderate Republicans.

The Interregnum

The promises made by Goldwater and other candidates to
direct the campaign through the offices of the National Committee were not publicly known. Some newspapermen interpreted the decision to operate through the national headquarters
as proof that Goldwater's followers planned to "seize control" of
the Republican Party. The truth was that Goldwater's small staff
had made no plans beyond the Convention. Put together hastily
after Goldwater's announcement in January, the staff—which was
never as large or as well financed as Nelson Rockefeller's—concentrated its entire energy on capturing the nomination. For
nearly six weeks after the Convention, the momentum of the
Goldwater cause drained away during an organizational hiatus
and public relations vacuum while the campaign staff was reorganized and expanded for the national election. Meanwhile,
staff members of the Goldwater for President Committee were
preparing files and equipment for their removal across Farragut
Square from their offices on Connecticut Avenue to the National

Committee offices in the Cafritz Building. Denison Kitchel conferred for four days with various aides and with representatives of the newly hired advertising agency; seven basic themes were planned for emphasis in the campaign. Kitchel then flew to California, along with G. Warren Nutter, an economist from the University of Virginia and the new chief speech writer, to discuss the tentative decisions with Goldwater. Throughout the campaign, Kitchel longed in vain for a week with no other demands in which the campaign's progress could be reviewed and its direction charted.

A less complete review was planned as part of the regular campaign schedule. Each week, the candidates were to be on the campaign trail from Tuesday through Saturday, returning to Washington late Saturday evening. While the candidates rested on Sunday, their chief staff lieutenants were to meet to review campaign progress. The candidates would spend part of Monday taping television programs; Goldwater and Miller could then meet in a relaxed manner to review key decisions with their closest associates. After the formal campaign was launched, the meetings were held at 2 P.M. on Sundays. Dean Burch usually presided. The regular members of the group included Kitchel; Lou Guylay, Director of Public Relations; Wayne Hood, Director of Campaign Organization; John Grenier, Executive Director of the National Committee; Edward McCabe, Research Director; Clif White, Executive Director of the Citizens for Goldwater-Miller; Leonard Hall of New York, former national chairman; Ohio State Chairman Ray Bliss; William Warner and Robert Smalley of the vice-presidential campaign staff; Ralph Cordiner, Finance Director; and Cordiner's two principal associates.

The meetings were broadly representative of the effort of the political organization and should have served as a means of co-ordinating the total effort. In practice, however, the meetings were always concerned with some immediate crisis in finance or in scheduling, and there was no opportunity for an objective review of the campaign's direction. The relaxed sessions planned for Mondays, among Goldwater, Miller, and their most intimate advisers, never really worked. Goldwater was often detained by the demands of the television producers; Miller was occasionally ill; and the staff was too exhausted for much objective thinking.

Long before this mechanism for high-level coordination was established, Dean Burch and John Grenier faced the urgent task of organizing the political technicians for action. Burch had learned only on the day of Goldwater's nomination that he would be designated the national chairman. Immediately, a flood of demands by local party organizations and communications media poured in regarding campaign schedules, press accommodations, and the thousand details that constitute a national political campaign. Yet the structure for answering such questions was largely unplanned. One result: Volunteer workers from the Draft Goldwater Committee, recruited originally because of their affinity for conservative ideas, were given technical assignments at National Committee headquarters for which ideological purity was inadequate preparation.

The members of the existing staff waited for new assignments or confirmation of their previous duties. Each day brought a new crop of rumors. But one of the methods of exchanging those rumors was inadvertently abolished. Every division of the National Committee habitually sent a secretary to bring the mid-morning coffee. The secretaries met in The Huddle Coffee Shop, in a corner of the Cafritz Building garage. This time-honored practice may have helped give the lower-echelon staff a sense of cohesion; staff members from other buildings had made regular pilgrimages to The Huddle during the 1960 campaign. In the interest of efficiency, Dean Burch ordered the installation of several coffee urns within the National Committee offices. His decision was a sensible one, but the long-time employees resented it as yet another change in established patterns.

Between presidential campaigns, the second floor of the Cafritz Building houses nearly every function of the Republican National Committee. But it can hardly begin to fill the space needs of a campaign-time organization. As newly leased space became available, the second floor underwent extensive remodeling. The walls were repainted, and new partitions were installed to separate one segment of floor space from another. Some of the most devoted Goldwaterites removed pictures of past Republican heroes—including Abraham Lincoln and Dwight D. Eisenhower

—from the walls. An energetic administrative assistant destroyed National Committee files for the years before 1960.

The offices had grown shabby, having been occupied by the National Committee staff since 1952 without major remodeling. But the presence of painters and carpenters added greatly to the confusion of organizing for the campaign. The redecoration seemed to confirm the claim that the Goldwater managers were preoccupied with putting their own stamp on the Republican Party, while important campaign matters went undecided.

The established staff members found other reasons to resent the authority of their new superiors. Two weeks after the National Convention, in an effort to control costs, use of the mimeograph machine was denied to all members of the staff, even for the most routine tasks, until the stencils could be approved by an assistant to the Acting Director of Public Relations. Although no permissions were refused, the delay in obtaining them served to increase tensions within the staff. The Goldwater managers, at least at the middle levels, did not appear to accept the concept of National Committee employees as party civil servants.

Professionals had criticized the 1960 campaign because of poor communication between Nixon's staff and the regular party organization. The problem would presumably be solved by running the Goldwater campaign under a single roof. But the mutual lack of confidence between the regular staff and the Goldwater circle created a similar problem. The National Committee personnel gossiped among themselves, waiting for decisions. The news of the resignation of this or that co-worker fed their feelings of insecurity. And the Goldwater people also talked among themselves, taking little interest in the established programs of the National Committee.

One person, William E. Miller, was potentially capable of forging a link of understanding between the two organizations. The National Committee staff had been his staff. It spoke in his name, and its programs were undertaken with his approval. But Miller's self-conscious political style is that of the "team player." He has a well-developed sense of positions in the party hierarchy and their attendant roles. Relations were always cordial between Miller and Burch, but the haste and confusion of the campaign left no time for polite consultation. Miller volunteered no advice, and it was rarely solicited.

Miller did invite key employees of the National Committee to work on his personal campaign staff, thus retaining the experience and energy of persons who were not members of the Goldwater circle. William S. Warner, after being replaced as Executive Director of the National Committee by John Grenier, became Miller's campaign manager. Warner organized a small staff that, with only one exception, was made up of Republican professionals. Experienced in managing the technical details of campaigning, they had little difficulty making decisions, such as the selection of an official campaign photograph, that the Goldwater workers agonized over. A joke that expressed the resentment the established staff members felt toward the Goldwaterites was the suggestion that perhaps Miller could have been elected regardless of the fate of the other half of the ticket.

Room at the Top

The reorganization of the National Committee took shape weeks after the Convention, when Dean Burch and John Grenier had been installed in their new offices. It was their responsibility, as Burch later expressed it, to serve as the "mechanics" of the campaign—to design and operate the political machinery for implementing the decisions of the issue-oriented wing of the campaign staff.

Little effort was made to consult the experienced party civil servants already at their desks. Incumbent employees waited for their files and equipment to be moved from the second floor of the Cafritz Building. Before long, an organizational chart was produced. Such devices had been little used at the National Committee, because "somebody always gets mad if their square isn't big enough." But Goldwater and his finance officials were committed to the careful control of campaign costs, and a businesslike budget required the allocation of functions among personnel in the organization.

The spaces at the top of the chart were filled by the leaders of the preconvention Goldwater organization: Denison Kitchel, Dean Burch, John Grenier, Wayne Hood, and Edward McCabe.

One aspect of the chart, in Kitchel's opinion, haunted the campaign: The scope of the authority Dean Burch was expected to wield was never made clear. Goldwater and Kitchel had always intended the national chairman to serve also as campaign manager, but, because the finance directors insisted on a relatively independent organizational position, it seemed as if Burch's authority were limited to National Committee affairs. As a result, many felt they had to contact Denison Kitchel (who traveled with Goldwater) when their problem or request could have been handled by Burch.

New workers were recruited; the National Committee payroll listed more than 600 people at the peak of the campaign. Units providing mechanical support for the work of the Committee were little changed. The mail room, with its mass of duplicating machines, presses, and files of address plates, began working overtime after the Convention. Its staff labored practically around the clock until Election Day. The accounting and payroll office was expanded to handle its sharply increased volume. Personal offices were established on the third floor of the Cafritz Building for Senator Goldwater and Congressman Miller. The most important changes were made in the heart of the Committee: the Public Relations Division, the Research Division, and the various enterprises operating under the banner of the Campaign Division.

The Public Relations Division. The choice of a public relations director for the Goldwater campaign was one of Kitchel's major preoccupations even before Goldwater announced his candidacy. Kitchel decided to approach Lou Guylay, who had served at the Republican National Committee as public relations director for the Eisenhower and Nixon campaigns. Guylay was unwilling to commit himself to Goldwater in advance of the Convention, as he wished to maintain his availability to serve Richard Nixon, if Nixon should become the nominee. The preconvention campaign functioned without a professional public relations director; Guylay did accept the position after the Convention. He brought a wealth of experience—and political acquaintanceships—to the position. The advertising agency with which Guylay was associated —Erwin Wasey, Ruthrauff, and Ryan—was given the National Committee account. The Leo Burnett Agency of Chicago, hired by Chairman Miller, was discharged, and most of what it had accomplished in laying the groundwork for the national campaign was lost. In view of the crucial nature of the relationship between client and agency, however, it seems unlikely that any candidate would have retained Burnett.

The Research Division. The techniques of establishing contact with the public are the realm of public relations; the preparation of candidates' speeches requires the support of a sound research organization. Much of the research support for Goldwater's candidacy before the Convention was supplied on a part-time basis by scattered individuals. Campaign finance on a presidential scale made it possible to bring some of them together. But the National Committee already housed a Research Division that was highly respected by scholars and journalists, although its work, emanating as it does from the National Committee, has had little relevance for the propagandists of specific policy positions. The Director of Research from 1960 until the 1964 Convention was Dr. William Prendergast, a political scientist, a former congressional candidate from Maryland, and an adherent of moderate Republicanism who submerged his personal preferences to function as an effective party civil servant. Kitchel hoped that Prendergast would remain as a deputy research director under Edward McCabe after the Convention. John Grenier relayed the offer to Prendergast but would not promise employment after the campaign. Prendergast resigned.

The impact upon the Research Division was electric. Two secretaries resigned immediately, feeling their loyalty was to Prendergast, not to John Grenier. No sooner had Prendergast departed than the quarters his staff had occupied were commandeered. Prendergast's staff, including an expert in election analysis, two researchers examining the public records of Lyndon Johnson and Hubert Humphrey, and half a dozen others, was installed on the ninth floor of the Cafritz Building, six floors above the headquarter's nerve center. With Prendergast gone, there was no senior staff member to channel the work of the researchers to the campaign decision-makers. The group functioned for several weeks as a service agency, filling the requests of state organizations for specific information. Only in September, when

Goldwater's own research unit was organized, was the Prendergast staff integrated into the national campaign.

The "candidate support unit" of the research staff was established near Goldwater's third-floor office, where it prepared material for Goldwater, Miller, and Nixon. Such preparation
included screening speech material, locating needed facts, preparing speech drafts and checking their accuracy, organizing expert task forces to prepare position papers, and writing the
individual statements requested by specialist publications such
as farm journals and trade-association publications.

Edward McCabe had served without pay as Goldwater's research director since 1963. McCabe had little interest in, or training for, the management of the day-to-day research operation
required by a national campaign. Charles Lichenstein was hired
as McCabe's deputy to fulfill that responsibility during the New
Hampshire primary. Lichenstein is a political scientist with undergraduate and graduate degrees from Yale. His chief interest
is political theory, which he taught for a time at Notre Dame. He
served on the Nixon staff during the presidential campaign of
1960 and the California gubernatorial contest of 1962. In 1963,
he served as the staff research director of the Republican Critical
Issues Council, which was headed by Dr. Milton Eisenhower.

As Deputy Research Director of the Republican National Committee, Lichenstein was the functioning head of the candidate
support unit. He was the only person in that unit with extensive
political experience. Lichenstein had assumed a major responsibility for organizing public relations activity, particularly in relation to television, during the California primary campaign. His
success in that task led to his assignment as liaison between Goldwater and the technicians who prepared Goldwater's television
shows. This duty proved so time-consuming that Lichenstein's experience was frequently not available to direct the research
enterprise.

The Goldwater research unit worked as a group for the first
time at the San Francisco Convention. The leading research specialists who worked in the Cafritz Building were Professor G.
Warren Nutter; W. Glenn Campbell, an economist and the director of Stanford University's Hoover Institution on War, Revo-

lution, and Peace; and Richard A. Ware, a political scientist by experience and training and the secretary of the Relm Foundation of Ann Arbor, Michigan. All were on leave of absence from their respective institutions. All had been acquainted with Goldwater for several years and had been leading members of McCabe's academic correspondence network. These men were oriented toward issues, particularly in the realms of economic and defense policy. None were professional specialists in voting behavior or the techniques of survey research, and, indeed, there was no such specialist in the unit. During the campaign, however, officials of the Opinion Research Corporation (ORC) presented oral reports, using extensive graphs and charts, at the regular Sunday staff meetings. The oral form of presentation was chosen in the belief that none of these men would have the time or inclination to digest written reports. A private opinion research organization, ORC, had been retained by Goldwater during the primary campaigns. But the attitude of Goldwater and his advisers toward opinion research was, at best, ambivalent, at worst, uninformed.

Far from being concerned with the reactions of public opinion, Barry Goldwater steadfastly held to unpopular opinions. His attitude, which can be paraphrased as "If the party wants me, they'll nominate me; if the people want me, they'll elect me," was often the despair of his staunch supporters. Little concerned with the projection of an "image," Goldwater even resisted efforts to improve his speech delivery. His campaign organization, based on the recommendations of Raymond Moley, included an implicit hostility to the use of pollsters and to the worries of minor politicians. Goldwater was led by circumstances to redefine policy positions that had been rather casually stated. The more his concern for the management of nuclear war was attacked, the more he felt compelled to discuss it. Neither Goldwater nor any of his closest associates felt that issue positions should be determined by first sampling the public pulse, although they felt that survey research could provide clues as to which aspects of Goldwater's position should be emphasized. By the campaign's mid-point, as ORC data, in agreement with other indicators, pointed to the public's concern for the social security system and to its worry about the use of nuclear weapons, the Goldwater staff decided it was learning nothing new from the polls, and ORC activities were curtailed to save money.

Although some of his supporters would have used any device to win, Goldwater and his closest friends probably regarded the close marriage of opinion data and political-strategy planning as a Machiavellian device to be disdained by responsible leaders.

Scattering the Campaign Division. The organizational work of the National Committee had long been based on a coalition-building strategy. The Campaign Division, headed by "AB" Hermann, was charged with contacting specific voting groups and organizing the contacts of state parties with these groups, which included Negroes, farmers, veterans, laborers, Americans of foreign extraction, senior citizens, and even professors. Hermann was also in charge of special projects such as voter registration and big-city organization.

Instead of offering appeals to interest groups, whose members are found in every part of the nation, the Goldwater campaign was organized on a regional basis—just as the drive for the nomination had been organized. The head of field operations was Wayne Hood, the director of campaign organization. Hood, formerly a supporter of Senator Robert Taft, had been the Wisconsin state chairman in the early 1950's, and he had served as executive director of the Republican National Committee in 1952. His political activities since then had been confined to the Finance Committee. The Goldwater movement inspired his reentry into active politics.

For campaign purposes, the nation was divided into seven regions, each headed by a regional campaign director. Hood's political contacts had grown rusty, and all but two of the regional directors he appointed had had little political experience prior to their involvement in the Goldwater for President Committee. A major function of the regional directors was to persuade state parties to follow the suggestions of the national headquarters. A regional director might be welcomed and trusted in one state and hardly greeted in a neighboring state where he was regarded as an outsider with little understanding of the local situation.

Hood's organization symbolized the difficulties of the Goldwater managers. Unable or unwilling to welcome into their ranks Republicans who had not supported Goldwater's nomination, they were forced to run the campaign through the persons they knew —Goldwater adherents—regardless of whether those persons had power and influence within their state parties.

The Nationalities Division, like the Arts and Sciences Division, was kept with the regular staff. Congressman Edward Derwinski of Illinois headed the Nationalities Division; its staff director was Professor Lev Dobriansky of Georgetown University. The Nationalities Division had a well-developed program for contacting American voters of foreign descent. Their appeal had long been based on the claim that a Republican administration was most likely to roll back the Iron Curtain and liberate the "captive nations." This appeal was consistent with a main theme of Goldwater's campaign. Money was provided; the staff was expanded; and a stream of press releases appeared announcing the appointment of persons with foreign-sounding names to head the local organizations affiliated with the Nationalities Division. Additionally, Barry Goldwater, long accustomed to campaigning among the Spanish-Americans of Arizona, taped some Spanish-language television commercials; these were used primarily in California.

An Arts and Sciences Division had been formed in 1960 in an attempt to combat the "anti-intellectual" label pinned on the Republican Party. In five years' time, it built up a mailing list of 10,000 people in American higher education identified as Republicans, and it stimulated twenty-four state parties to undertake at least token organizational efforts among intellectuals. In 1964, the Arts and Sciences Division was transferred from the Campaign Division to the Research Division in the belief that its role would support the research task. Its campaign assignment was to organize "Scholars for Goldwater," and it was established as a working organization, not a mere letterhead structure. The Goldwater scholars were asked to report on the progress of campaigns in local areas, give speeches endorsing Goldwater in their local communities, and perform other campaign services. But Senator Goldwater's interest in academicians was reciprocated by only a few hundred of the 10,000 Republican educators.

An office of the old Campaign Division that did not appear on early versions of the Goldwater organization chart was that of director of the Big City Program. Dean Burch later explained that time was required to find the right person for the position. In September, Sherman Unger, a young Ohio attorney with experience in the Nixon campaign, was appointed. He had two assistants.

When the voter-registration drive was abandoned as a national activity and assigned to the precinct-canvass operation, its staff director resigned. The directors of activities among farmers, veterans, and organized labor also resigned, feeling that their functions had been abolished when their fields of responsibility were assigned to the citizens' organization (see pages 35–36). Dean Burch would later explain that little could be accomplished by a one-man office, and it hardly seemed worthwhile to continue minuscule operations aimed at such vast enterprises as capturing the farm vote or the labor vote.

The Southern Division. Despite Burch's misgivings, the experience of the National Committee had demonstrated that one person with a broad range of acquaintances and with respect in the special constituency he sets out to organize can accomplish a great deal. The Southern Division had been, in essence, the activity of one man, I. Lee Potter. He had the aid of a secretarial staff and ample travel funds. In later years, he was aided by a former newspaperman, Hal Dunham, who prepared the barrage of literature sent to the growing list of southern Republicans and handled other public relations duties for the Southern Division. Potter stimulated the organization of a functioning Republican Party in the South—a party prepared to challenge the Democrats on their home ground.

Lee Potter's staff was disbanded; the South became only one of seven regions. A Tennessee legislator, Sam Claiborne, became southern regional director, but John Grenier was considered the effective leader of the campaign effort in the South. Hal Dunham joined the Miller staff, and Potter was assigned to the Tour Committee, where he was placed in charge of advance scheduling for former President Eisenhower and former Vice-President

Nixon. Potter's vast experience and knowledge of the South were shelved.

Potter's replacement was intended to symbolize the coming of age of southern Republicanism. No longer would the South be regarded as missionary territory. It was free to join the Republican Party on the same basis as any other region. This symbolic meaning was lost on Potter's friends, who regarded his replacement as yet another sign that the Goldwater managers were preoccupied with remaking the party organization.

No place was found for the Minorities Division in either the National Committee structure or Citizens for Goldwater. This division had, for two decades, maintained contact between the national Republican Party and local Negro leaders and organizations. Before the Convention, plans for appealing to the Negro vote were well advanced. These plans were based on attacking Lyndon Johnson's early record on civil rights legislation. But Goldwater's vote against the Civil Rights Act was of recent vintage, and the plans of the Minorities Division did not fit the Goldwater strategy.

The director of the Minorities Division was Clay Claiborne, an able Negro politician from New Jersey. Although his division was disbanded, Claiborne was appointed a special assistant to the National Chairman. This appointment, a press release duly announced, symbolized the determination of the Goldwater campaign not to abandon any group of voters, by default, to the opposition.

Claiborne was assigned an office several floors removed from the center of National Committee activity. The materials prepared earlier under Claiborne's direction were withheld from publication, presumably in the belief that attacking Johnson's civil rights record would offend Goldwater supporters in the South. With this project stalled, Claiborne had little to occupy his time. Toward the end of the campaign, however, a campaign tactician conceived the notion of wooing Negroes away from the Johnson-Humphrey ticket in key states by stimulating support for Martin Luther King as a write-in candidate. As is the case with many ideas born late in a losing campaign, the idea was probably never mentioned to Goldwater or Denison Kitchel.[6] An order was given to arrange the printing of handbills that would urge this course of action upon Negro voters. The handbills were printed in New Jersey and distributed there and in other industrial states. But Claiborne did not return to his National Committee office until after the election. He had no interest in further assignments.[7]

Friction points between party civil servants and newcomers to the Cafritz Building were eventually worn down by the sheer necessity of working together. Staff unity was achieved by Barry Goldwater when, in the middle of the campaign, he invited the entire Washington-area campaign staff to a Monday-morning breakfast at a downtown hotel. Hundreds of campaign workers, professional and volunteer, crowded in to hear a relaxed and beaming Goldwater recount the experiences of the preceding campaign trip and tell his favorite jokes, such as that concerning the lonesome television tower in Austin, Texas. That Goldwater could take this time away from the preoccupations of the campaign and the regular demands of his Monday schedule astonished the professionals. No presidential candidate in their memory would have devoted the time or scarce campaign funds to the entertainment of the entire staff.

Feedback

By definition, a meaningful political campaign involves communication between the candidates and the voting public. A minority party must do more than reinforce existing electoral attitudes. It must create new attitudes favorable to the positions and personalities of its own candidates.

For these reasons, a candidate must have some mechanism for determining the effectiveness of the communication process. The traditional source of information is the campaign organization. Through contacts at the grass-roots level, campaign workers should gain some sense of the impact of the campaign on individual voters and communicate this sense to the campaign managers.

In his talks at regional campaign workers' schools a month after the Convention, John Grenier described the national campaign headquarters as a "command post." He pictured it as the nerve center of the campaign, where tactical decisions would be made and communicated to the local organizations. But he did not describe the sources of information upon which the basic decisions were to be made.

A campaign worker who did not know of the Moley memorandum complained that Goldwater's advisers paid little attention to "feedback" from the campaign organization. Local party workers are anxious for the national candidate to espouse those policies that will have the strongest impact in their own constituencies. They are little concerned with the unity and coherence of the national campaign. But the candidate may resist the pressures that would make him seem all things to all men. Such a refusal was a long-standing component of Barry Goldwater's political position.

Farm price supports provide an example of the internal party problems that resulted. As Goldwater prepared to campaign in their districts, Republican congressmen requested that he say a kind word for the leading local crop. A staff member paraphrased the typical reaction to the typically negative response: "I've been for peanuts for fifteen years. I don't give a damn whether Barry Goldwater thinks it's a sound public policy. If he can't be for peanuts, he better not come into my district." National Chairman Dean Burch received such requests. Accepting his role as one of binding together the disparate elements of the party, he asked the speech strategists to abandon ideological purity, once in a while, for the sake of local political interests. His requests were refused.

Goldwater, still adhering to the Moley memorandum, deliberately emphasized the integrity of his conservatism by stressing exactly those aspects of his position that were least likely to please a particular audience. In Knoxville, Tennessee, on September 16, 1964, he referred to his conviction that parts of the TVA complex should be sold to private enterprise. Two days later, in Appalachia, he attacked President Johnson's "phony" poverty bill. The Goldwater appeal was to the voter as a citizen presumably able to choose conservatism for the good of the nation, regardless of immediate self-interest. On October 26, in his speech at an enthusiastic rally in Madison Square Garden, Goldwater declared, "If I had to cater to every special interest in the country to get elected, I wouldn't want the job."

This attitude was reflected in the reorganization of the Republican National Committee, which had been dedicated to the principle that, regardless of the party's position on issues, contact at least should be made with special groupings within the electorate. The reorganization placed such activities outside the regular party structure by assigning them to the Citizens for Goldwater-Miller organization.

A large number of letterhead—or press-release—organizations of Goldwater supporters were administered by Citizens for Goldwater-Miller. Some members of these organizations were attracted by aspects of Goldwater's personality and his general policies; they hardly expected Goldwater to support some specific policy that would benefit their group. Some shared an avocational interest with the candidate. Such a group was Pilots for Goldwater, which raised a substantial sum for the campaign. Members of the National Committee staff who specialized in political organization among the elderly, organized labor, and farmers were transferred to the Citizens organization, although their "constituencies" had registered strong disagreement with various Goldwater positions. Senior citizens were alarmed at the talk of modifying the social security system; labor groups were reminded by their leaders of Goldwater's support for local "right-to-work" laws. Similarly, Negroes were told repeatedly that Goldwater had voted against the Civil Rights Act. The approach to any massive interest group would normally involve some policy pledge in return for its support. The Citizens organization was in no position to offer such a pledge. Such organizations are never expected to have a life beyond the campaign. They have no authority to speak on behalf of the candidate or any other member of the regular party. The task of heading the Citizens organization was given to Clif White. Of all those involved in winning the nomination, White had the broadest friendships within the regular Republican Party. His judgment was perhaps the most likely to be trusted by professional Republican politicians. Yet he was given the task of dealing with those workers and voters who favored Goldwater but preferred not to enroll in the Republican Party.

Barry Goldwater maintained his intention of presenting "a choice, not an echo." But he was not insensitive to public reaction. The main intent of his half-hour television shows was to portray him as he is: friendly, quiet, and candid. The shows were a conscious effort to counter the "trigger-happy" image. This charge, first leveled at Goldwater during the primary campaigns, had been gleefully adopted by the Democrats, and many of Goldwater's supporters remain convinced that much of the American press consciously conspired to reinforce that image.

The Democrats described Goldwater as psychologically unfit for the nation's highest office. President Johnson called him a "ranting, raving demagogue." Goldwater's opponents were uninterested in a campaign dialogue on the issues he tried to raise. As a result, Goldwater abandoned the original plan of developing seven basic campaign themes. Instead, he was forced to make every public appearance a demonstration of his fitness for high office.

Problems of Control

A candidate who is obviously ahead easily controls the actions of his supporters. They are not inclined to question his political judgment. The trailing candidate is not so lucky. As the campaign wears on, groups of his campaign workers, convinced their candidate is getting bad advice, may take matters into their own hands. Federal law limits the amount that can be spent for political purposes by a single committee ($3 million per calendar year). Intended to limit the total sums devoted to campaigning, the law has never been effective. It has merely stimulated the multiplication of campaign organizations. Adherence to the spirit of the law requires that each organization have separate directors. There is no legal compulsion for these various directorates to obey the national campaign managers.

The National TV for Goldwater-Miller Committee was organized in Los Angeles to work with members of the motion-picture industry and other media. A staff member explained, "Some of the big money we wanted to tap was out there." But the TV Committee became an independent power because of small contributions. Its mailing address was appended to appeals for funds by Raymond Massey, which were flashed on the screen at the conclusion of Goldwater's half-hour shows. In the closing days of the campaign, the TV Committee was rich enough to schedule television programs—including one that featured a speech by actor Ronald Reagan—without consulting the Republican National Committee.

The most famous example of the difficulties of campaign control was the incident of *Choice,* a film produced under the supervision of Rus Walton, public information director for the Citizens for Goldwater-Miller. Distressed by Goldwater's defensive posture, Walton and his associates sought some exciting method of regaining the offensive. The film, prepared for national television, was made up of clips of street rioting, frenzied dances, and other less attractive elements of modern American society. A speeding automobile, similar to one driven by President Johnson, was intended to link his administration with the theme of national moral decay. One brief sequence of a girl in a topless bathing suit made the newspaper headlines when the film received premature publicity. But many felt its most striking feature was the portrayal of whites battling Negroes.

Goldwater had done his best to keep racial prejudice from playing a role in the campaign. He had conferred with President Johnson, before the campaign began, about methods of eliminating race as an issue. Although the concept of a film portraying a decline in the quality of American life had been approved by the candidate, neither Goldwater nor Denison Kitchel knew what methods would be used to dramatize the theme of *Choice.* When Kitchel saw the film, he vetoed it. Plans for its distribution had progressed so far, and so many people beyond Kitchel's authority had become involved, that only Goldwater's personal and public intervention could make Kitchel's veto effective. Goldwater saw the film without knowing of Kitchel's prior action. His decision was spontaneous. "It is not salacious," he snapped. "It is racist." The film was withheld.

The most common problem of control, however, resulted from the nature of American political parties. Any work done by state organizations for the national ticket is voluntary. No sanctions compel obedience to the suggestions of national headquarters. When a canvass of eligible voters was organized by the National Committee and administered by local party workers, the director of this effort, in her progress report to Burch, noted that Iowa and

Maine "did not adopt our canvass report" and that Michigan was "not working for Goldwater."

"A Great Organization—on Paper"

The Goldwater campaign suffered from inadequate planning. Too many weeks were spent at tasks that should have been completed before the Convention. One result of the hurry to make up for lost time was that ideologues from the Draft Goldwater Committee were given assignments for which they had no particular qualifications. The Tour Committee suffered initial organizational difficulties that led Denison Kitchel to complain that he could not obtain a copy of the candidate's schedule. As with other aspects of the campaign, plans for the candidate's public appearances were confused in the early weeks of the campaign. No tentative schedule had been prepared before the Convention; in the Convention's aftermath, some local organizations were less than hospitable. A staff member traveling with the Miller plane has preserved a note from a friend on the Tour Committee: "There is some uncertainty here as to whether you're expected in Marietta, Ohio, or Marietta, Georgia."

In spite of these handicaps, the Goldwater campaign organization amassed an impressive record of technical accomplishment. A communications system of extraordinary capacity was installed. Machines located in regional headquarters could receive 1,050 words per minute; materials were transmitted to lesser headquarters by teletype. These devices fitted nicely into the Grenier concept of national headquarters as a command post. But the virtuosity of the equipment was a considerable temptation. During the initial weeks of the campaign, more material was transmitted than could readily be absorbed. Some state headquarters adopted the habit of paying scant attention to communications from the national headquarters.

The Goldwater campaign fielded an enormous number of devoted workers. Precinct workers contacted several million more households than did the Democratic precinct staffs. As in any campaign, the field organization was spotty. Some state organizations worked hard for the national ticket. Others, including Michigan and New York, concentrated on state campaigns. In

such states, Citizens for Goldwater-Miller directed the effort for
the national ticket. In California, various organizations battled
each other for influence in campaign direction. No internal dissent, however, could obscure the devotion of many thousands of
local activists to the cause of Barry Goldwater.

Though the largest single campaign-expense item was television, it was difficult to use the medium effectively. In all, $5.5
million were spent, giving Goldwater the greatest television exposure of any candidate in history. But the audiences for the
Goldwater television appearances were seldom large. As with
other candidates, Goldwater's largest audience was for the acceptance speech, which was carried as a public event by all networks.
Later audiences never approached that peak. The acceptance
speech, the context in which it occurred, and the criticisms that
followed it combined to damage Goldwater's image among the
crucial voting group made up of liberal Republicans and independents. No paid use of the medium by the Republicans could
completely repair that damage.

The Republican National Committee had scored a professional
triumph during President Eisenhower's 1956 campaign, by scheduling television time in advance, which permitted the networks
to plan their regular offerings around the Republican programs.
This precedent was not followed in 1960. Richard Nixon wanted
to preserve the appearance of a free choice at the Convention; he
felt that it would be presumptuous to make use of the facilities of
the party before receiving its nomination. Determined that the
opportunity should not be missed a second time, National Committee staff members and the Leo Burnett Agency made plans to
repeat the 1956 triumph in 1964. But, these plans were abandoned by the Goldwater campaign leaders because of financial
worries in the crucial early stages of the campaign.

Political advertising must be paid for in advance. Network
television is costly: Half an hour in the evening required, in 1964,
at least $120,000. Final plans cannot be made until the money to
pay for the time is in hand. Since Goldwater's financial managers
would not borrow money to make advance payments for television time, the network time segments reserved by the Leo Burnett

Agency were not used. One of these was at the conclusion of the Democratic National Convention. Because of financial uncertainties, Goldwater's television programs were often planned on forty-eight hours' notice; yet, an additional charge then had to be paid for pre-empting new time. This cost was not to be reckoned in dollars alone. A representative of the advertising agency complained that displacing "Petticoat Junction" did not leave the show's fans in a receptive mood for Goldwater's speech.

As the 1964 Convention had approached, the staff of the Republican National Committee had attempted to plan the presidential campaign in a manner that would be acceptable to whoever became the nominee. By February, Chairman Miller had been able to report on the progress of those plans. But most of them were never implemented. Implementation would have required the agreement of all the "serious candidates," and none of the candidates were willing to discuss such plans, either among themselves or with the National Committee staff.

The regular staff of the National Committee provided experts in several technical areas, and the loss of momentum after the Convention could have been prevented, at least in part, if the staff had been permitted to take certain actions before the Convention made its choice. Television scheduling was a case in point. However, a more important loss to the total campaign effort followed from the reluctance of the Goldwater managers to utilize National Committee expertise even after the Convention, due to their fears that the loyalty to Goldwater of certain party civil servants was less than absolute.

The mechanical side of National Committee operations eventually functioned smoothly, when the initial hostility between the elements of the newly combined organization had dissipated and the massive organizational changes initiated by Dean Burch and John Grenier were completed. Campaign literature flowed out to the local parties; press releases flowed into the mails; reporters accompanying the candidates were made comfortable; and the campaign planes landed at the designated airports. Edward Peete, veteran manager of the Republican mail room, stated that he had never seen such dedicated labor in a presidential campaign. The Goldwater volunteers spared no energy in laboring for their hero.

But, what was the tangible result of these labors? What was the impact upon the electorate of the Republican organizational effort? Private surveys done by ORC for the National Committee agreed substantially with the Harris and Gallup polls. Goldwater's selection as the Republican nominee made him the choice of just over 30 per cent of the electorate. Slightly more than 60 per cent preferred President Johnson, and less than 10 per cent reported themselves as undecided.

Psychologists have described the phenomenon of "selective perception." In political terms, this means that voters who have formed a decision—and their basic party identification is its chief determinant—pay attention only to arguments that reinforce their predetermined conclusions. Selective perception may distort or blot out cues from the environment that are contrary to these predetermined conclusions. Barry Goldwater adapted this concept to the language of electronics and labeled it "filtered listening." He repeatedly begged his listeners to tune out their filters, so that they might hear his views without interference from those who would distort them.

There were several aspects of the campaign that fed the hope of Republican workers for a miraculous victory. The most impressive was the outpouring of small contributions. A corollary was the army of field workers who conducted a record-breaking door-to-door canvass of voter preferences. With so many willing to support Barry Goldwater with money and volunteer labor, it was easy to assume that untold millions would at least vote for him. The canvass revealed a large number of undecided voters, rising to more than 30 per cent in states as diverse as Maine, Minnesota, New Jersey, and Virginia. Republican workers commented that "people aren't talking about this one" and continued to hope for a silent vote favoring Goldwater. Finally, the traveling campaign staff was heartened by the size and enthusiasm of crowds in the closing weeks of the campaign.

Election night showed a Johnson victory of nearly as great a magnitude as the opinion surveys had predicted. It also indicated that those who were already convinced had provided the main audience of the Goldwater campaign. The classic campaign function is to inspire the workers in the field and encourage the organizational effort—door-to-door canvass, transportation of voters to the polls, baby-sitting for overworked mothers—that can make the difference in a close election. Such efforts made the difference in the California primary. The circumstances of the national election were not so favorable.

The Search for New Directions

Reporting the vote was the province of the television networks. Computers announced the verdict as the polls closed in the East. Dean Burch issued a plea for voters in the West to regard the outcome as not yet settled, but the verdict was increasingly clear: Johnson by a landslide. In addition to his native Arizona, Goldwater carried the five states of the Deep South. Four of them had voted Dixiecrat in 1948. Goldwater conservatism was placed under a lengthening shadow of suspicion: No matter how high-minded its leaders, voters in the Deep South apparently approved it as a masquerade for racism. Others saw it as a purely negative, and even dangerous, force in American life.

Although split-ticket voting was widespread, the magnitude of Goldwater's rejection toppled Republican candidates and office-holders across the nation. Half a thousand state legislative seats passed into Democratic hands. Rising GOP stars, including Charles Percy in Illinois and Robert Taft, Jr., in Ohio, were drowned in the deluge.

Defeat brought recriminations. Republicans in large industrial states called for an immediate public demonstration that Republicanism does not equal the image of Goldwaterism. The polls were hardly closed before John Martin, Michigan's national committeeman, called for the resignation of Dean Burch. Militant conservatives announced that the election represented a moral victory for their cause and the foundation for future electoral triumphs. State party leaders were confronted with a dilemma: Barry Goldwater had brought into the party a force of dedicated workers; those who accepted the procedures of the party should be welcomed; but the general public should form a new image of Republican leadership, so that Democrats could not, in future, run against the memory of Barry Goldwater, as they had once campaigned against the memory of Herbert Hoover.

Dean Burch became the focus of the contest for Republican organizational leadership. (See Chapter 6.) Calls for Burch's resignation came from many quarters. Feeling that the retention of Burch was necessary to keep many of Goldwater's followers in the party, Goldwater and Miller jointly refused to bow to these pressures. Members of the Republican National Committee, with whom the decision rested, were besieged with telephone calls from the factional leaders. They received pamphlets threatening the formation of a third party if Burch should be replaced. National committeemen who complained of being bypassed by local Goldwater managers during the campaign were now sought out by them. Burch.called a meeting of the National Committee for January 21.

Each side continued its nose-counting and its claims of victory. By early January, Goldwater announced that, although Burch could count on the support of a majority of the national committeemen, he could not command a workable majority. A face-saving compromise was reached. Ray Bliss, Ohio's state chairman, agreed to accept the position the following April, when Burch would resign. Goldwater announced his firm support for Bliss. A movement among southern national committeemen to nominate one of their own number in opposition to Bliss was squelched, largely through Goldwater's own efforts. At the January meeting, the National Committee members made the required decisions by voice vote, and every vote was unanimous.

In his speech to this National Committee, Barry Goldwater reaffirmed his party regularity. He pledged that he would never permit his name to be associated with a third party movement. He asked that Republicans cease blaming one another for the outcome of the election and blame only himself, for he was ultimately responsible for the decisions of the campaign. Goldwater spent part of his talk on what he felt was a major lesson of the campaign. He pointed out that Ray Bliss would be the eighteenth Republican National Chairman in twenty-nine years. It was time, he said, for the national committeemen to cease their traditional practice of leaving the choice of a chairman to the presidential nominee. The National Committee should elect a full-time, salaried national chairman who would enjoy their confidence and, he implied, the confidence of any potential nominee. Continuity would then characterize the party effort.

Students of the American political scene have remarked that the structure of our political parties remains remarkably stable, in the midst of rushing technological and economic change. After the Landon defeat of 1936, the Republican Party elected John Hamilton as its first long-term, salaried national chairman. The practice was abandoned in 1940. The Goldwater defeat of 1964 has restored the practice. Unified by defeat, Republican governors, congressmen, and former presidential nominees joined in forming a Coordinating Committee that would attempt to give the Republican Party the appearance of speaking with a single voice. The Republican National Finance Committee approved a combined budget for the National Committee and the Senate and House campaign committees of $4.5 million dollars. As the Goldwater era ended at national headquarters, there were noticeable signs of new vitality in the Republican Party. Reports of the demise of the two-party system seemed premature.

2

■

MYTH AND REALITY:
THE 1964 ELECTION

■

Philip E. Converse, Aage R. Clausen, and Warren E. Miller

On Election Day, 1964, the aspirations of Senator Barry Goldwater and the conservative wing of the Republican Party were
buried under an avalanche of votes cast for incumbent President
Lyndon Johnson. The margin of victory, approaching 16 million votes, was unprecedented. Historical comparisons with other
presidential landslides are left somewhat indeterminate by the
intrusion of third parties. However, it is safe to observe that
Johnson's 61.3 per cent of the two-party popular vote put his
plurality in the same general range as those in the striking victories of Franklin Delano Roosevelt in 1936, Warren G. Harding
in 1920, and Theodore Roosevelt in 1904.

Before the fact, the election was also expected to be the most

The collection of data from a national sample of the electorate around the
time of the 1964 election was made possible by a grant to the Survey Research
Center of the University of Michigan from the Carnegie Corporation of New
York. This piece is reprinted by permission of the Survey Research Center.
One version appeared in the *American Political Science Review,* June, 1965.

intensely ideological campaign since 1936, in no small measure because of Goldwater's reputation as a "pure" conservative. After the fact, doubts existed as to whether this expectation had been fulfilled. Goldwater supporters, in particular, expressed disappointment that President Johnson had refused to join battle on any of the fundamental ideological alternatives that were motivating the Goldwater camp. However, as we shall see by comparing data on the 1964 election with parallel data from either 1960 or, as is more impressive, the relatively tense election of 1952, the mass public had some sense that "important differences" between the two major parties were heightened in 1964. And, certainly no one questioned the importance of ideological differences in the factional dispute that split the Republican Party along liberal-conservative lines with an enduring bitterness unmatched in decades.

Indeed, three prime elements of the 1964 election—faction, ideology, and the contest for votes—became intertwined after the manner of a classic script. That is, the "outer" ideological wing of a party captures its nomination, leaving a vacuum toward the center of gravity of national opinion. This vacuum is gleefully filled by the opposing party without any loss of votes from its own side of the spectrum. The outcome, logically and inexorably, is a landslide at the polls.[1]

With a script so clearly written in advance, the outsider would naturally ask why any party controlled by rational strategists should choose a course likely to lead to such a massive repudiation. The answers to this question in the 1964 case are not particularly obscure, although they can be made at numerous levels. One answer, of course, is that Republican Party strategists were themselves in deep disagreement as to just what script was relevant. Many, of course, recognized the classic script and predicted the eventual outcome, with all of its attendant losses for other Republican candidates, with deadly accuracy.

But the factional dispute within Republican ranks not only involved an ideological clash; it also involved major differences in the perception of that political reality which becomes important in winning votes and elections. The Goldwater faction was told by its Republican adversaries, as the conservative wing had been told for years, that a Goldwater could not conceivably defeat a Democratic president, and would instead greatly damage the party ticket at all levels. The Goldwater group countered that a victory for their man was entirely plausible despite the danger signals of the spring polls and the normal difficulties of challenging an incumbent. It is not clear how sincere or widespread this confidence was: Some statements sounded as though the Goldwater candidacy had little chance of winning but would at least provide a forum for the conservative philosophy, along with control of the Republican Party. But, even in their more pessimistic moments, the Goldwater people argued that, while victory might be difficult, there was no reason to believe that Goldwater would do worse than any other Republican challenger or encounter the electoral disaster the liberals were predicting.

Similarly, at the San Francisco Convention, his opponents vehemently charged that Goldwater was a "minority candidate," even among Republicans in this country. In another direct clash of perceptions, Senator Goldwater is said to have remarked to a group of midwestern delegates, "What the minority [the convention liberals] can't get through their heads is that this is a true representation of the Republican Party."[2]

In this article, we wish to examine the relationship between such conflicting perceptions and what is known of the relevant reality in the context of the 1964 election. Our information comes primarily from sample-survey studies of the mass public that formed the electorate in 1964, and whose reactions represent one level of political reality about which so many conflicting opinions and predictions were made. While the most important aspect of that reality was unveiled by the election outcome, there has remained some of the customary latitude of interpretation as to its full significance. And, with respect to the interplay between the stratagems of party elites, on one hand, and the grass-roots American voters, on the other, the chronology of the 1964 election does, indeed, provide a fascinating composite of sheer myth, genuine but discrepant reality worlds, and self-fulfilling prophecies.

The Myth of the Stay-at-Home Republicans

The first theory of electoral reality on our agenda may be rapidly disposed of, for it lies more simply and unequivocally in the realm of myth than any of the others we shall treat. It should not be overlooked, however, both because of its historical persistence and because of its enshrinement in the battle cry of 1964 Goldwater supporters: "A choice, not an echo!"

In the quadrennial competition between the liberal and conservative wings of the Republican Party for the presidential nomination throughout the 1940's and 1950's, the conservatives were consistently bested. One of the prime contentions of the liberals was that all of the entries of the conservative wing were so distant from the "middle of the road" that they had no hope of attracting the independent votes necessary for victory over the Democrats. At an ideological level, the conservative wing coined the epithet "me-tooism" to ridicule the liberals for their refusal to reject, root and branch, Democratic innovations of the New and Fair Deal eras. The liberals, it was charged, were slowly selling out the fundamental principles on which earlier days of GOP ascendancy had been based.

This accusation of ideological flabbiness was not, however, compelling in itself without some further comment on the problem of winning votes. As a consequence, a theory became widely current among conservative Republicans that GOP difficulties in maintaining much contact with the White House were, in fact, directly tied to the "me-tooist" flavor of its presidential candidates. Republicans running for that office tended to lose not because there was any lack of potential Republican votes (as the superficial observer might have thought) but because many of the "real" Republicans were so offended by me-tooism that they simply didn't bother to vote at all. Nominate a true Republican rather than a Tweedledee, the theory went, and enough of these stay-at-homes would return to the polls to put him into the White House.

As such theories go, this contention is remarkably verifiable. That is, the critic of this approach need not argue that few Republicans were disappointed by the nominees of their party, for disappointment in itself is irrelevant to the argument. The question is simply whether or not Republicans, however disappointed, did continue to turn out and vote even for me-tooist candidates through this period—a matter much easier to ascertain. Nor is there any point in arguing that there were *never* any stray Republicans who, in the last analysis, vented their frustrations by refusing to go to the polls. Undoubtedly there were some. But the theory hinges less on whether such people existed than on the contention that they existed in significant numbers: not merely several hundred or several thousand, or even a few hundred thousand, but in the millions needed to overcome the persistent Democratic majorities.

Such a pool of potential voters would be large enough to be discriminated reliably in most sample surveys. And we know of no reputable sample surveys at any time in this period that give any shred of reason to believe that this significant pool of stay-at-home Republicans existed. Indeed, relevant findings point massively in the opposite direction. From 1944 on, for example, one can contrast turnout rates between Democrats and Republicans of comparable strengths of party identification. And one finds that, in election after election featuring me-tooist Republican nominees, turnout rates were consistently higher—often much higher—on the Republican side. Indeed, each time we isolate that polar minority who not only had an intense commitment to the Republican Party but whose commitment was of a highly sensitive ideological sort, we find that turnout typically reached proportions staggering for the American system—90 per cent, 98 per cent—levels almost implausible in view of registration difficulties, travel, sickness, and other accidents that can keep the most devoted American from the polls upon occasion. More impressive still, we find that, in 1952, Republicans who reported during the campaign that they would have preferred the "conservative" Taft over the "liberal" Eisenhower—exactly those Republicans to whom the theory refers—actually turned out at much *higher* rates to vote for Eisenhower in the election (94 per cent) than did the set of Republicans who indicated satisfaction with Eisenhower's nomination (84 per cent).[3]

These brief observations do not begin to exhaust the evidence, none of which lends any support whatever to the theory of a silent pool of frustrated conservative Republicans. Hence, it is scarcely surprising that the Goldwater cause in 1964 was not buoyed up by some sudden surge of new support at the polls, which other strategists had overlooked; for, the hitherto silent people expected to provide such a surge existed principally in the imaginations of conservative strategists who, in time of adversity, needed desperately to believe that such allies were there. It is less of a wonder that this theory was generated, particularly before sample-survey data took on much scope or stature in the 1940s', than that it persisted with greater or lesser vigor into the 1960's, in the face of repetitive contradictory evidence readily available to any proponents with an edge of interest in the facts.

The Minority Candidate of a Minority Party

On the eve of the Republican Convention, an irate Goldwater supporter wrote to the Paris edition of the *Herald Tribune*, upbraiding it for the doubts it had expressed as to the extent of Goldwater sentiment beyond the convention delegates themselves, and pointing out that a massive groundswell of support had built up for Goldwater throughout the country "west of Madison Avenue."

The charge made by the liberal wing of the GOP that Goldwater not only was not attractive to Democrats and Independents but was not even the majority preference of Republicans was a particularly severe allegation in view of the constraints under which the Republican Party has been obliged to operate in recent years. It has been the consensus of observers for quite some time that the Republican Party is a minority party. Our relevant data collections, made at frequent intervals since 1952, have left little question in our minds both as to the minority status of the Republicans and as to the stability of that status during this epoch. For most of this time, our estimates would suggest that, in terms of underlying loyalties, the Democrats could expect to receive—all other things being equal—something in the neighborhood of 54 per cent of the national popular vote. If any change has been occurring in this figure in the past fifteen years, it is that this Democratic majority is slowly increasing.[4] In practical terms, this means that a Democratic candidate need not have much attraction for grass-roots Republicans: He can win easily if he can carry the votes of a reasonable share of Independents and has general appeal for Democrats. A Republican candidate, on the other hand, can only win at the national level by drawing nearly monolithic support from Republicans, attracting the votes of a lion's share of Independents, and inducing unusual defection among the less committed Democratic identifiers. This was the Eisenhower formula and one that Nixon nearly succeeded in following in 1960. More generally, the liberal wing of the Republican Party sought candidates with this kind of broad appeal throughout that period. In this light, the question of Goldwater's popularity was serious, for if a minority party nominates a figure enjoying only minority support within his own party, it is an obvious invitation to disaster.

In the spring and early summer of 1964, the opinion polls lent much weight to the contention that Goldwater enjoyed no broad support even among Republicans. The Goldwater supporters tended to counter this kind of evidence by either (1) ignoring the polls, (2) questioning the validity of the polls (some Goldwater placards read, "Gallup didn't count us!"), or (3) questioning the immutability of the early poll readings. Of these reactions, certainly the last mentioned was entirely appropriate. That is, in the very early stages of a push toward the presidency, even a person who has been something of a "national" figure—as a senator or a prominent governor—for a considerable period may not be recognized by very large portions of the public. Until he has received much more intense national exposure in the limelight of presidential primaries and the nominating convention, "straw polls" as measures of his popularity can be highly misleading and unstable, particularly if the polling pits such a candidate against figures with more long-standing national prominence and "household" names.[5]

However, survey data gathered over the course of 1964 can be put together with "hard" data from the presidential primaries to provide an illuminating picture of Goldwater's general popularity and, in particular, of the reactions of grass-roots Republicans to him. In January, 1964, before the beginning of the spring primaries, we asked a national sample of the electorate:

  • Many people are wondering who will run for President on the Republican side this fall. . . . If you had to make a choice, which Republican leader do you think would be best for our country in 1964?
  • Who would be your second choice?
  • Are there any of the leading Republicans that you think would make very bad candidates?

Table 1 summarizes the responses to this sequence of questions.

TABLE 1.

PREFERENCES FOR THE REPUBLICAN PRESIDENTIAL NOMINATION
AMONG SELECTED SEGMENTS OF THE ELECTORATE, JANUARY, 1964

| | Segments of the Electorate | | | |
Candidate	Per Cent Mentioning[a]	Score Across Total Electorate[b]	Score Within "Minimal Majority": All Independents and Republicans[b]	Score Among All Republicans[b]
Nixon	42	+25	+32	+37
Lodge	10	+11	+13	+13
Romney	11	+ 9	+11	+10
Rockefeller	49	+19	+10	+ 1
Scranton	11	+ 7	+ 6	+ 5
Goldwater	54	− 8	− 5	+ 9

[a] The percentage entered represents the proportion of individuals in the total sample mentioning the Republican leader indicated, either as one of two best or one of two very bad candidates.

[b] Each mention of a leader as the "best" candidate received a score of +2. Each mention as second best received a score of +1. The first-mentioned "bad" candidate received a score of −2. Any negative second mentions were scored −1. The entries in the table represent the net balance of positive or negative scores for the candidate, expressed as a proportion of the maximum possible score an individual would have received had he been awarded all of the "best" choices given by the indicated segment of the electorate.

The open-ended nature of the questions ensured that the respondents rated only the Republicans they thought of as plausible candidates at the time of the sampling. The table excludes a thin scattering of other mentions. Since the scoring used reflects both the breadth and the intensity of the support, a Republican receiving relatively few mentions could not achieve a very high score. Thus, for example, another possible scoring could have shown Henry Cabot Lodge vastly outdistancing all other aspirants, as his references were almost unanimously positive, whereas the other Republicans suffered numerous descriptions as "very bad candidates." However, at this time, he was not commonly regarded as an aspirant for the nomination, and the scoring was deliberately designed to put this warm but limited positive feeling toward him in perspective.[6]

The table speaks for itself as to Goldwater's attractiveness as a candidate. Clearly, Goldwater's problem was not that he was still too little known: He was mentioned by a wider proportion of the electorate than any of his competitors. But, for much of the electorate, he was an object of antagonism even in January, 1964. And, among grass-roots Republicans, where his strength was concentrated, he remained fourth in a field of six.

The sequence of Republican primary elections in the succeeding months tended, with some local variation, to fit the lines suggested by these January reactions. The data shown in the table presaged the startling Lodge write-in victory over both Goldwater and Rockefeller among New Hampshire Republicans in March, as well as his numerous subsequent strong showings. They also presented ample warning of the amazingly poor Goldwater record in the primaries throughout the spring, including his scattered victories; for example, in the seemingly congenial conservative state of Nebraska, Goldwater, though he stood alone on the ticket, managed to win only about half of the votes, as a flood of Nixon and Lodge write-in votes were cast. The table even renders intelligible the crucial Goldwater victory in California, where write-ins were not permitted, where the sole opponent was Rockefeller, and where Democrats had a hotly fought primary of their own. Indeed, there is room to wonder whether any presidential aspirant has ever contested so many primaries with so disastrous a showing and still captured the nomination of his party's convention.

No evidence from polls of the period, moreover, suggests that Goldwater's popularity showed any sudden increase, even among Republicans, in the short interval between the final primary and the San Francisco Convention. In interviewing our sample of the national electorate in September and October, we asked respondents to recall their reactions to the decisions of the Republican Convention by indicating the identity of the candidates they had preferred at the time the Convention began and by reporting their gratification, indifference, or disappointment at the ultimate nomination of Goldwater. While these responses suffer the inevitable frailties of any retrospective account that goes back over an evolving situation, the social and political lines of support for, and antagonism to, the various major contestants in July, as reported during the campaign, bear so close a resemblance to the lines of support and antagonism visible in the January, 1964, data as to make it unlikely that the September and October responses were badly distorted by selective recollection, *post hoc* rationalization, and the like.

It is most instructive, perhaps, to set these popular reactions to the 1964 Republican Convention against a fairly comparable set of data collected in 1952, after the conservative wing had lost its bid to nominate Senator Taft for the presidency, for, in its bitterness, the 1952 struggle came closer to matching that of 1964 than did either of the intervening conventions. In 1952, we asked respondents, irrespective of partisan allegiance, whether they would have preferred to have seen any other candidate nominated in either of the major-party conventions held in Chicago. Thus, Republican identifiers could focus their remarks on the Democratic Convention in a way that the 1964 question did not permit. However, partisans tended to comment primarily on the outcome of their own party's nominating convention.

Among Republican identifiers in the fall of 1952, about one in five—20 per cent—recalled having preferred Taft to Eisenhower at the time of the Convention. Another 8 per cent had preferred some third candidate. The vast majority of the remaining 72 per cent either indicated that they had been indifferent to the choices at either party's convention or expressed gratification at the selection of Eisenhower as the Republican candidate. Some other Republicans responded that they would have preferred a candidate other than Stevenson from the Democratic Convention. Presumably, however, these citizens were satisfied with the Republican Convention, and it seems reasonable to conclude that a maximum of some 30 per cent of all Republicans in 1952 recalled any disappointment over their party's nomination.

The picture from 1964 is remarkably similar in one respect and drastically different in another. Among Republican identifiers in this latter year, slightly less than 20 per cent recalled having preferred Goldwater at the time of the Convention. This figure is only 1 per cent lower than the proportion of Taft supporters among Republicans in 1952. What was different, of course, was that, in 1952, Taft lost the nomination on the first ballot, whereas, in 1964, Goldwater won it handily on the first ballot. Although, in our 1964 data, a large segment (30 per cent) of Republican identifiers indicated that they had held no preference for a specific candidate at convention time, very nearly half of our Republicans did recall some preference other than Goldwater. Thus, these grass-roots Republicans with non-Goldwater choices outnumbered the Goldwater supporters within Republican ranks by a margin of better than two and one-half to one. A clear majority (60 per cent) of those with other preferences, when asked, "Were you particularly unhappy that Goldwater got the nomination, or did you think that he was nearly as good as your man?" expressed their lingering unhappiness about the outcome.

In sum, then, it is hard to turn up any bit of evidence to challenge the conclusion that Goldwater was, to a rather startling degree, a minority candidate within a minority party. If his camp actually believed that the San Francisco delegates represented a true cross-section of grass-roots Republican sentiment, then they grossly misunderstood the situation. There was, however, at least one extenuating circumstance: The support among Republican citizens for candidates other than Goldwater was split badly among his four or five leading competitors. Thus, while any of several pairs of other candidates had, by the time of the Convention, grass-roots party support that would have outnumbered the Goldwater faction quite readily, the fact remains that the 20 per cent Goldwater support represented a plurality for any single candidate.

However this may be, disappointment at the Convention's outcome in 1964 had radically different consequences in November from the consequences comparable disappointment wrought among Republicans in 1952. As we have seen, the former Taft supporters in 1952 turned out at the polls in near-perfect proportions and cast a very faithful Republican vote for Eisenhower. In 1964, however, the widespread defections among Republicans— necessary to account for the Johnson landslide—tended to follow rather closely the lines of lingering discontent with the nomination.

These recollections of San Francisco varied according to the different camps in which rank-and-file Republicans had located themselves at the time. So, for example, about three Lodge supporters in four reported they were unhappy with the Goldwater nomination; for Rockefeller supporters, the figure was closer to two in three. Slightly over half of the Nixon supporters, however, indicated that they thought Goldwater was "nearly as good" as their man. With minor departures, similar patterns marked the ultimate defections to Johnson among these diverse Republicans. Since Nixon's supporters were, like Goldwater's, more frequently "strong" Republicans than the adherents of some of the other camps, lower defection rates were only to be expected. However, defections to Johnson among Republicans who had preferred Nixon at convention time remained about double what could be expected from past norms for Republicans of this particular mixture of strengths of identification. Over three times as many Republicans for Lodge and Scranton defected to Johnson as parallel "normal" expectations would suggest, and—perhaps surprisingly— defections among Republicans who expressed no preconvention favorite at all were in this range as well. Most extreme were the Rockefeller and Romney supporters, with defection rates at the polls exceeding expectation by a factor greater than four.[7]

These differences across the several non-Goldwater camps are intriguing, in part because they appear related to relations of the various GOP leaders to the Goldwater candidacy. That is, of the set of major Republicans under discussion, Nixon took greatest pains to maintain relations with the Goldwater group before the Convention, and he undertook to help unify the party behind Goldwater after the nomination. Therefore, it seems fitting that dismay at the nomination was least in his camp, and defections relatively limited. Neither Rockefeller nor Romney made any major show of reconciliation after the nomination, and, subsequently, they went to some lengths to dissociate themselves from the Goldwater aspects of the Republican campaign.

Yet, if it were true that nothing more than a "follow-the-leader" response is needed to account for these variations in defection rates among Republicans, the data would cast a somewhat different light on the question of the conflicting perceptions of Goldwater's voting strength that were held by the liberal and conservative wings. For, in such a case, the Senator's problem would have been less one of gross overestimates of his strength than of self-fulfilling prophecy on the part of the disgruntled liberal leaders. In other words, they first refused to support Goldwater on grounds that he could not win enough votes and then proceeded to withhold, in large quantities, the votes of their "followers," to ensure exactly this outcome.

No airtight way is available to determine whether Republican defections at the presidential level might have been reduced significantly had Rockefeller or some of the other liberals effected a more genuine reconciliation with Goldwater to unite the party for the campaign. Nevertheless, if we were to compare the issue positions and ideological persuasions of 1964 Nixon Republicans with those of Rockefeller or Romney Republicans and find no substantial differences, we might be tempted to judge that differences in leader behavior did play some independent role in minimizing or maximizing Republican defections in November. Preliminary analyses suggest rather clearly, however, that substantial ideological differences did exist across the range of Republican factions. Republicans enthusiastic about Goldwater showed a rather unique (or "extreme") pattern of ideological positions. Nixon supporters, while unmistakably different, looked more like the Goldwater people than did the adherents of any of the other camps. Next in order, moving away from the Goldwater position, were the Scranton and Lodge followers, and the Rockefeller and Romney adherents show slightly more liberal positions still. Ideological differences, therefore, plainly existed between grass-roots supporters of the various factions, and these differences were, indeed, correlated with defections from a Goldwater vote. This does not exclude the possibility that the defections might have been lessened by a genuine "unity" move on the part of more liberal Republican leaders. It indicates, nevertheless, that the desertions were rooted not only in leader-follower behavior but also in a more personal sense of ideological distance between many rank-and-file Republicans and the Goldwater faction—a distance that would have produced increased defections quite apart from examples set by the leadership.

However this may be, it was a significant feature of the election that the customary postconvention reconciliation between party factions was, in the 1964 Republican case, lackluster at best and, at many levels, simply nonexistent. Many of the liberals wished to avoid identification with the Goldwater platform. At the same time, Goldwater seemed to do less than most candidates to make it easy for the dissident brethren to return to the fold. Among several possible reasons, one may have been that, in the blueprint laid out by Goldwater strategists for a November victory, the support of most of these leaders did not appear to be critical.

Campaign Strategy: The South as Republican Target

The strategy of the Goldwater camp for a November victory was both simple and relatively selective. Goldwater felt, to begin with, that he could hold on to essentially the same states that Nixon had won in 1960. This meant a clean sweep of the populous states of the Pacific Coast, most of the Mountain and Plains states, and a scattering of states east of the Mississippi. Goldwater believed that, to reap the additional electoral votes needed for victory, the way lay open, under proper circumstances, for the Republican Party to make further major inroads in the once solidly Democratic South. The plan implied that Goldwater could afford largely to write off the populous industrial states of the Northeast and some, if not all, of the Midwest—a matter that greatly reduced the importance of the dissident liberal Republican bloc. And, in making of the South a fulcrum for victory, this approach represented a dramatic departure from any past Republican strategy.

Such a strategy was not only unusual, but, against the long sweep of American electoral history, it might even be thought of as implausible. Yet it was no hastily devised scheme. For years, Goldwater had participated in the congressional coalition between conservative Republicans and southern Democrats. The same drive for ideological neatness that led him to call for the reorganization of American politics into "Conservative" and "Liberal" parties impressed upon him the grotesque incongruity of a Democratic South. The South had no reason to be a Democratic bastion; by all of its affinities and traditions, it should long since have become Republican. Part of the problem lay with the national Republican Party, which, under the control of the northeastern bloc, had failed to present national-level candidates who made it clear that Republicanism was the natural home of the southern voter. This had been a frustrating fact since Goldwater's entry into national politics—a period during which political observers had frequently predicted an imminent partisan realignment of the South. But gains in the region, while very obvious, had remained rather modest. In discussions of Republican difficulties in recapturing majority status in the land, Goldwater had opined that the party had to learn to "go hunting in the pond where the ducks are"—the South. As bitterness began to mount in that region toward the civil rights pressures of the Kennedy Administration, the time seemed more ripe than ever for the presentation of a purely conservative Republican candidate who could appeal to the southern ethos in a most direct way and, thereby, break the Democratic hold on the region in one dramatic and decisive stroke.

This long-planned strategy had suffered two temporary but alarming setbacks. The assassination of President Kennedy suddenly placed a southerner in the White House and removed from power the most feared personal symbols of federal intrusion. The continuation of the Kennedy beginnings by the Johnson Administration, however—particularly in the 1964 civil rights bill—helped to reset the stage. So did the increased signs of Negro unrest, and the new element of "white backlash," in the North as well as in the South, that seemed apparent in the spring primaries. The capping touch was Goldwater's vote against the civil rights bill. This vote, to be sure, represented no condoning of segregationism per se but, rather, a blow for states' rights against the encroachment of the federal government. Nevertheless, white supremacists in the South had so long paraded under the states'-rights banner as to leave little room for fear lest the Goldwater gesture go unappreciated. The liberal wing of the Republican Party, having worked for years to prevent the Democrats from "gaining position" on the civil rights issue, was further horrified as it envisioned the GOP suddenly transformed into the "party of the white man" at just the moment when the Negro vote was becoming effectively mobilized.

The second setback threatened when Governor Wallace of Alabama decided to enter the presidential race as a states'-rights candidate. This was especially alarming, for Wallace would have competed for exactly the votes that Goldwater had been wooing toward the Republican column. However, Wallace's subsequent withdrawal left the field open again for the original victory blueprint, and the implementation began in force. Mid-campaign accounts of the Goldwater organizational efforts spoke of a high-powered, modernistic campaign apparatus in the South, stocked with volunteer labor in numbers that would have been unbelievable for the earlier Eisenhower and Nixon campaigns. While this southern machine had been humming efficiently from the start, the Goldwater organization in the West was described as effective but less advanced; in the Midwest, it was chaotic; and, in the Northeast, next to nonexistent. At few, if any, points in recent political history have so many campaign resources—both in issue positions taken and in organizational efforts made—been devoted to the cultivation of a single region. The first discordant note came when, during the campaign and, apparently, as a result of new poll data, Goldwater remarked to reporters that he was not as strong in the South as everybody seemed to think.

After the votes were counted, what was the success of this strategy? The verdict must come in two parts. From one point of view, the strategy was a brilliant success, and it left its imprint on the geographical voting returns with greater strength than any other short-term forces in the 1964 election. One crude way of separating these immediate or new effects from those better attributable to long-standing loyalties is to create a different kind of electoral map, entering state by state or region by region the departure of a particular presidential vote in a more Republican or more Democratic direction than the normal voting of the area involved. A map so constructed for 1964, with pro-Goldwater deviations regarded as "high ground" and pro-Johnson deviations as "low," would show one primary "tilt" or gradient across the nation. The very lowest ground would appear in the northern reaches of New England, and the gradient would move upward with fair regularity all the way west to the Pacific Coast. The same gradient would appear, but much more sharply tilted still, as one moved southward to the Gulf of Mexico. In other words, Goldwater's regional emphases were, indeed, profoundly reflected in the vote.

As soon as one leaves the relative question of the regional and the geographic, however, one perceives that the strategy was a dismal failure. For, while the whole continent tilted in the expected direction, the strong Democratic tide nationally left virtually all of the country submerged under what, from a Goldwater point of view, was "sea level"—the 50-50 mark in popular votes. In terms of electoral votes, Goldwater was stranded on a few islands that remained above the tide on the outer southern and southwestern fringe of the nation. These islands represented stunning "firsts," or dramatic historic reversals in states like Georgia, Alabama, Mississippi, and South Carolina. But their historic interest did not bring Goldwater any closer to the presidency.

Indeed, while Goldwater scored sharp Republican gains through the "Black Belt" of the deepest South, his assault on the South as a whole produced rather pathetic results. All observers agree, for example, that the South has been drifting away from its old status as a one-party Democratic bastion for at least two decades, if not for five or more. Hence, Goldwater could have hoped to profit from four years more of this drift than Nixon, and a decade more than Eisenhower. Second, all observers are equally agreed that not only in the Black Belt but well north into the border states of the South, civil rights was the prime political issue, and there is no doubt where the mass of the white population stood on the matter. Our data from the late 1950's and the early 1960's have consistently made clear that the potential of this issue for dramatic partisan realignment in the South had been muffled because of lack of clear belief on the part of the mass population, prior to 1964, that either of the two major national parties offered much hope to the southern white. It was exactly this ambiguity that Goldwater set out to remove by providing a distinct party differentiation on civil rights at the national level. When these two ingredients are seen together, the actual 1964 election results from the South as a whole may seem astonishing, for Goldwater actually did less well in the region than either Nixon, in 1960, or Eisenhower, in 1952 and 1956. One has to return at least to 1948 to find a comparably poor showing by a Republican presidential candidate, and there are reasonable treatments of the 1948 Thurmond vote that would send one back to 1944 for a parallel. Given the fact that Goldwater wooed the South so straightforwardly and injected into the 1964 picture the new and potent ingredient of clear party differentiation on civil rights, this retrogression of Republican popular voting strength for a presidential candidate back to levels of the 1940's may seem quite incomprehensible.

A possible explanation, although one that we can summarily reject, would be that the clear party differentiation on civil (or states') rights that Goldwater tried to communicate failed to come across to the mass voters.[8] Perhaps to the dismay of the liberal wing of the Republicans, however, the communication was nearly perfect. In our 1960 election study, a measure of association between the two parties and the policy extremes of the civil rights controversy showed values of .02 and .05 (the Democrats only very slightly associated with a pro-civil rights position) on two different civil rights policy items.* In 1964, the perceived association in the same terms on the same two items had risen to values of .54 and .50. The change in *volunteered* identifications of the two parties with the issue, among the much smaller subset of people so concerned that they brought the matter up themselves, showed even more dramatic change. In 1960, these civil rights–concerned people tended somewhat to associate Kennedy with a pro–civil rights position and Nixon with more of a "go slow" approach (an association of .30). For Johnson and Goldwater in 1964, the association had mounted to .84, approaching consensus. The same volunteered materials include images of the parties, as well as of the candidates, and it is a matter of some interest to know in what measure Goldwater's 1964 position "rubbed off" on the Republican Party as a whole. In 1960, the civil rights association appeared to lie more clearly with the Kennedy-Nixon pairing (.30) than with any differences between the two parties, for these volunteered references to the parties showed an association of only .08. The comparable figure for the two parties in 1964 was .86. In short, we cannot explain why Goldwater pro-

---

* The statistic is such that, if all citizens in the sample agreed that the Democrats represented one side of the issue and the Republicans the other, the figure would be 1.00 (perfect association). The figure .00 would indicate that there was no aggregate association whatsoever.

duced a retrogression of Republican presidential voting strength in the South by suggesting that his key civil rights position failed to get across.

The southern vote for Goldwater becomes intelligible if we add three elements to the consideration. First, while the issue of civil rights lent an important new pro-Goldwater force to the situation, various strong short-term forces that had pushed the southern electorate in a pro-Republican direction in 1952, 1956, and 1960 were no longer present. We have argued elsewhere that the popular vote for Eisenhower and Nixon in the South was a very misleading index of the degree of solid Republican advance there.[9] While our data do show the Republican Party inching forward in the affections of mass southern voters, the pace has been slow; the South remains a preponderantly Democratic region. In 1952 and 1956, the Southern presidential vote swung far to the Republican side of normal for the region, just as it did in all other parts of the United States. In 1960, with the Eisenhower appeal gone, most other regions moved back toward the Democrats, as expected. This return toward normal was almost invisible in the South, since a new and offsetting short-term force —Kennedy's Catholicism—had arisen, which was peculiarly repugnant to the southern population with its concentration (Louisiana excepted) of devout and fundamentalist Protestants.[10] Thus, if any other of the Republican aspirants had run in 1964, we might have expected a delayed return toward a much more normally Democratic vote in the South. From this point of view, the injection of a new civil rights differentiation by Goldwater did not occur in a void but was something of a replacement for other forces that had kept the southern vote extended in a remarkably pro-Republican direction for three consecutive presidential elections.

Once we take this into account, the Republican retrogression is less perplexing, although, intuitively, we would expect civil rights to have an impact on the southern voter more potent than either Eisenhower's appeal or fear of a Catholic president. It is here that the second and third considerations enter. While Goldwater's civil rights position drew southern whites toward the Republicans, Negroes both South and North moved monolithically toward the

Democrats. Although southern Negro voting was still limited by registration difficulties, it increased over 1960 and was almost solidly Democratic for the first time.[11] If this sudden new increment of Negro votes could be removed from the southern totals, the Goldwater vote proportion would, undoubtedly, appear to be a slight progression, rather than a retrogression, in relation to the Eisenhower and Nixon votes.

Finally, it must be recognized that civil rights, though the primary issue in the South, was not the only one. Beyond civil rights, southerners reacted negatively to the Goldwater positions much as did their fellow citizens elsewhere. Many southern white respondents said, in effect, "Goldwater is right on the black man, and that is very important. But he is so wrong on everything else I can't bring myself to vote for him." From this point of view, the civil rights issue did, indeed, have a powerful impact in the South: Without it, the 1964 Goldwater vote probably not only would have slipped to normal Republican levels but also would have veered, as elsewhere, to the pro-Democratic side. Aside from the Negro question, the more general ideological appeal to what Goldwater saw as southern "conservatism" did not have major impact.

Much the same comments hold for the failure of "white backlash" to develop outside the South in the way many expected. Our data show that civil rights attitudes did not lack impact elsewhere. But, for many nonsouthern whites who resented the advance of the Negro cause and the "summer of discontent," the election involved other important issues as well, and Goldwater's positions on these struck such voters very negatively. Thus white-backlash feelings were translated into Goldwater votes by Democrats only where fear of the Negro was so intense as to blot out virtually all other considerations. Voters fitting this description existed in fair number and geographic concentration in the deepest latitudes of the South. Elsewhere, they were thinly scattered.

The Election "Post-mortem"

Up to this point, we have referred only vaguely to the many negative reactions Goldwater occasioned in all sectors of the country, which tended to dim out the isolated attractions he did present.

The Goldwater "image" was, indeed, phenomenally unfavorable. We have measured such images in the past—among other ways, by simply tallying the numbers of favorable and unfavorable references made by respondents to broad questions inviting them to say what they like and dislike about each of the candidates. Typically, American voters have tended, on balance, to speak favorably even about candidates they were about to send down to defeat. Adlai Stevenson, in his second try, in 1956, displayed the least favorable image shown in our studies prior to Goldwater's candidacy. Only about 52 per cent of all responses to Stevenson were favorable. Less than 35 per cent of the Goldwater responses were favorable.

Just after the 1964 election, Goldwater observed that "more than 25 million people" voted "not necessarily for me, but for a philosophy that I represent." At another time, in assessing the magnitude of his defeat, he chastised himself for having been a personally ineffective spokesman for that philosophy. This seems particularly odd when viewed against the descriptions of Goldwater before his nomination, in which even opponents concurred that, at long last, the right wing had found an articulate spokesman with a magnetic personality.

The candidate references we collect are a mixture that includes observations concerning the personality and leadership qualities of the individuals themselves as well as reactions to policy positions they represent in the public eye. Ideally, we could take this image material and split it cleanly into references to personal attributes as opposed to references to policy positions, in order to judge the accuracy of the proposition that what the public repudiated was the spokesman and not the philosophy. Speaking practically, such divisions present many difficult coding decisions.[12]

Nevertheless, we have sifted the references to Johnson and Goldwater into categories more or less purely reflecting "policy" as opposed to "personality" significance. Among the purest policy references, Johnson's were favorable by an 80–20 margin—visibly ahead of the 69–31 balance of his total image. Mentions of Goldwater policies ran less than 30–70 favorable, thereby trailing the rest of his image slightly. In general, the farther one moves from pure policy to pure personality, the more Johnson's advantage declines. His "wheeler-dealer" style and the aura of conflicts of interest that dogged him during the campaign came through to dilute his attractiveness. Against this backdrop, Goldwater's personal "integrity" and "sincerity" drew praise. Throughout, the data suggest that Johnson was carried along to an image nearly as positive as Eisenhower's best less by his personal characteristics than by the policies with which he was associated (many of them identified by respondents as continuations from the Kennedy Administration). For Goldwater, if anything, the reverse was true.

Aside from civil rights and a faint flutter of approval brought by Goldwater's latter-day stand against immorality, none of his major positions were attractive to voters outside the most hard core Republican ranks. In general, the mass of public opinion has been, for several decades, quite unsympathetic to traditional Republican thinking in areas of social welfare and other domestic problems. A major Goldwater theme involved attacks against the increasingly heavy hand of "big government," yet this struck little in the way of a responsive chord. Most Americans in the more numerous occupational strata do not appear to feel the governmental presence (save for local civil rights situations) in any oppressive or day-to-day manner and, as a consequence, simply have no motivationally significant reactions to the area. Among those more aware of the practices and potentials of federal government, a slight majority feel that, if anything, governmental services and protections are inadequate rather than excessive. Thus, for better or for worse, such contentions on Goldwater's part had little popular resonance.

Goldwater's failure to make much capital of domestic policy was not uncharacteristic of a Republican presidential candidate. What was new for a Republican, however, was his performance in the area of foreign policy. To a degree often overlooked, the 1950's were a period during which, from the point of view of many Americans inattentive to the finer lines of politics and reacting to the parties in terms of gross associations and moods, there prevailed something of an uneasy equilibrium between the two major parties. Much more often than not, for these Americans, the Democratic Party was the party of prosperity and good times, but also the party more likely to blunder into war. The Republican Party, conversely, was more skilled in maintaining peace, but brought with it depression and hard times.

The foreign policies proposed by Goldwater and refracted

through the press and other commentators shifted this image more dramatically than one might have thought possible (Table 2). Setting aside the large mass of voters who, throughout the

TABLE 2.

PERCEPTIONS AS TO THE PARTY MOST LIKELY TO KEEP THE
UNITED STATES OUT OF WAR IN THE ENSUING FOUR YEARS
(in Per Cents in Each of Three Election Years)

	1956 (Eisenhower-Stevenson)	1960 (Nixon-Kennedy)	1964 (Goldwater-Johnson)
Democrats would handle better	7	15	38
No party difference	45	46	46
Republicans would handle better	40	29	12
Don't know; not ascertained	8	10	4
	100	100	100

period, did not see any particular differences between the parties in foreign-policy capability, the balance of expectations in the area favored the Republicans by better than a 5–1 margin in 1956. This margin deteriorated somewhat in the late stages of the Eisenhower Administration but remained as an imposing 2–1 edge. During the Goldwater campaign, it was reversed to a 3–1 margin favoring the Democrats.

Thus, to the many ways of describing the public's repudiation of the Goldwater candidacy, another may be added: Between a party of prosperity and peace and a party of depression and war, there is little room for hesitation.

Levels of Public Opinion and Bases for Misperception

From at least one point of view, it is less interesting that Goldwater lost the 1964 election than that he thought he had a chance to win. What most of our descriptions of the election year had in common was a sort of chronic miscalculation of electoral reality: miscalculations of standing strength, of new strength that might be won, and of what appeals were necessary to win that new strength. Since "electoral reality" is, at many points, a nest of uncertainties, and since we are told that, in the face of uncertainty, personal needs are likely to color perceptions the more strongly, there is little that is surprising in the fact that Goldwater overestimated his strength and drawing power. But, as these misperceptions by Goldwater and his aides went grossly beyond what many observers felt were the margins of uncertainty, they deserve closer comment.

Rather than write off these perceptions as figments of imagination, let us suppose that, to persist in the way many electoral misperceptions of the right wing have persisted, there must be some sustaining reality bases; and let us ask, instead, what such bases might be. For "public opinion" is a protean thing, and we shall discover that there are perfectly sound ways of measuring public opinion during the 1964 campaign that, instead of illustrating Johnson's towering lead in the opinion polls, would actually have shown Goldwater enjoying a slight margin.

As is well known, public opinion was spoken of, and roughly gauged, long before the operations of public opinion polling were developed. What was gauged was opinion from a variety of kinds of sources: informal reactions to events among ancillary elites around the centers of government; the writings of intellectuals and newspaper editors; representations from leaders of interest groups, and the like. While it was apparent that this conglomerate of opinion came disproportionately from relatively elite and informed sources and, hence, need not have coincided with what the "real public" thought, beyond mass elections themselves there were (and *are,* for those who totally distrust the polls) few further ways of understanding what the public below an elite level was thinking. One of those few ways of "digging down" into the real population was letters of opinion: letters sent from unassuming constituents to public officials and "letters to the editor" composed by nonprofessional writers reacting to daily events or, in no few cases, to the opinions of the editor himself. This was one level of public opinion that seemed to be generated below the elite level and that could be monitored regularly on a wide geographic base by the observer interested in opinion beyond the localisms of municipal government.[13]

In our 1964 interview schedule, we spent some time investigating the behavior of our respondents with respect to the writing of politically relevant letters. We ascertained, first, whether they had ever written such a letter either to any kind of public official or to the editor of a newspaper or magazine. Then, dealing with the minority who could recall ever writing such a letter, we went on to ask about the frequency of such activity—whether any of the letters had been written in the past four years and, if so, roughly how many such letters the respondent would estimate he had written to each of the two types of targets over that recent period.

Many aspects of these data remain intriguing despite their general predictability. Thus, for example, the materials demonstrate handsomely that the large bulk of letters to public officials or the printed media come from a tiny fraction of the population, who tend to write with very repetitive frequency. Thus, we found that only about 15 per cent of the adult population reports ever having written a letter to a public official. Of the total stream of such letters from the grass roots, two-thirds are composed by about 3 per cent of the population. Where letters to newspapers or magazines are concerned, the constituency is even more restrictive: Only about 3 per cent of the population recalls ever having written such a letter, and two-thirds of such letters are turned out by not more than 0.5 per cent of the population.[14] Needless to say, there is fair overlap between those who write to the printed media and those writing to public officials, so that the observer monitoring both lines of communication would tend to count the same people twice.

Furthermore, as these few people write more and more letters over time, they are counted again and again, and this of course is the phenomenon that interests us. What we have done is to reconstruct our data on various preferences relevant to the 1964 election *not* by a raw head count, which is what a mass election represents, but, rather, with each individual's preference on an item weighted by the number of letters that he has reported writing to either target in the four preceding years. This provides a basis, within reasonable limits, for a fair replication of the different kinds of "public opinion" as it might be assessed by a hypothetical observer.[15]

Figure 1 contrasts public opinion in the head-count sense with public opinion as measured in terms of letter writing. We suggest

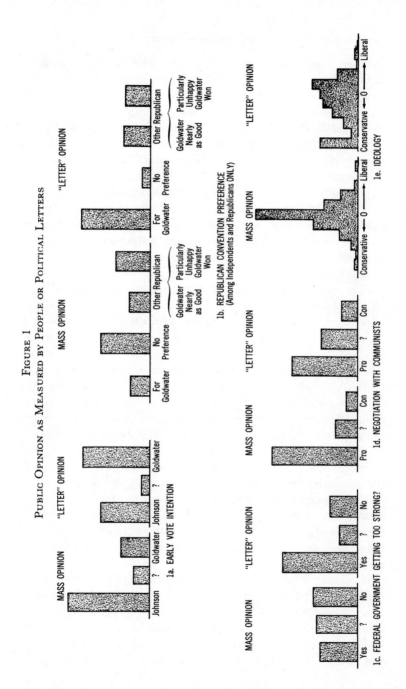

FIGURE 1

PUBLIC OPINION AS MEASURED BY PEOPLE OR POLITICAL LETTERS

that this figure may usher us into the reality world on which many of Goldwater's assessments and stratagems were based. This is not to say that Goldwater had no other bases from which to calculate public opinion. He had, among other things, public opinion as measured by the polls, and he did not entirely discredit this information. Yet, as we have noted, there was evidence that poll data perplexed him, not simply because they customarily brought bad news but also because they failed to square with his intuitive impressions as to what the public was thinking. To the extent that these impressions came from a variety of sources not very different from the letter writers among the public (that is, from party activists, campaign personnel, and colleagues), it is not hard to believe that they may have been displaced from the head count of public opinion in much the same ways.

If, for the moment, we accept letter writing as a valid indicator of public opinion, we see a rather marvelous change in the state of political affairs. In Fig. 1*a*, instead of trailing Johnson sadly in the anonymous crowd in mid-campaign, Goldwater holds a visible lead. Moving back to the time of the San Francisco Convention, Fig. 1*b,* Goldwater is no longer the candidate of a small minority among Republicans and Independents but is, rather, the toast of an absolute majority, even counting "no preferences" against him. In Fig. 1*c*, we discover not only that a vast majority of the public is interested in the problem of the growing strength of the federal government,[16] but also that those upset by this growing strength outnumber their opponents by a ratio approaching 3 to 1. In Fig. 1*d*, the displacement of "letter opinion" from public opinion is much less, in part because the item wording brought a response involving relatively little disagreement. However, it is clear that Goldwater's "hard" inclinations in foreign policy were somewhat overrepresented as well by the letter-writing public.

However, in some ways, Fig. 1*e* contains more grist than any of the others. First, the very form of the distributions of ideological preference differs rather dramatically. Where public opinion is concerned, nearly half the population falls in the "zero" category, making no affective distinction whatever between conservatives and liberals.[17] In addition, the clustering around this zero point is very tight: Over three-quarters of the population is located within one category of the zero-point. The distribution of "letter opinion," however, is quite different. The central mode of indifference or ignorance shrinks dramatically, and voices from more extreme positions on the continuum gain in strength. Other analyses show that virtually all letter writers rank very high on scales we have used to measure ideological sensitivity. Hence, those who remain toward the middle of the continuum in the right half of Fig. 1*e* are not there through indifference or ignorance: They understand the ideological alternatives and deliberately place themselves near the middle of the road. And, as the bimodal shape of the distribution suggests, political discourse becomes most notably a dialogue between very mild liberals and ultraconservatives.

It is to the world of "letter opinion," or one like it, that the Goldwater campaign, in its original design, was addressed. At least until its late stages, the campaign assumed an electorate with near-total ideological comprehension and sensitivity. Any appeal to the southern conservative tradition in an abstract vein was, indeed, joyfully received in the South and created great ferment among a part of the southern population. Except as such a theme became concretized in day-to-day problems with Negroes, however, the part of the population affected was tiny, even though in the letter-writing and related senses it was so visible as to appear to be "most of the South," politically speaking.

Similarly, the distribution of the population in this world of "letter opinion" helped maintain persistent overestimations of strength. Empirically speaking, the center of Goldwater support lay roughly in the third bar of the figure on the conservative side. It weakened rapidly with any further steps toward the center, and was relatively solid in the outer two bars of the graph. If one looks at "letter opinion" with this zone in mind, it would appear that the base of standing Goldwater support was very substantial. Goldwater hoped to "firm up" the support on his side of the center sufficiently to create a majority, and, according to this figure, it would have taken only a modest extension of influence to achieve this. In the world of public opinion relevant for mass elections, however, the distribution of actual and potential support was radically different. Rather than starting from a solid base of support on the conservative wing, the initial springboard was scarcely populated at all. To win a majority, a much deeper penetration into the center would have been required.

In the measure that we have delineated in Fig. 1*e*—the kind of political environment familiar to many practicing politicians—we can also better understand the first of our puzzles, the myth of the stay-at-home Republicans. For ultraconservatives who found a wide measure of social support and particularly of resonance for their views in the world of public opinion that they understood, it must indeed have been perplexing that uniquely at election time, and uniquely in vote totals, this vigorous support had a habit of evaporating. How could one interpret this gross discrepancy between what one heard and read about public sentiments and what happened at the polls? The easiest explanation was that staunch conservatives in large numbers simply refused to go to the polls, however vigorously they would express themselves otherwise. And, as soon as a useful reason was worked out to explain why this willful nonvoting should occur, a theory was born. It persisted, in part, because it was a handy tactical weapon, but, in some part, it persisted because the discrepant realities that helped to catalyze the theory also persisted. For the theory's proponents, the election of 1964 was a sobering reality test.

It should be apparent that the phenomena we have examined in this chapter have a significance that stretches considerably beyond the 1964 election, beyond questions of the credibility of public opinion polls, beyond the playing of games with the epistemologies of practicing politicians, fascinating though each of these subjects may be.

But the more important implications flow from the reflection that, while the opinion worlds we discussed may be discrepant from one another in many regards, and it behooves us not to confuse them, it is not a simple matter of fact versus fantasy. Both worlds are real and have real effects on the political process. Save for the obvious fact that the reality of "one man, one vote" governs the mass election with greater or lesser modification, while other public-opinion realities like the letter-writing world tend to hold sway otherwise, we know all too little empirically about the counterpoint between the two in actual political systems, and the normative significance of motivation-weighted votes is largely unexamined.

However this may be, if the reality of one of these worlds was manifest on Election Day, 1964, then the reality of the other was equally apparent at the San Francisco Convention. For it is obvious that the intense levels of political motivation that underlie the letter writing of the ultraconservative wing are part and parcel of the ingredients that led to the gathering at a Republican convention of a delegate majority so markedly discrepant from either the rank and file of the party or its customary leadership. What had been lacking around the country in bodies was made up for in dedication, but the outcome of the Convention was in no sense less real because of that. From this juxtaposition of two worlds, the oddities of the 1964 election grew.

3

.

DEEP SOUTH REPUBLICANS: PROFILES AND POSITIONS

.

BERNARD COSMAN

There was a time, not too long ago, when Deep South Republican leadership occasioned little interest except perhaps as "palace or bureaucratic politicians, since their chief preoccupation was not with voters but with maneuvers to gain and keep control of the state party machinery."[1] For decades, Deep South Republicans attended the party's national conventions in the hopes of giving their votes to the winner. A Republican in the White House would reward his Deep South faithful with patronage, and national patronage was the cement that held together the subregion's Republican organizations. It was not surprising, therefore, that Deep South GOP leaders tended to identify closely with the presidential party and its candidates. Nor was it surprising that they should de-emphasize grass-roots activity. One

This is a revised version of Bernard Cosman, *The Case of the Goldwater Delegates: Deep South Republican Leadership* (University, Alabama: Bureau of Public Administration, University of Alabama, 1966). Reprinted by permission of the Bureau of Public Administration, © 1966.

reason for the latter was the hostility of Deep South electorates to Republican candidates. Another equally important reason was that, by discouraging grass-roots activity, those who controlled the party were in a better position to restrict the number of party members and, thereby, to minimize the danger of losing control of federal patronage—a pitfall inherent in any serious attempt by Republicans to break the Democratic monopoly in the subregion.

The popular image of the Deep South Republican leader as a patronage seeker who carried the party organization around in his hat never quite fitted the reality of the southern situation, particularly after 1933, the year in which federal patronage dried up. In the 1930's and 1940's, a business leadership began to displace the old-time patronage type. Then, in the early 1950's, Eisenhower supporters poured into several of Dixie's Republican parties, bent on winning delegate votes for the General's candidacy.[2] Some of these "new Republicans" stayed on to occupy top party-leadership posts. Yet, in spite of changes in the character of the party's governing elite, the popular image of Dixie's GOP leadership lingered until, in 1964, it was dispelled, dramatically and decisively, by two events: the Republican National Convention and the November general election.

The Deep South Republican leaders who met in San Francisco in July, 1964, represented a burgeoning Republican strength in the subregion. From 1962 through mid-1964, the proportions of the vote received by GOP candidates for governor or senator reached new highs in Alabama, Louisiana, and South Carolina.[3] In Mississippi, the party fielded a gubernatorial candidate for the first time in this century, and he polled a respectable 38 per cent of the vote. In addition to seeing the emergence of Republican voters within Deep South electorates, the early 1960's also were a time of accelerated organizational development. A report prepared by the Republican National Committee revealed that, in April, 1964, party organization (as measured by the presence of an active chairman and vice-chairman) had spread to more than three-fourths of the counties in four of the Deep South states— Alabama, Georgia, Mississippi, and South Carolina. Louisiana, the fifth Deep South state, was to reach this level of organizational development by the end of the year. Admittedly, these signs of a

Republican buildup in the Deep South could be read only as first steps toward a more competitive politics in the subregion, though the stepped-up organizational activity of the early 1960's did suggest that the party's leadership was seeking to construct viable state and local organizations capable of challenging Democrats where it counts, at the grass roots.

The hope of Deep South Republican leaders for further party growth in 1964 was Senator Barry Goldwater of Arizona. It is by now widely known that Deep South Republicans played prominent roles in the formation of the Draft Goldwater movement and in the Senator's successful drive for the GOP presidential nomination.[4] Several Deep South GOP leaders had been present at a series of meetings of Goldwater supporters held in 1962 to plan a draft-Goldwater organization. In April, 1963, a National Draft Goldwater Committee was formed in Washingon, D.C., with Peter O'Donnell of Texas as its chairman. In the months that followed, a team of southern Republican state chairmen began the task of building a preconvention organization for Senator Goldwater at the grass roots. With John Grenier of Alabama as its regional coordinator, the southern arm of the National Draft Goldwater Committee, which, in the Deep South states, overlapped the regular party structures,[5] recruited a hard core of delegate support for the Goldwater candidacy; then, at San Francisco, it made that support effective through a convention organization that, in proficiency, rivaled the Kennedy model of 1960.[6]

The extent of the Deep South's commitment to Senator Goldwater at San Francisco became a matter of record when, on the first ballot for the presidential nomination, he received ninety-five of the ninety-seven Deep South delegate votes. Behind this nearly unanimous support for Senator Goldwater was an enthusiasm for the man and a dedication to his candidacy seldom replicated at such a high level by followers of recent American political leaders. Deep South Republicans attended their party's National Convention determined to nominate the Senator from Arizona and, having succeeded, they returned home to work for his election and that of his running mates at the grass roots. In short, the Deep South Republican leaders of 1964, unlike their earlier counterparts, were out to alter the political landscape of their subregion and, they hoped, that of the nation. Illustrative of their high hopes and great expectations for the Goldwater candidacy were these reactions, among Alabama delegates, to the Senator's nomination:

• This is the finest thing that has happened in America since I have been old enough to be aware of what happens politically. People will have a choice and I think they will return the government to the people.

• It's a new day for America, returning to constitutional government for which our forefathers planned.

• It is like witnessing the birth of a new party.

• For the first time the South will have a great voice in affairs and courses of the party. For the first time we have a candidate, in reality a true southern candidate.

• Goldwater will be elected and it will be the first time we will have a friend of the South in the White House in my lifetime.[7]

The November election produced mixed results for Deep South Republican leadership. On the one hand, their high hopes and great expectations for a Goldwater victory were denied by the national electorate. But, while Senator Goldwater lost decisively, Republicans flourished in the Deep South. Alabama, Georgia, Louisiana, Mississippi, and South Carolina supplied the Republican presidential party with forty-seven of its fifty-two electoral votes and the congressional party with seven of its ten new members in the House of Representatives. Less widely publicized, but nonetheless impressive, advances were made by the GOP at the grass roots. The most spectacular outbreak of grass-roots Republicans occurred in Alabama, where, in addition to the election of five new congressmen, ninety-four of the party's candidates were elected to local offices.

The outcome of the Republican National Convention and of the 1964 election have called attention to the Republican Party in the Deep South and invited renewed interest in the course of its development, particularly as regards its leadership. Deep South Republican leaders have been controversial, largely because of their identification with the militant conservatism of Senator Goldwater. Indeed, it has been their firm and unyielding com-

mitment to Goldwater that has caused both the spectator elites
and the mass public to picture them in emotional, value-laden
terms, which have ranged from the severity of "extremist" and
"racist," on the one side, to the approbation implied by "patriot"
and "dedicated American," on the other. To be sure, profiles of
Deep South Republican leadership drawn in the heat of the party
battle not infrequently hinted of caricature. The fact is, we have
lacked empirical data that might replace possibly impressionistic
portrayals of Deep South leadership with more accurate descriptions of their characteristics and attitudes.

Research Procedures

In relying upon delegates and alternates to the 1964 Republican National Convention as the source for our data about Deep
South Republican leadership, we have assumed that these GOP
delegations[8] were at least broadly representative of the party's
governing elite in the subregion—an assumption seemingly confirmed by the organizational experience of respondents. Delegate
and alternate respondents were drawn from all levels of the party
hierarchy, with the heavier weight of their experience at the middle (county and district committees) and upper (state central committee) levels of the party organization (see Table 1). Moreover,
more than one-third of the respondents had run or were running
for public office.

Not shown in Table 1 but included among the respondents
were four of the five incumbent state chairmen, one acting state
chairman, two past state chairmen, four state finance directors,

TABLE 1.

PROPORTIONS OF DELEGATE AND ALTERNATE RESPONDENTS
HOLDING OR HAVING HELD PARTY OFFICE

Office	Per Cent	Number
Precinct committeeman	32	42
County chairman	36	47
County committee	63	83
Congressional district committee	39	51
State central committee	47	62
Candidates for public office	37	49

four national committeemen, and one national committeewoman. In short, while the Deep South delegations did not provide a random sample of the subregion's GOP leadership, there was no reason to suppose that members of these delegations were atypical of incumbent party leadership in Dixie, especially its top-drawer leadership.

The data that served as the basis for this inquiry were obtained from questionnaires mailed to each Deep South Republican delegate and alternate during the summer of 1964. Of the total of 186 delegates and alternates, 131 returned usable questionnaires— a rate of return of slightly better than 70 per cent.[9] The proportions of questionnaires returned by each state delegation varied considerably: from 96 per cent for Mississippi (25 out of 26) to 58 per cent for Louisiana (23 out of 40). For South Carolina, Georgia, and Alabama, the figures were, respectively, 75 per cent (24 out of 32), 73 per cent (35 out of 48), and 60 per cent (24 out of 40). Given these differential rates of response, it was encouraging to find that, except for Mississippi, the proportion of delegate and alternate respondents coming from each Deep South state closely resembled the proportion contributed by each state to the total number of actual convention delegates from the Deep South (see Table 2). Respondents from Georgia, Mississippi, and South Carolina were overrepresented in our sample, whereas respondents from Alabama and Louisiana were underrepresented. Only in Mississippi, however, did the differential exceed four percentage points.

Other types of check data on which we could gauge the representativeness of respondents relative to the actual delegate and

TABLE 2.

PERCENTAGES OF DELEGATES AND ALTERNATES
FROM EACH DEEP SOUTH STATE

State	Actual	Respondents
Alabama	21.5	18.3
Georgia	25.8	26.7
Louisiana	21.5	17.6
Mississippi	14.0	19.1
South Carolina	17.2	18.3

alternate population were the ratios of delegates to alternates and of men to women. In both cases, the comparisons were favorable. Delegates comprised one-half of the full delegation population and just under one-half (49 per cent) of the respondent population.[10] The ratios of men to women in the full delegation population and among respondents were approximately the same, 3 to 1.

The questionnaire used in this study, while necessarily brief, included items relating to the respondent's personal background, party affiliation, perceptions of political parties, and attitudes toward domestic social-welfare issues. In seeking to tap delegate and alternate attitudes, and in order to permit comparisons between their attitudes and those of larger populations, we replicated several of the questions asked in national samples, particularly those developed and used by the Survey Research Center of the University of Michigan (SRC).

In analyzing the completed questionnaires, we will consider, in turn, the personal profiles of the delegate and alternate respondents, two elements of their political profiles—their party affiliations and their perceptions of the role of political parties—and, last, their attitudes toward domestic social-welfare issues. In a concluding section we shall seek to relate delegate and alternate attitudes to party strategy.

Personal Profiles

We begin our analysis of the delegate and alternate questionnaire by focusing on those items that, when taken together, provide information about each respondent's personal profile: Race, sex, age, place of birth, mobility, education, occupation, income, religion, and class status will be considered, in that order. It should be noted that the personal characteristics of Deep South delegates and alternates are described in the aggregate for the subregion rather than for each state delegation, although the sharper differences in the personal characteristics of state delegations have been accounted for. Also to be noted is the limited opportunity for comparison. No data were available for Deep South Republican delegations previous to those of 1964. Paul T. David and his associates did present information about the sex and median income of southern delegates to the 1948 and 1952

Republican national conventions in *The Politics of National Party Conventions*.[11] Chapter 14 of that work, "Characteristics of Delegates and Delegations," constitutes the single most important source of information about the personal characteristics of delegates, especially those who attended the 1948 national conventions. The personal data on non-Deep South delegations cited in this section were drawn from that chapter.

Race, Sex, and Age (131 Respondents). Deep South Republican delegates and alternates were, in each instance, white, usually male, and most often under fifty years of age. Male respondents numbered ninety-eight; females, thirty-three. In percentages, this worked out to 75 per cent male, 25 per cent female.[12] The data on age confirm the general impression that Deep South Republican leaders were relatively young; the modal age category was thirty to thirty-nine and 85 per cent ranged between ages of twenty-one and forty-nine. These data on age contrast rather sharply with the figures for 1948, the only year for which information about the age of delegates has become available. In that year, the average age of all Republican delegates was fifty-two; and that of all Democrats, fifty.[13]

Place of Birth (129 Respondents). Most delegates and alternates were native southerners. Almost three-fourths (74 per cent) listed a birthplace within one of the former eleven Confederate states and well over half (57 per cent) gave a location within their present Deep South state of residence.[14] Of the respondents born outside the region, the largest proportion, 11 per cent, listed their birthplace as the Midwest; 6 per cent had been born in the Northeast; 4 per cent, in a border state; 3 per cent, in the Far West; and 2 per cent in a foreign country.

Mobility (131 Respondents). Although more than half of the delegates and alternates had been born within their home state, less than two out of five had never lived outside that state. A detailed breakdown of delegate and alternate mobility reveals that forty-nine (37 per cent) were "lifers"; that is, they had never lived outside their present state of residence. Another thirty-one (24 per cent) had resided outside their home state but never in a nonsouthern state. Of the remaining fifty-one delegates and alternates, seven had lived in nonsouthern states for less than one year, fifteen for from one to five years, two for from six to ten years, and twenty-seven for more than a decade. Though these fifty-one Deep South Republicans had, at one time or another, resided in nonsouthern states, the Deep South's delegations were not top-heavy with recent immigrants from the North. Only thirteen delegates and alternates had arrived in their present Deep South state of residence during the preceding decade; five of these, in the preceding five years.[15]

Education (126 Respondents). Deep South Republican delegates and alternates were an exceptionally well-educated group. Nearly three-fourths (74 per cent) of the respondents reported they had college degrees; of this group, just under one-third (31 per cent) had undertaken work beyond the undergraduate level. About one out of five respondents (18 per cent) listed some college, while less than one in ten reported that their formal schooling had ended at the elementary (0.7 per cent) or secondary (7 per cent) level.

Occupation (124 Respondents) and Income (121 Respondents). The superior educational achievement of the delegates and alternates is related to the fact that disproportionate numbers reported occupations in the more prestigious professional, managerial, and proprietary categories, and incomes in the upper brackets. Paralleling the education data are data indicating that almost three-fourths (74 per cent) of the respondents belonged in the professional, managerial, and proprietary categories. The next largest proportion (20 per cent) were the twenty-five delegates and alternates self-identified as housewives. Only six respondents (5 per cent) listed farming as their vocation. None could be classified as laborers. A closer inspection of these occupational categories—excluding housewives—reveals that the largest proportion of respondents were business executives, 27 per cent; they were followed by merchants, 20 per cent; lawyers, 16 per cent; doctors, dentists, optometrists, 8 per cent; insurance salesmen, 8 per cent; farmers, 6 per cent; and engineers, 5 per cent. Other delegate and alternate occupations were accountant, airline pilot, geologist, artist, and teacher. Two delegates were retired military officers.[16]

By far, the largest proportions of delegates and alternates had high incomes. Specific income distributions were four out of ten (43 per cent) in the $20,000-or-more bracket, two out of ten (17 per cent) in the $15,000–$19,999 bracket, and three out of ten (29 per cent) in the $10,000–$14,999 bracket. Approximately one out of ten (11 per cent) of the delegates and alternates had incomes under $10,000, and, with but a single exception, these were housewives.[17]

Religion (128 Respondents). Three-fourths of the delegates and alternates identified themselves with higher-status Protestant denominations: Episcopalians, 29 per cent; Methodists, 24 per cent; and Presbyterians, 22 per cent. Baptists constituted the next largest proportion—10 per cent—and were followed by Catholics, 6 per cent, and Jews, 2 per cent. The Lutheran, Unitarian, and Church of Christ denominations had two identifiers each. There were also one Quaker and one Christian Scientist.[18]

Summary. From the foregoing, we can begin to construct, at least in broad outline, a composite personal profile of Deep South Republican leadership as represented in the subregion's delegations to the 1964 Republican National Convention. A Protestant white male born and raised in the South and living in his home state for more than a decade, the "typical" Deep South Republican delegate or alternate was somewhere in his late thirties or early forties. It is likely that he had a college degree and had made a thriving thing of it in the subregion as a professional, manager, or proprietor with an annual income well above $10,000. In brief, many of the Deep South delegates and alternates were of the upper-income, professional-managerial category that, for several decades, has provided the Republican presidential party with its most reliable support outside the South and, more recently, within the South.[19]

The general condition of affluence characteristic of the Deep South delegates and alternates was to be anticipated on the basis of previously available data on the personal characteristics of national-convention delegations; it was also predictable because, as a practical matter, delegates and alternates had to pay their own convention expenses. For this latter reason alone, affluence is a characteristic that Deep South Republican leaders share with many of their nonsouthern counterparts, both Republican and Democratic. It is also apparent that, because of their affluence, Deep South delegates and alternates—again, like those from outside the subregion—do not represent a socioeconomic cross-section of either the subregional or the national electorate. While a variety of data might be cited to make the point, one indicator may suffice here for purposes of illustration; that indicator is subjective class identification. In its 1964 presidential-election survey, the SRC found that 56 per cent of the American electorate claimed working-class status, while another 39 per cent said that they were of the middle class. The remainder of the sample was divided among those who identified with the upper class (1 per cent), those who rejected the idea of class (2 per cent), and those who did not know to what class they belonged or whose class was not ascertained (2 per cent).

In marked contrast to the subjective class identifications of adult Americans in 1964 were the subjective class identifications of the Deep South Republican delegates and alternates.[20] Although 56 per cent of the national sample chose to identify with the working class and 39 per cent with the middle class, only 2 per cent of the Deep South delegates and alternates selected the working-class alternative; by far the largest proportion (67 per cent) chose the middle-class alternative. A striking differential occurred between the proportions of the two groups that identified with the upper class: Nearly one-third (31 per cent) of the delegates and alternates identified with the upper class, as opposed to less than 1 per cent of the national population. Not only were Deep South Republicans of higher status than many adult Americans—as determined by objective measures of status, such as income and education—but a surprisingly large proportion willingly attested to the fact when asked about their class status.

Political Profiles

Attention to the personal profiles of Deep South delegates and alternates has emphasized the broad similarities between many of their personal characteristics and those generally attributed to delegates and alternates from outside the subregion. When, however, we focus on the political profiles of the Deep South Republicans—specifically, their party affiliations and their perceptions of the role of political parties—then characteristics emerge that are not only similar to those of southerners from other parts of the South but that may well be peculiar to all southern Republicans, especially followers of Barry Goldwater.

Party Affiliations (125 Respondents). First, as regards party affiliation, it was found that Deep South delegates and alternates divided almost evenly between those who had always been Republican (51 per cent) and those who had once identified with the Democratic Party but who later switched to the GOP (49 per cent). Probably, the proportion of delegate and alternate switchers was unusually large relative to that of nonsouthern delegations, but this would not be surprising, since a significant amount of political conversion was to be anticipated among Republican delegations from states where overwhelming proportions of the electorate had, for decades, identified with the Democratic Party.

Whether or not a delegate or alternate had once been a Democrat appears to have depended, in significant measure, upon parental party affiliation. Thus, of delegates and alternates who had once been Democrats, almost two-thirds (61 per cent) reported that both their parents had been Democrats, while somewhat less than one-sixth (15 per cent) recalled that both their parents had been Republicans. By way of contrast, of those delegates and alternates who had always been Republicans, more than one-half (58 per cent) had Republican parents and less than one-seventh (13 per cent) had parents who were Democrats. Another, and perhaps more dramatic, illustration of parental influence upon the delegation members' initial choices of party can be obtained through consideration of the party affiliations of delegates and alternates whose parents both identified with the same political party. Thirty-seven out of forty-six delegates and alternates whose parents had been Republican stated that they themselves had always been Republicans, while thirty-seven out of forty-five delegates and alternates whose parents had been Democrats reported that at one time they too had been Democrats.

A close relationship between parental and offspring party affiliation is not, of course, peculiar to Deep South Republican delegates and alternates. Numerous studies of family imprint upon offspring party attachment have shown that, when the father and mother agree politically, the children are likely to adopt the political coloration of their parents.[21] Once acquired, party affiliation tends to persist through time, particularly when the individual's life style and life experiences coincide with those of his parents. When, however, parental and offspring life styles diverge, there is a strong possibility that the offspring will feel cross-pressured; at times, the forces creating cross-pressures can be of sufficient strength to separate him from his family's political ties. It is generally conceded that, during the Great Depression, large numbers of Republican Party identifiers experienced cross-pressures as a result of the economic adversity of the period and the promise of the New Deal; many of these Republicans resolved the conflict in favor of the Democratic Party. Of particular interest to this inquiry are the reasons why almost half of the Deep South Republican delegate and alternate respondents whose first allegiance had been to the Democratic Party had subsequently switched to the GOP.

Fifty-eight of the sixty-one delegate and alternate converts gave their reasons for switching to the Republican Party. Their explanations lend support to the proposition that higher-status southerners have been suffering from extreme disenchantment with the national Democratic Party and for that reason have been switching to the GOP. Nineteen delegates and alternates stated that their conversion to Republicanism had been a reaction against the national Democratic Party because of its "socialism," "liberalism," "Communist coddling," "wild spending," or "fiscal irresponsibility." Another seven delegates and alternates cited, as their reason for switching to the GOP, particular Democratic presidents and their policies: "Roosevelt's court packing plan" or his "inability to cure the Depression"; "Truman's seizure of the steel mills" or his "Korean policy"; or "Kennedy's invasion of Mississippi." Four delegates and alternates took the position that the national Democratic Party had deserted its southern supporters. Their reactions were "They left us." "The Democratic Party changed not I." "The Democratic Party no longer stands for the democratic principles of our forefathers." "The Democratic Party went off and left us when it became socialistic."

One probable course of action for individuals who are displeased with the national Democratic Party because of its liberal orientation is to adopt the party whose philosophy has been more in line with their own conservative views. Twenty-two delegates and alternates emphasized this by attributing their change in party affiliation to their own conservative political orientation and their perception of the Republican Party as the political grouping most representative of the conservative viewpoint. Typical of the responses of delegates and alternates who linked their conservatism directly to the GOP were the following:

- *A delegate from Alabama:* "The Republican Party more nearly represents my conservative political philosophy."
- *A delegate from Louisiana:* "I am a Goldwater conservative and the GOP offers the only real place to put my belief into practice."
- *A delegate from Mississippi:* "I changed when I began to think for myself and realized that the 'R' [Republican Party] was the conservative party."
- *An alternate from South Carolina:* "After studying both parties, [I found that] the GOP as a whole came closer to my political beliefs."

Six delegates and alternates indicated that they had switched to the Republican Party neither because of displeasure with the national Democratic Party nor because of their conservative views and their preference for the GOP as the more conservative of the two parties. Two of these, both delegates, attributed their change in party affiliation to the desirability of establishing the two-party system at the state level. Another stated that he had abandoned the Democratic Party in the hope of "giving the South a voice in national politics." Two delegates explained that they had been drawn into the Republican Party by friends. Another noted that she had switched parties when she "married a Republican and started thinking." Yet, once we have accounted for these six delegates and alternates, the point to be re-emphasized is that nine out of ten Deep South Republicans attributed their change in party affiliation to disapproval of the national Democratic Party or to conservatism.

Role of Political Parties. A second element of the political profiles of the delegates and alternates is their perceptions of the role of the political party. Better than nine out of ten delegates and alternates disagreed with the statement "The role of the political party is to reconcile different interests rather than take clear stands on issues." Seven out of ten disagreed strongly. Only eleven delegates and alternates agreed with the statement, and, of these eleven, only two (both delegates) agreed strongly. Interestingly enough, these two delegates did not vote for Senator Goldwater at San Francisco. The inference from these responses is that the negative reaction of Deep South Republicans to the conception of the party as a mechanism for reconciling differing interests may well have been tied in with their unyielding commitment to Senator Goldwater.

Senator Goldwater had frequently and vigorously criticized the Republican presidential party and its candidates for having played Tweedledum to the Democratic Tweedledee. The Senator's specific criticisms had been directed against the moderate wing of the party. From the time of Wendell Willkie's nomination, in 1940, moderate GOP leadership, based primarily in the Northeast, had urged that, if the Republican Party were to win the presidency, its nominee would have to appeal not only to the conservative end of the political spectrum but also, more importantly, to the great mass of voters at the center. To weld the moderate center to the conservative right required that GOP presidential aspirants profess at least a mild degree of enthusiasm for major New Deal and Fair Deal programs at home and for American involvement abroad. Goldwater rejected the strategy of the center and, in announcing his candidacy for the Republican presidential nomination, he promised that he would offer a conservative "choice, not an echo."[22]

That the Deep South delegates and alternates shared Senator Goldwater's determination to provide a conservative choice was readily apparent from their responses to the question "What persuaded you to become a delegate or alternate to the 1964 Republican National Convention?"

A delegate from Alabama replied: "Because I am interested in seeing the Republican Party offer [an alternative to the] left-wing socialism offered by the Democrats [I want the] conservative program offered by the Republicans under Barry Goldwater."

A second Alabama delegate responded: "I feel the Republican Party must find itself and not continue as a me-too party trying to outdo the Democrats. The Republican Party is the only hope for conservative government."

A delegate from Georgia commented: "To help change and shape the posture of the Republican Party so that it can once again offer a choice not an echo."

Another delegate from Georgia noted: "The national Democratic Party is a threat to the vitality of our nation and the people should be given a choice."

A delegate from Louisiana reacted: "The direction of our party is in serious need of definition—I seek to help in that direction by supporting Senator Goldwater."

A Mississippi delegate explained: "I have worked for four years for Barry Goldwater and the conservative cause. It is time we have a choice."

A South Carolina delegate stated: "My desire is to nominate Senator Goldwater and give the electorate a choice between two philosophies of government."

These responses indicated that Deep South Republican delegates and alternates for Goldwater desired a national Republican Party that could serve as a means of aggregating the opinions of like-minded conservatives. This conception of the Republican presidential party is, of course, at odds with the present-day reality of the American presidential party as a loosely organized and decentralized brokerage institution, more intent on building majority support than on upholding particular principles or advocating narrowly distributed points of view. Nor does the concept of the Republican Party as a mechanism for assembling conservative opinion seem to take into account the present distribution of party identifiers within the electorate, a distribution that—according to numerous studies of mass opinion—favors the Democratic Party.[23] Yet, despite what may appear a somewhat unrealistic conceptualization of the role of the political party—particularly of a minority party—the fact remains that the Deep South delegates and alternates did have their way at San Francisco. Moreover, their candidate swept the five Deep South states in November. It is within the context of these two events and the continued Republican stirrings at the Deep South grass roots that we shall now consider the domestic attitudinal profiles of Deep South Republican leaders.

Domestic Attitudinal Profiles

What kinds of opinions did the Deep South Republican delegates and alternates seek to implement through state and national Republican parties and through the candidacy of Senator Goldwater? This section will attempt to provide an answer for one category of delegate and alternate opinions: those in the broad area of domestic social welfare. In focusing our attention on the domestic attitudinal profiles of the Deep South Republicans, we will examine the direction and intensity of their opinions, the interrelationship of their opinions with those of the mass public, and their attitudes toward settled domestic issues and toward states' rights.

Opinion Direction and Intensity. It is by now a commonplace finding of survey research that Republican Party identifiers usually take a more restrictive view of the scope of governmental welfare activity than do Democratic identifiers. One question that the SRC employed to illustrate this difference in outlook of party identifiers toward domestic welfare policy was the following: "Some people think that the national government should do more in trying to deal with such problems as unemployment, education, housing, and so on. Others think that the national government is already doing too much. On the whole would you say that what the government has done has been about right, too much, or not enough?"[24]

When Deep South Republican delegates and alternates were asked this question, the overwhelming proportion (94 per cent) responded that they felt the national government was doing too much; under 5 per cent thought that the present level of governmental activity was about right; and less than 1 per cent favored expansion of governmental activity. Given the unimodal shape of this opinion distribution, we may readily infer one rather obvious reason why Deep South Republican delegations united in support of Senator Goldwater: Both shared a decidedly conservative outlook toward the proper scope of governmental social-welfare activity. We may ask to what extent this conservative outlook embraced more specific domestic social-welfare issues.[25]

The distribution of the Deep South Republicans' opinions on a series of domestic-issue propositions is displayed in Table 3. There, one can see that delegate and alternate opinions were overwhelmingly conservative. Upward of eight out of ten respondents opposed federal action with regard to employment guaranties, medical care, public power and housing, aid to education, school integration, and voting rights. Of these issues, the job-guaranty proposition evoked the largest proportion of conservative responses, and voting rights the smallest. To be specific, 95 per cent of the delegates and alternates disagreed with the statement that "The government in Washington ought to see that everyone who wants to work can find a job." A slightly smaller proportion (93 per cent) disagreed with the statement "The government in Washington ought to help people get doctors and hospital care at low cost" and then agreed that "The government in Washington should leave things like electric power and housing for private businessmen to handle." As for public education, 89 per cent of the delegates and alternates preferred leaving support for education entirely to state and local governments, while 84 per cent agreed that "The government in Washington should stay out of the question of integrating the public schools." A smaller proportion, 82 per cent, favored leaving the matter of voting rights for Negroes to state and local governments.

In addition to establishing the direction of delegate and alternate opinions on these domestic-issue propositions, certain of the data in Table 3 also provide information about the intensity of these opinions, that is, with reference to the issue propositions relating to job guaranty, medical care, public power and housing, and school integration. For each of these issue propositions, the delegates and alternates were asked whether they agreed, strongly agreed, disagreed, or strongly disagreed. To measure the intensity of their opinions, we had to assume—as did the late V. O. Key, in his *Public Opinion and American Democracy*—that "strongly agree" responses, on the average, differ in intensity from "agree" responses.[26] By making this assumption, we could

TABLE 3.

DIRECTION OF OPINION OF DEEP SOUTH REPUBLICAN DELEGATES AND ALTERNATES ON SELECTED DOMESTIC SOCIAL-WELFARE ISSUES

Question	Strongly Agree	Agree	Disagree	Strongly Disagree	No Opinion
Job guaranty[a]	1%	3%	23%	72%	1%
Medical care[b]	1%	5%	14%	79%	1%
Power and housing[c]	77%	16%	4%	1%	2%
School integration[d]	76%	8%	8%	7%	1%

Question	Federal	State and Local	No Opinion
Support for education[e]	9%	89%	2%
Voting rights[f]	17%	82%	1%

a "The government in Washington ought to see that everyone who wants to work can find a job."

b "The government in Washington ought to help people get doctors and hospital care at low cost."

c "The government in Washington should leave things like electric power and housing for private businessmen to handle."

d "The government in Washington should stay out of the question of integrating the public schools."

e "Do you think that the national government should provide grants to the states for the construction and operation of public schools, or do you feel that support for public education should be left entirely to state and local governments?"

f "Do you think the question of voting rights of Negroes should be left to state and local governments or should the federal government take action in this field?"

combine, for each question, the "strongly agree" and "strongly disagree" responses to obtain a crude measure of intensity of opinion. The results were: job guaranty, 73 per cent; medical care, 80 per cent; public power and housing, 78 per cent; and school integration, 83 per cent. This treatment of the data reveals that upward of three out of four delegates and alternates held strong opinions on these four issue propositions. The degree of opinion intensity varied with the issue, increasing from the job-guaranty proposition to the power and housing and medical-care propositions. Not surprising was the fact that school integration elicited the largest proportion of strong opinions from these Deep

South respondents. V. O. Key had turned up a similar finding for the national population; using as his data source the 1956 sample of the SRC, Key had found that the school-integration question generated a larger proportion of strong opinions than any other domestic-issue proposition (64 per cent). Somewhat smaller proportions of the SRC's sample (respectively, 60 per cent and 56 per cent) had felt strongly about the job-guaranty and medical-care questions, while less than half of the sample (45 per cent) had sharp opinions about the power and housing proposition.[27] In examining these levels of national opinion intensity, one will notice the marked differences between the strength of the opinions held by Deep South Republicans and that of those held by the cross-section of the nation's adults. For each issue proposition, a larger proportion of delegates and alternates than of adult Americans held strong opinions. The differential was particularly sharp on the medical-care and power and housing questions; in both cases, the differential exceeded 20 percentage points. Doubtless, the higher intensity of the opinions held by Deep South delegates and alternates related in part to their high level of political participation. For, generally speaking, people who strongly espouse their opinions are more likely to engage in activities designed to implement them than are people with opinions only lightly held.[28] On the average, political activists are most likely to succeed in their implementing activities when the direction of their opinions finds support within the general population. A relevant question for this inquiry is that of the extent to which the opinions of Deep South Republican delegates and alternates derived support from mass opinions.

Interrelationship of Delegate Opinion and Mass Opinion. In relating the attitudinal characteristics of party leaders to those of larger populations, we would anticipate differences not only with respect to intensity of opinion but also with respect to political involvement, issue familiarity, and attitudinal structure, all of which are more highly developed and technically consistent among party leaders than among the general public. Evidence on this last point has been provided by Herbert McClosky and his associates, who studied the interrelationship of the attitudes of delegates and alternates to the Republican and Democratic conventions in 1956 and the attitudes of party members within the electorate. They found that Republican and Democratic leaders exhibited divergent attitudes on many issues that caused little disagreement within the ranks of their followers.[29]

Even though our data for 1964 were limited to the Deep South Republican delegations, the opportunity to relate delegate and alternate opinions to the opinions of larger populations did exist. Figure 1 may be consulted, first, on this point. It depicts the interrelationship of delegate and alternate opinion and public opinion on the medical-care, public power and housing, and school-integration questions. Similar questions had been put to national samples, in 1956, by the SRC. Because our data sources differ in point of time, the comparisons of Fig. 1 must be read and interpreted with extreme caution. The direction of mass opinion may have changed since 1956, although our basic assumption was that the direction of national opinion on the three questions had not undergone revolutionary change during the intervening eight years. To some extent, we can test the soundness of this assumption with more recent poll data. For the moment, however, let us consider the data of Fig. 1. There, one can see the dramatic contrasts between the patterns of delegate and alternate opinion and those of public opinion, as well as the less pronounced, but nonetheless substantial, differences in the directions of these opinions. Whereas Deep South Republican opinions assumed distinctively unimodal patterns, with the heavy weight of each distribution cast in the conservative direction, the opinions of adult Americans more nearly approximate bimodal conflict patterns in which the direction of opinion varies depending on the issue. On medical care, the direction of public opinion was liberal, inasmuch as most respondents favored the proposition. On the other hand, on the power and housing and the school-integration questions, the larger proportions of respondents were clustered at the conservative end of the scale, although, on these two questions, the proportions of adult Americans holding conservative viewpoints were considerably smaller than the proportions of delegates who took conservative positions.

We can give certain of our data more timeliness by relating the opinions of Deep South delegates and alternates to the public's

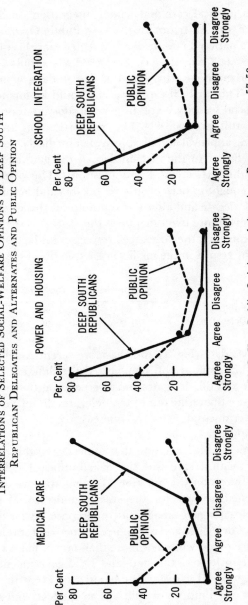

FIGURE 1

INTERRELATIONS OF SELECTED SOCIAL-WELFARE OPINIONS OF DEEP SOUTH
REPUBLICAN DELEGATES AND ALTERNATES AND PUBLIC OPINION

Data source for public opinion: V. O. Key, *Public Opinion and American Democracy*, pp. 57-58.
Percentage bases exclude those with no opinion and, in the case of the public's opinions, the
"Depends" category.

opinions on medical care and school integration. In the case of medical care, the American Institute of Public Opinion (Gallup Poll) asked a national sample of adult Americans this question, in January, 1965: "Congress has considered a compulsory medical insurance program covering hospital and nursing home care for the elderly. This medical care program would be financed out of increased social security taxes. In general, do you approve or disapprove of this program?"[30] The proportions of the nation's adults voicing approval and disapproval of medical care are shown below, in relation to the distribution of delegate and alternate opinion on the SRC medical-care question ("The government in Washington ought to help people get doctors and hospital care at low cost"). Delegate and alternate opinions on this question have been compressed into two categories: the "agree" responses in the "Approve" category, the "disagree" responses in the "Disapprove" category. The results in the medical-care question were

	% Approve	% Disapprove
Public	63	28
Delegates	6	93

Both the SRC data (Fig. 1) and the more recent American Institute of Public Opinion poll emphasized the differential outlook of the public and the delegates and alternates on the medical-care question. More than nine out of ten delegates disapproved of this type of governmental activity, whereas six out of ten adult Americans approved.

Another piece of information that underscored this differential outlook on medical care was the distribution of delegate and alternate opinions on the question "Do you approve of the plan to provide medical care for the elderly under social security?" Only two delegates gave an affirmative response. By far the largest proportion of delegates and alternates, 75 per cent, preferred private insurance plans, while few more than one in ten (11 per cent) would prefer to look to the state and local governments for the provision of medical care for senior citizens. From these figures and from the distributions of opinions on the SRC and American Institute of Public Opinion medical-care questions, we may conclude, with some assurance, that (at least on the medical-care issue) delegate and alternate opinion was considerably more conservative than public opinion.

There is an opportunity to obtain a more precise picture of the interrelationship of delegate and alternate opinion and public opinion on the school-integration issue. A Gallup Poll of November 13, 1963, reported the breakdown of Republican and southern opinions, as well as the distribution of mass opinion, on the question "Some people say that each state should decide what to do about integrating whites and Negroes. Other people say that if it is left to each state, Negroes will be deprived of their constitutional rights in many states. How do you feel—should each state have the right to decide what it will do about integration, or not?" Our Deep South delegates and alternates had been asked whether they agreed or disagreed with the proposition "The government in Washington should stay out of the question of integrating the public schools." Although the phrasing of the American Institute of Public Opinion question and the one used in the delegate questionnaire differed, presumably both questions sought to measure the same basic attitude, with the results shown in Fig. 2.

In Panel 1 of that figure, one can examine the contrasting distributions of public opinion and delegate and alternate opinion on the integration question. The public divided about equally between those who would leave integration to the states (43 per cent) and those who would not (48 per cent). On the other hand, the overwhelming weight of delegate and alternate opinion clustered in opposition to school integration. The contrast becomes less marked, however, as the attitudes of, first, Republicans (Panel 2) and then white southerners (Panel 3) are filtered from those of the general public and compared with delegate and alternate attitudes. Indeed, the differential that exists between the opinions of white southerners and Republican delegates and alternates in Panel 3 might well disappear if we had available a sample of Deep South white attitudes on the burning issue of the day in the subregion.[31]

The congruence of Deep South Republican opinion and white southern opinion on school integration should not be taken to

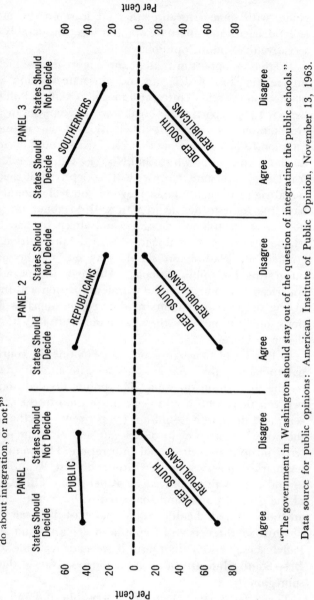

FIGURE 2

INTERRELATIONSHIP OF OPINIONS OF DEEP SOUTH REPUBLICAN DELEGATES
AND ALTERNATES AND THE PUBLIC

"Some people say that each state should decide what to do about integrating whites and Negroes. Other people say that if it is left to each state, Negroes will be deprived of their constitutional rights in many states. How do you feel — should each state have the right to decide what it will do about integration, or not?"

"The government in Washington should stay out of the question of integrating the public schools."

Data source for public opinions: American Institute of Public Opinion, November 13, 1963.

mean that a close articulation of their opinions would necessarily
prevail on social-welfare issues in which race was not salient.
V. O. Key, for example, after studying geographic distributions
of opinion, concluded that "apart from its attitudes on the Negro
question, the South takes positions in mass opinion on broad
questions of policy remarkably similar to those of the nation."[32]
Before reaching this conclusion, Key had related southern and
nonsouthern opinions on several social-welfare propositions, two
of which were on job guaranty and public power and housing. On
these issues, distributions of southern opinion resembled those of
the rest of the nation. In Table 4, southern opinions are related to

TABLE 4.

INTERRELATIONSHIP OF OPINIONS OF DEEP SOUTH REPUBLICAN DELEGATES
AND ALTERNATES AND SOUTHERNERS ON JOB GUARANTY AND
PUBLIC POWER AND HOUSING

Opinion	Job Guaranty		Power and Housing	
	Delegates and Alternates[a]	Southerners[b]	Delegates and Alternates[a]	Southerners[b]
Strongly agree	1%	53%	77%	43%
Agree	3%	16%	16%	13%
Disagree	23%	9%	4%	11%
Strongly disagree	72%	13%	1%	22%

[a] Percentage bases include those with no opinion.

[b] A "Depends" category is excluded. Data source for southern opinion: V. O. Key, *Public Opinion and American Democracy*, p. 104.

those of Deep South Republican delegates and alternates. Instead
of being congruent, the two sets of opinions differ significantly;
larger proportions of southerners than Deep South delegates and
alternates hew to the liberal position on both the job-guaranty
and power and housing questions, while smaller proportions of
southerners than of delegates and alternates assume a conservative
stance on these two questions.

The Settled Issues. Although the domestic issues examined to
this point did not divide the public into warring camps, the dis-

tributions of mass opinion on issues such as job guaranty, public power, and medical care more nearly fit conflict patterns of opinion than consensus patterns. Of a different character are the settled issues—those that evoke widespread agreement within the mass public and, therefore, are usually thought of as part of a broadly shared consensus in mass opinion. We may inquire as to where the Deep South Republican delegates and alternates stood on the settled issues. A partial answer to the question may be forthcoming if we focus on delegate and alternate attitudes toward social security and the income tax. Presumably, if these two public policies were put to the national population, they would receive widespread support. Admittedly, evidence to bolster this contention is scant. On social security, a series of Gallup polls, taken between December, 1935, and November, 1939, did reveal that upward of nine out of ten Americans favored "government old-age pensions for needy persons."[33] When Deep South Republicans were asked for their opinions about the social security system, slightly less than one in ten (9 per cent) urged its abolition; about four in ten (38 per cent) favored retention of the present system; while the largest proportion, almost half (48 per cent), held that social security should be placed on a voluntary basis. A congenial interpretation of this opinion distribution might emphasize that a vast majority of the delegate and alternate respondents (86 per cent) supported some form of social security. Probably, a more accurate appraisal of these data would count those Deep South Republicans who desired a voluntary social security program as opponents of the present system, thus leaving somewhat less than four in ten delegates and alternates (38 per cent) aligned in support of social security, a proportion well below the level necessary for us to conclude that an attitudinal consensus exists among the delegates and alternates on the desirability of social security.

It is not unfair to assume that, in the half-century since the passage of the Thirteenth Amendment, most Americans have become reconciled to the income tax as a necessary, albeit not always cheerfully accepted, public policy. The Deep South Republican delegates and alternates were asked whether they favored (1) reduction of the present tax rate, (2) elimination of different rates for different incomes, so that all would pay the same rate, (3) repeal of the income tax by constitutional amendment, or (4) leaving the income tax as it is. Delegate and alternate opinion divided as follows: 44 per cent favored rate reduction; 32 per cent, equalization; 16 per cent, repeal; and 2 per cent, no change. Following the line of our approach to the social security question, we may begin by noting that more than three-fourths (78 per cent) of the delegates and alternates supported a federal income tax, although a goodly number of these (32 per cent) desired basic change in the existing tax structure through elimination of its progressive feature. Though equalization of tax rates would constitute a fundamental alteration in public tax policy, a far more antagonistic and markedly less rational attitude toward the income tax was that favoring outright repeal—an attitude acknowledged by approximately one-sixth (16 per cent) of the Deep South delegates and alternates. When this segment of delegate and alternate opinion is considered together with those who preferred equalization, we find the Deep South Republicans split about equally between those who would either effect fundamental change in the income tax structure or eliminate it entirely and those whose preferences were for rate reduction or no change. In short, the income tax proposition, like the social security question, failed to generate a supportive consensus within Deep South delegations. Indeed, the reverse was true. More than half of the delegate and alternate respondents wanted drastic reform or elimination of the social security system, and just under a majority of respondents favored equalization or repeal of the income tax. Small though the levels of support for social security and the income tax may appear to be, the proportions of delegates and alternates who approved of these policies exceeded by a substantial margin the proportions of delegates and alternates who lined up behind any other governmental social-welfare activity.

States' Rights. A skeptic who has followed our discussion to this point may ask whether, in stressing the conservative cast of Deep South opinions, we have not overlooked an important attitudinal dimension of Dixie's Republican leaders. We refer to states' rights. Within the context of Deep South politics, states' rights has usually meant preserving the racial status quo, but it can also mean vigorous, positive state government. Instead of relying upon the federal government to provide jobs or medical care for the aged, it may well have been that Deep South Republican leaders preferred that these and other social-welfare matters be handled by state and local governments.

Our data on the subject of states' rights were not abundant. Five questions were put to the delegates and alternates that involved, to some extent, their assessment of the proper scope of state and local governmental welfare activity. Two of these questions dealt with public education and voting rights (see Table 3). Both questions afforded the respondent two alternatives—one was national action; the other, state and local action. Confronted with these alternatives in the areas of education and voting rights, huge majorities of the Deep South Republican delegations favored state and local action rather than national action. When, however, the range of alternatives broadened to include the possibility of private activity, disproportionate numbers of delegates and alternates gave as their preference private activity. One question that provided respondents with the full range of alternatives concerned the maintenance of full employment. Delegates and alternates were asked whether public works programs to maintain full employment should be the responsibility of the federal government, state and local governments, or private industry. More than two-thirds of the delegate and alternate respondents (68 per cent) preferred private action; 13 per cent desired state and local action; 15 per cent wanted the states and localities and private industry to work together on the matter; and a scant 3 per cent thought that public works should be the responsibility of the federal government. Another question sought to tap delegate and alternate opinion in the area of public housing. The question was "Do you approve of the use of state and local funds for public housing or do you generally feel that the provision of housing can be better taken care of by private effort?" In this question, the choice narrowed to but two alternatives: state and local activity, on the one hand, and private effort, on the other. Eight out of ten delegates and alternates (80 per cent) opted for private effort; less than two out of ten (18 per cent) approved of the use of state and local funds for public housing. A third question that embraced the possibilities both of increased state and local governmental welfare activity and of private action was the medical-care item cited earlier in our discussion of the interrelationship of the opinions of delegates and alternates and those of the public. In that question, the delegates and alternates had been queried as to their attitudes toward medical care for the elderly through social security. One alternative open to them was state and local action. Only 11 per cent elected this alternative. A whopping majority (75 per cent) favored placing reliance upon private insurance plans.

In sum, when the delegates and alternates were given a choice between public and private social-welfare activity, the heavy weight of their opinion turned up on the side of private action. To be sure, the questions we asked by no means exhausted the subject of states' rights as seen by the Deep South Republican delegates and alternates in 1964. At the same time, the direction of delegate and alternate opinions in the areas of employment, public housing, and medical care offered little support for a contention that Dixie's Republican leaders were receptive to state and local governmental welfare activity. Indeed, it would appear that, for most of these Republicans, the best government governs least.

Attitudes and Party Strategy

The principal findings of this study may be telescoped as follows: The Deep South Republican leaders, as represented in the subregion's delegations to the 1964 Republican National Convention, emerged from the data as white, high-status Protestants, most of whom had been born and reared in the South—many, in their home state. Approximately half were former Democrats who had been attracted to the GOP because of their displeasure with New Deal, Fair Deal, and New Frontier democracy or because of their belief in the GOP as the more conservative of the two major political parties. Consequently, it was not surprising to find that the delegates and alternates preferred a Republican presidential party that would provide a conservative choice instead of the echo many felt the party had been offering under eastern leadership. The conservative preferences of Deep South Republican leaders became readily apparent when their domestic attitudinal profiles were examined. Upward of three-fourths of these Republicans offered restrictive views of the proper scope of governmental social-welfare activity, which differed both in direction and intensity from distributions of public opinion and even, in two instances, from patterns of southern opinion. Only on the race issue did the attitudes of the Deep South Republican leaders converge with those of a larger population—in this case, white southern opinion. Social security and the income tax drew the heaviest proportions of positive responses from the Deep South respondents, but, even on these settled issues, less than half of the delegates and alternates registered favorable opinions. Nor was there a surge of states'-rights sentiment within the Deep South delegations, although, when confronted with a choice between federal and state governmental activity, overwhelming proportions of the subregion's Republican leaders stated their preference for the latter alternative.

In some ways, the profiles of Deep South Republican leaders bear a resemblance to what is known of the characteristics of members of the nonparty groups of the far right. Murray Clark Havens studied the implementing activities of these groups in a number of Texas communities and he found their membership heavily weighted with individuals drawn from among the better-educated and more prestigious occupational categories.[34] Havens was careful in advancing generalizations relative to the nonparty groups of the far right that he analyzed, inasmuch as the bulk of his data was acquired, of necessity, from people at least once removed from these organizations. He was also careful to point out the importance of differentiating from the radical right those individuals and groups that "accept the legitimacy and the legal validity of the policies of which they disapprove and of the political system through which these policies were established."[35] In the main, the Deep South Republicans met this test. This is not to deny that Deep South GOP delegates and alternates shared with many members of far-right groups both a high degree of enthusiasm for the candidacy of Senator Goldwater and an intense dissatisfaction with the course of national policy. But, unlike those who inhabit the right-wing fringe of American politics, Deep

South Republicans chose to channel their implementing activities through a major political party rather than through closed associations.[36]

Withal, apart from the similarities between certain known characteristics of members of groups on the far right and those of Deep South Republicans, the profiles of the subregion's delegates and alternates underscore both the opportunities and dilemmas confronting their party in the subregion. On the one hand, there are opportunities. With their intense concern for the direction taken by public policy over the last three decades—a concern evident in their attitudinal profiles—these Republicans have sought to effect a change in course. As a first step, they began to build party organizations at the grass roots in states where, theretofore, there had been no grass-roots party machinery and where, today, the majority party frequently lacks even the rudiments of a permanent precinct organization. At the same time, they gave their full support to a Republican presidential candidate who could be expected to implement their aspirations for policy change, if elected, and—equally important—whose candidacy would strengthen the party at the Deep South grass roots. As it turned out, Goldwater lost in a landslide, but he carried the Deep South states in a manner reminiscent of 1948, when the States' Rights Party claimed the bulk of the Deep South's electoral votes. Both the Goldwater voting pattern and that of the States' Rights Party exhibited a distinctive regional coloration. There was, however, at least one important difference. In 1948, Deep South electorates went off to a third party; this time, majorities supported the GOP. As a result, whatever measure is used—votes, contests made and won, organization, money contributed, motivation, or even conversion of Democratic officeholders to Republicanism—the conclusion must necessarily be that the GOP in the Deep South emerged from 1964 stronger than ever before.

One might submit that 1964 was an anomalous election for Deep South states in that many voters who ordinarily might have been expected to vote for Johnson temporarily defected to Goldwater because of the latter's more congenial definition of states' rights. Yet, Republicanism has not vanished from the subregion with Goldwater's disappearance from the GOP ticket. Indeed, the fact that post-Goldwater Republicans have elected seven state legislators in Georgia, mayors in both Columbus and Hattisburg, Mississippi (both converts from the Democratic Party), and a scattering of other local officials in that state, plus a new Republican congressman in South Carolina (also a convert from the Democratic Party), attests to the continued vitality of the GOP in the subregion and emphasizes the determination of its managers to persist in their efforts to construct a strong second party. The question of what kind of second party it will be is one of the dilemmas of Deep South Republicanism.

In a word, this dilemma is one of strategy. Shall the party continue its appeal to white electorates on the basis of states'-rights doctrine—defined to include both a traditional appeal and a restrictive interpretation of the proper scope of governmental social-welfare activity—or should it begin to modify its appeals by seeking out other possible alternative approaches to the subregion's voters? Our reading of the profiles of Dixie's party leaders at one point in time, together with the party's recent electoral successes, suggests a continuation of the states'-rights strategy, at least in the short run or until that strategy produces an unfavorable outcome.

By adopting states' rights as their standard, Deep South Republicans have been able to capitalize on the wave of discontent with the national Democratic Party that has swept the subregion. Party managers are unlikely to tamper with a winning formula, particularly when that formula embraces what appear to be their own preferences. The GOP in the Deep South emerged from the 1964 general election as a party of the traditional South.[37] This characteristic had been apparent earlier at the leadership level, inasmuch as there were no Negroes in the Deep South delegations. The absence of Negroes from these delegations occasioned no particular surprise, in light of Goldwater's repeated emphasis upon states' rights, his vote against the civil rights bill of 1964, and the fact that the Deep South GOP leadership was almost solid for Goldwater. For these reasons, Negro Republicans were unable to work up any real enthusiasm for the candidacy of the Arizona Senator. Nor did the Goldwaterites in the subregion display any real interest in cultivating the Negro vote. The point was vividly

illustrated in Georgia, where Republican district and state conventions selected an all-white delegation to a Republican national
convention for the first time in fifty years. In explaining why
there were no Negro Republicans in the Georgia delegation, the
state chairman emphasized that "the only significance this has is
that . . . the leadership . . . that won . . . are people who believe in the philosophy expressed by Senator Goldwater, and
there have not been many—or any—Negroes in the forefront of
this effort."[38]

Given a states'-rights strategy, and candidates to implement
that strategy, it was not startling to find Negroes missing from
the subregion's Republican delegations. It was, however, of more
than passing interest that the attitudinal preferences of Dixie's
GOP leaders should coincide with this dimension of their party's
strategy. About three-fourths of the delegates and alternates
strongly agreed with the proposition that "The government in
Washington should stay out of the question of integrating the public schools"; approximately eight out of ten (82 per cent) thought
the question of voting rights for Negroes should be left to state
and local governments. In brief, the states'-rights solution to the
burning issue of the day in the Deep South not only would appear
to represent the views of majorities of the subregion's white electorate but also would seemingly embody the preferences of the
majority of southern Republican leaders. The latter is a point to
be remembered by those who might abruptly dismiss the traditional states'-rights appeals of Dixie's state Republican parties as
little more than a concession to the distribution of popular attitudes on racial issues. Similarly, the economic dimension of the
states'-rights strategy has a firm basis in the attitudinal preferences of many of the Deep South Republican leaders: One might
expect attitudes toward governmental social-welfare activity to be
particularly stable over time, since they parallel the socioeconomic
attributes of those who hold them.

This discussion of the dilemma of strategy comes down to the
speculation that the attitudinal profiles of Deep South Republican
leaders who attended their party's National Convention in 1964
indicate the likelihood of continued states'-rights appeals to Deep
South electorates. Of course, we have tapped delegate and alter-

nate opinion at only a single point in time. Attitudes may undergo change or, at least, modification. Indeed, party managers may
be displaced—as in 1964, when Eisenhower backers were turned
out at the state level by Goldwater enthusiasts. Furthermore,
forces are impinging upon Dixie's GOP leaders that have the potential to bring about changes, if not in their attitudes, at least in
the direction of their political strategy. Urbanization and indus-
trialization continue to alter the socioeconomic face of the subregion and to create the raw materials for a class-based politics
rather than a politics of sectionalism. As these raw materials are
activated, they will present new requirements and provide new
opportunities to the subregion's politicians. But the processes of
social and economic change are slow, and political change has a
way of lagging behind other changes.

Consequently, of immediate relevance to the GOP is the expansion of the Deep South's electorate. More citizens of the region are registering to vote—a development attributable not only
to the increase in the number of Negro voters but also to the rising number of lower-middle- and lower-income white voters.
Neither group has been active in the past.[39] Their entrance into
the Deep South electorate poses problems for the GOP, as it does
for the Democratic Party. From the Republican standpoint, the
adoption of a states'-rights strategy has meant that Negro voters
find little that is attractive in the Republican Party.[40] Lower-
middle- and lower-income white voters, on the other hand, may
continue to derive much satisfaction from the racial dimension of
the states'-rights strategy, but one may wonder to what extent this
category of white voters is charmed by conservative economic
views. If racial tensions abate, the GOP may find it necessary to
manufacture new and, perhaps, radically different types of appeals, unless the party is willing to write off altogether both the
Negro vote and that of lower-status whites.

In addition to forces at work within the Deep South, pressures
that emanate from outside the subregion are reaching its GOP
leaders. In this regard, the future of the Republican Party within
the Deep South probably is bound up with that of the party in
the nation. Survey research has demonstrated that most voters
who have perceptions of parties derive these perceptions pri-

marily from the national parties, rather than from state or local parties.[41] Seemingly, the Republican presidential party cannot afford to cater to the traditional South on racial grounds and, at the same time, get back into the business of winning votes elsewhere in the nation. A move away from the right toward the center is the reasonable expectation for the GOP presidential party in the immediate future. It is unlikely that Deep South Republican leaders will again get a presidential candidate who mirrors their views as closely as did Senator Goldwater. This is not to say that the presidential party will write off the Deep South. Given the need for congressional seats (as well as for electoral votes) both the presidential party and the congressional party may tolerate their Deep South supporters. And indeed, having made a breakthrough in the subregion, they may go a step beyond and seek to stimulate further Republican development in the Deep South on grounds other than a traditional states'-rights appeal.[42] What strategies the national party adopts in its attempt to rebuild the Republican party-in-the-electorate will in large measure effect developments in Dixie. Conversely, how Deep South Republican leaders respond to national strategies and to the changes taking place in their region will be a critical factor in the national party's future.

In 1966, Deep South Republican parties generally employed a states'-rights strategy with mixed results. In Mississippi, Republicans were defeated in races for the U.S. Senate and for the House seat they had won in 1964. In Alabama, the GOP retained three of the five House seats won with Goldwater, but major efforts to win the governorship and a Senate seat failed. In Georgia, Republicans added two House seats to the one already held and won a plurality of the gubernatorial vote, but they lost the governorship. The Georgia Constitution prescribes that when no candidate receives a majority the legislature will choose the governor. Not unsurprisingly, the Georgia General Assembly chose the Democratic candidate. In South Carolina, Republicans retained the House and Senate seats occupied by former Democrats turned Republican, but the Republican candidate for governor was defeated. Republicans won no major offices in Louisiana. Today, all those contests having been decided, the strategic dilemma remains. In the near future, there may well be a necessity for choice and for accommodation, both of which will provide a severe test of the skills of Deep South Republican leadership. Future choices and outcomes are not predictable; yet, it will be essential to observe the course of Deep South Republicanism. What happens to the GOP in Dixie will be significant for both the subregion and the national two-party system.

4

■

MONEY AND VOTES:
PARTY FINANCE, 1964

■

HERBERT E. ALEXANDER

The financing of the presidential campaigns of 1964 contrasted sharply with the voting patterns: The victory of Lyndon Baines Johnson was built on a narrow financial, but broad electoral, base; the Barry Goldwater candidacy had a broad financial, but narrow electoral, base. The contrast was put in more vivid terms by John M. Bailey, chairman of the Democratic National Committee, when he said the Republicans "wound up with a vote deficit and a financial surplus," while the Democrats had a vote surplus and a financial deficit.[1]

Political costs, in 1964, escalated at all levels, from the national to the local. To take one outstanding example: There were dramatic increases in television and radio costs between 1960 and 1964. Broadcast costs are easily measurable, thanks to the surveys of political broadcasting conducted by the Federal Communica-

This is a revised version, done for this volume, of Herbert E. Alexander, *Financing the 1964 Election* (Princeton, N.J.: Citizens' Research Foundation, 1966). Used by permission of Herbert E. Alexander.

tions Commission (FCC). Other political costs, by category of
expenditure, are not so easily ascertained. Since 1956, there has
been no congressional investigation of campaign funds—as there
had been in earlier presidential election years—which would
gather data and summarize findings. Accordingly, the only systematic attempt to obtain data from official fund reports was made
privately[2] and only for national-level committees that filed reports
(as legally required) with the Clerk of the House of Representatives. These reports furnish basic data on costs of the presidential
campaigns. But they fail to reflect expenses incurred at the state
and local levels on behalf of the national party tickets—and they
lack much more, as will be seen. Hence, a statement of national
costs from these sources alone gives an incomplete and possibly
distorted view. If the reader bears in mind this caveat, 1964 financial patterns can be described and conclusions drawn.

The 107 committees operating at the national level reported
spending $34.8 million in 1964 (see Table 1). This was more than

TABLE 1.

SUMMARY OF POLITICAL SPENDING AT THE NATIONAL LEVEL, 1964
(in Thousand of Dollars)

Committees[a]	Gross Reported Disburse-ments[b]	Known Debt	Total Cam-paign Costs	Transfers to Candi-dates and Com-mittees	Direct Expendi-tures[c]
18 Republican	$17,187	$ —	$17,187	$1,163	$16,026
32 Democratic	10,973	1,000	11,973	3,216	8,757
31 Labor	3,665	—	3,665	2,940	725
26 Miscellaneous	1,963	—	1,963	889	1,074
107 Total	$33,788	$1,000	$34,788	$8,208	$26,582

a The number of national-level committees increased from seventy in 1960,
but the same criteria were used in identifying them.

b Data derived from reports filed with the Clerk of the United States House
of Representatives.

c Details on all categories of expenditures were not obtained from the campaign-fund reports. Hence direct expenditures were determined by subtracting
from total campaign costs all transfers of funds out. Though the totals in
this column may be subject to error, enough evidence is available to indicate
that the totals represent fair approximations.

TABLE 2.

RATIOS OF NATIONAL-LEVEL DIRECT SPENDING PLUS DEFICITS,
1956, 1960, AND 1964 (in Per Cents)

	1956[a]	1960	1964
Total on behalf of Democrats:	41	51	37
Democratic committees:	37	47	34
Labor committees:	4	4	3
Republican committees:	59	49	63
	100	100	100

[a] Derived from Alexander Heard, *The Costs of Democracy* (Chapel Hill: University of North Carolina Press, 1960), p. 20, and *1956 General Election Campaigns*, Report to the Senate Committee on Rules and Administration, 85th Cong., 1st Sess. (Washington, D.C.: Government Printing Office, 1957), Exhibit 4, p. 41. 1956 deficits are listed by the Gore Committee as bills unpaid as of November 30, 1956. Heard's figures for Republicans and Democrats are for the full calendar year 1956, but labor figures are for January 1–November 30, 1956.

twice the $17.2 million spent in 1956, and represents a 39 per cent increase from the $25 million spent in 1960.[3]

Major-party national-campaign costs in 1964, other than spending by labor and miscellaneous nonparty committees, were $29.2 million, or 41 cents per voter spent by both parties in competition for the 70,642,496 votes cast in the presidential election. A study comparing costs in the presidential years 1912–28 showed that, though direct expenditures of the two national committees rose from $2.9 million, in 1912, to $7.2 million, in 1928, the cost per presidential vote cast remained between 19 and 20 cents—at the same time that the price level rose 40 per cent. Costs in 1952 were 18 cents per presidential vote cast, and, in 1956, 19 cents.[4]

The fairest index reflecting fully the dollar value of presidential-campaign activities at the national level in past years has been direct expenditures plus deficits in the "Direct Expenditures" column; accordingly, in dollar terms, the comparison is between Republican spending of $16 million and Democratic spending of $8.8 million plus labor spending of $726,000. Using this index for 1964, as shown in Table 2, one finds that Republican expenditures at the national level exceeded those of the Democrats and labor combined, reinstating an advantage the Republicans held

in 1952 and 1956, but not in 1960, when Democratic and labor
spending totaled more than Republican spending.[5] For 1964, the
ratio of Republican advantage over the combination was 63:37,
which was a higher ratio than in 1956. Given their greater gross
receipts and expenditures in 1964, the ratio favors the Republican; however, significant Democratic spending by state groups
and congressional candidates utilizing national-level Democratic
money is not included in this computation. In effect, the index
eliminates duplication for both parties by subtracting from total
costs the expenditures that go to other committees or candidates
for spending. This requires subtracting $3.2 million of Demo-
cratic transfers—an unusually large amount. In 1964, labor also
transferred more than twice as much money as in 1960, while
somewhat decreasing direct spending. Since the Republicans transferred only $1.2 million—about the same amount as in 1960—
their direct national spending for campaign activities in 1964
was proportionately greater.

Despite the seeming Republican advantage in spending, the
Democrats never, in recent times, conducted such a well-financed
national campaign as in 1964. The financial base of Democratic
support, in the main, comprised a wide geographical and occupational diversity of large contributors. About 69 per cent of the
dollar value of total individual contributions came in sums of
$500 and over, most of it raised through the President's Club and
fund-raising dinners. In fact, of the 6,700 individual contributions of $500 or more on record with the Clerk of the House of
Representatives, 3,400 were Democratic contributions.[6] Compared
with the Republican financial base, which included unparalleled
numbers of small contributors, the Democratic base was narrow
indeed; it could be considered broad only in relation to times
past, when only a handful of very large contributors financed
campaigns, and to the Republicans' smaller number of large contributors.

At the national level, the Republicans continued to receive
financial support from many of their usual sources, but they
broadened their appeal dramatically through massive direct-mail
drives and effective television appeals for funds. Neither method
had theretofore been very successful in national fund raising, but,

in 1964, the Republicans received an unprecedented 32 per cent of their total income from direct mail and almost 14 per cent from television appeals.[7] The Republicans raised $18.5 million, over $7 million more than in 1960. Most of these additional funds came from an unusual outpouring of 650,000 contributions of less than $100 each, raised by direct-mail and television appeals. Only 28 per cent of the dollar value of Republican individual contributions came in sums of $500 or more.

Compared with 1952, the Goldwater financial support was notable. In that earlier year, the Eisenhower candidacy drew wide electoral support in the general election; yet the Republican National Committee claimed only 17,500 contributors and the national Citizens for Eisenhower-Nixon claimed about 20,000 contributors.[8] It was remarkable, indeed, that so much was raised from so many, in view of the widespread belief that Senator Goldwater would not win the election—a condition that usually hinders fund-raising appeals. In addition, some normally Republican sources of funds were closed to Goldwater, and some actually aided the Johnson campaign. The Republicans were the "out" party, usually considered a disadvantage, especially in seeking contributions from special interests. And the campaigns for the presidential nomination had been expensive, draining off more than $10 million that might otherwise have gone to the party during the campaign.[9]

To some extent, the large number of contributors to national-level Republican committees must have reflected the political polarization within the Republican Party in 1964. Goldwater supporters tended to give directly to Washington to avoid normal Republican state finance channels whereby funds would be shared with moderate candidates for other offices. Nor were moderate Republicans anxious to have portions of their funds shared with the national campaign; hence, individual moderate candidates, and not state party committees, benefited from these contributions.

During the period of Democratic ascendancy from 1932 to 1952, the Republicans had consistently spent more money in presidential campaigns than the Democrats. During the Eisenhower campaigns, this pattern continued. In 1960, though the GOP incurred a small deficit, the Democrats went deeply into debt to equal Republican spending. In 1964, the Republicans again surged ahead, ending with a surplus. Though they raised more than ever before, the Democrats, in 1964, went into debt.

Republican experience in 1964 was marked by the breakdown of the unified fund-raising structure that had been developed in recent decades. On the one hand, there was little change from 1960 to 1964 in the number of large contributors, though, in geographic terms, there were indications in 1964 of increased financial support in the South and Southwest, and decreased support in parts of the North and East. On the other hand, an unparalleled number of small contributors responded to massive direct-mail drives and television appeals. The response was due, in part, to the special appeal of Senator Goldwater, but it was also attributable to the large investment of time, energy, and money that the Republicans, since 1962, have consciously devoted to building a national sustaining fund. The 1964 Republican surplus gave the Goldwater camp its one clear and unqualified achievement—financial soundness. In a sense, the Republicans were caught by their own platform, though, fortunately, they did not need to indulge in deficit party financing while attacking deficit governmental financing.

Experience in recent years, particularly in 1964, has served to put in perspective some widely held notions about aspects of political finance:

1. That large amounts in small sums could not be raised by direct mail. (This was proved erroneous by the immediate and developing success of the Republican National Committee's sustaining fund from 1962 on.)
2. That large amounts in small sums could not be raised through televised appeals for funds. (The Goldwater campaign had extraordinary success with such appeals.)
3. That money is difficult to raise for a candidate with unfavorable poll results. (The Goldwater campaign experienced unsuccessful polls and successful fund raising.)
4. That the "out" party is disadvantaged in fund raising. (Republicans at the national level reported raising more than the Democrats reported.)

5. That the drain of funds into expensive prenomination contests cuts into fund-raising ability in the general election campaign. (The Republicans in 1964 spend much more than the Democrats did in 1960 in the prenomination period, yet raised more than could be effectively spent in the general election in 1964 and ended with a surplus.)

6. That Democrats attract fewer large contributors and fewer big businessmen than Republicans. (There was a dramatic switch in traditional sources of party income in 1964.)

While some of these propositions may have resulted mainly from a unique Goldwater phenomenon, or from the Johnson-Goldwater confrontation, the fact that they happened at all confirms that, given certain conditions, such results are possible; as more is learned about the conditions under which such exceptions occur, presumably even exceptions to a rule could prove susceptible to imitation.

The Preconvention Costs: The Candidates

There is no federal requirement that prenomination expenses be disclosed, and laws in states holding presidential primaries are not uniform; hence, data for this study had to be obtained from candidates and other participants voluntarily. Though there are gaps in the information, some data for the campaigns of all major Republican candidates were obtained from responsible participants in each campaign. The following sections summarize known facts about preconvention-campaign funds and evaluate the impact of financial matters on events leading up to the conventions.

Goldwater. The first formal conference in what became the movement to nominate Barry Goldwater was held on October 8, 1961, in Chicago. Two months later, a $60,000 budget for 1962 was approved and, according to one report, $50,000 were raised.[10] Other meetings held in 1962 raised money, but also incurred expenses. From December, 1962 until January, 1964, the National Draft Goldwater Committee raised $751,000; this, added to the 1961–62 amounts raised and spent, probably represents the largest fund ever raised publicly prior to a candidate's announcement.

From Senator Goldwater's announcement of candidacy in January, until his nomination in July, an additional $2.75 million were raised, largely by the National Goldwater for President Committee, which supplanted the Draft Goldwater Committee. To this combined total of $3.5 million or more must be added $2 million raised separately, primarily in California for the California primary. This calculation, derived from most reliable sources, indicates that at least $5.5 million were raised and spent for the nomination of Senator Goldwater—and the calculation does not include amounts raised by numerous state and local groups throughout the country.

From January to July, 1964, the Goldwater national campaign raised more money ($4.75 million) than did the national Republican Party committees ($3 million), which were suffering from uncertainty as to who would be the presidential nominee. It is estimated that funds for the Goldwater candidacy for nomination came from more than 300,000 contributors. However, donations did not come steadily, and funds were scarce at times.[11] The large numbers of contributors were part of a mass volunteer effort that was, perhaps, the greatest asset Goldwater had.[12]

Unlike those running most presidential prenomination campaigns in both major parties, the national Goldwater command did not provide large sums for state primary campaigns; it did spend substantial amounts for publicity and organizational expenses in states selecting national delegates at state conventions. As will be seen, $50,000 were sent to California to aid the primary campaign there; the national-level Goldwater committees transferred $88,210 to New Hampshire; $60,900 were sent to Oregon. Small amounts were sent to other states (Texas received $4,500). Most additional funds for the Goldwater effort in these and other primaries were raised locally, though some wealthy Goldwater financial supporters from out of state are known to have contributed to his committees in both New Hampshire and Oregon. Thus, only about 7 per cent ($200,000) of funds spent by the Goldwater for President Committee from January to July, 1964, went to finance primary contests. (In 1960, about 52 per cent—$470,000—of total funds were transferred by the Kennedy national command to state primary campaigns.[13]) More than $260,000 were spent on travel for the candidate and his staff. From June, 1963, until the Convention, a little more than a year later, $152,000 were spent for public opinion poll surveys conducted by one opinion-research organization, and paid for by committees and individuals supporting Goldwater's candidacy.

The story of the Goldwater campaign in California requires separate telling. There, Goldwater supporters raised $2 million for the primary; of this, the state-wide Goldwater organization raised over $1 million, while another $1 million were raised at the local (county) level. But this was not all. From January 3, when Senator Goldwater announced his candidacy, until March 10, when the New Hampshire primary was held, Californians contributed, by one count, at least $150,000 to the national Goldwater campaign. After Goldwater's defeat in New Hampshire, and his decision not to contest personally the Oregon primary, the focus turned to California. National headquarters agreed not to solicit further in California, except for mass direct-mail drives, while California supporters—led by Henry Salvatori—agreed to assume responsibility for financing the primary campaign. National headquarters transferred only about $50,000 to California, though some national operatives campaigned in the state while drawing salaries and expenses from Washington headquarters. When Goldwater and his campaign organizers were in the state, California committees paid expenses; national headquarters paid for Goldwater travel into and out of the state.

Rockefeller. Spending on behalf of Governor Nelson A. Rockefeller of New York was in evidence long before he announced he was a candidate. A privately owned five-story brownstone building in New York City housed a sizable staff, which grew as announcement time approached and the campaign progressed, spreading into other quarters in New York and in Washington[14] as well. Rockefeller's campaign staff included high-salaried specialists in publicity, radio, television, research, women's groups, special committees, finance, and regional coordination; it also included state directors, and eventually there was some organization in all but seven states. Altogether, there were about 100 paid workers. Public opinion polling firms were employed extensively.

A California public relations firm, Spencer-Roberts and Associates, was hired to handle the primary campaign in that state. A family airplane was available to the candidate, and his Washington, D.C., home was used to dine congressmen and influential party members.

Reported estimates of Rockefeller expenditures ranged from $3.5 million to $5 million or more. According to close associates, admitted out-of-pocket Rockefeller expenditures were as follows: New Hampshire, $97,863; New England (having a bearing on the New Hampshire primary), $100,000; West Virginia, $80,000; Oregon, $477,135; California, somewhat over $2 million; the New York office (which had a bearing on all primary campaigns), $100,000; and the Republican Convention, $70,000. The total came to $2,929,135. These admitted expenditures of almost $3 million were exclusive of travel costs for the candidate and his party, the cost of personal staff—including much of the field staff throughout the country—and the cost of using the family airplane. With little overlap, such costs were additional and were paid for personally by the candidate and his family.[15] Rockefeller sources admitted that, of all financial resources bearing on the campaign, less than $100,000 were raised outside of the family for the Governor's candidacy.[16]

Scranton. The campaign of Governor William W. Scranton of Pennsylvania, which cost $827,000, consisted of activity for only about one month before the Republican Convention, plus some preannouncement maneuvering. Nine major committees, dispersed geographically from Connecticut to California, accounted for the receipts, which were received from individuals in all states except Arkansas and Mississippi. The national and state breakdown follows: National Scranton for President Committee, $431,284; Pennsylvania Scranton for President Committee, $216,164; Citizens for Scranton—Harrisburg, $52,009; Women for Scranton, $16,300; San Francisco Convention Committee for Scranton, $19,685; New York Committee for Scranton, $36,793; Greenwich Connecticut Committee for Scranton, $10,000; Connecticut Committee for Scranton, $16,300; Scranton Club, $28,500. The total amounted to $827,035.[17]

Much of the money came from Pennsylvania, where Frank C. P. McGlinn, a Philadelphia banker and long-time Republican fund raiser, and Thomas McCabe led the effort. The national finance chairman was Thomas S. Gates, Jr., formerly Secretary of Defense in the Eisenhower cabinet, who operated out of New York. Substantial sums were contributed by the Scranton family and by residents of Southern California, Connecticut, New Jersey, Indiana, and Michigan.[18] The suddenness of the Scranton candidacy left little time to raise sufficient funds for the short, concentrated effort, and commitments of considerable money had to be made quickly. Accordingly, money was borrowed, particularly for the network broadcasts. Funds were solicited during the broadcasts, and about $40,000 in small contributions were collected from one appeal. For several months after Goldwater's nomination, the Scranton campaign carried a deficit of $150,000; as new funds became available, bills were paid, and by early 1965, no debts remained.

Lodge. The campaign on behalf of Henry Cabot Lodge cost over $100,000.[19] Some active campaigners for Lodge such as Maxwell Rabb, a New York attorney, and the now famous team of Paul D. Grindle and David Goldberg, who organized the campaign in New Hampshire, received no salaries, and some paid their own expenses; one supporter, Irving Salomon, in the Far East on a business trip, paid his own expenses to Saigon to try to persuade Ambassador Lodge to return home from South Vietnam. The campaign was hobbled by the fact that Ambassador Lodge was not in the United States and would not return, which made communications with him difficult and costly.

Major amounts of funds for the Lodge campaign came from Boston and New York supporters, some of whom advanced money in the form of loans. Through fund-raising lunches and advances, money was raised in Massachusetts, New York, and New Hampshire for the New Hampshire primary. In New Hampshire, $32,000 were spent; deficits from that primary and from what national organization existed led to debts of $17,000 going into the Oregon primary. In Oregon, $54,300 were spent; of this, only $4,000 were raised in Oregon itself. For the over-all effort that started in December, 1963, a separate fund of about $10,000 was raised and utilized by a Washington, D.C., committee headed by public relations man Robert R. Mullen. The Lodge family apparently contributed some money later. By the end of the Oregon primary, the deficit was $9,600; by the end of 1964, this was reduced to about $4,000 in unsettled bills, since paid up.

Nixon. Another unannounced, absentee candidate was former Vice-President Richard M. Nixon. Available information indicates that more than $71,800 were spent on Nixon's behalf. Official reports from New Hampshire record $15,285 spent on his behalf, while $49,300 were recorded as raised and spent in Oregon. (Of the Oregon amount, $38,450 were contributed in sums of $500 or more by nineteen individual donors; a California group, the Friends of Nixon, contributed $10,000. J. Clifford Folger, a Washington, D.C., financier and experienced Republican fund raiser, was reported to have agreed to raise money for the Nixon campaign in Oregon,[20] and he and Mrs. Folger contributed a total of $5,000.) In Oregon, a telephone campaign was mounted in which 200,000 calls were made by two shifts of paid workers over a period of several weeks.[21] A campaign operative claimed that about $7,500 were spent for the Nebraska primary, in a three-day write-in campaign, with emphasis on mailings of 270,000 letters and radio spot announcements; newspaper reports indicate $20,000 were spent.[22] If more was spent on the Nixon candidacy, the amount had not been made public. There were repeated reports of difficulties in raising funds for Nixon in 1964.

Stassen. The quest of Harold Stassen for the Republican nomination for president cost over $70,000 and led him to primaries in New Hampshire ($44,833 for candidate and delegate candidates), Indiana ($10,000), and California ($15,000; here, a premium price was paid to a professional petition-circulation service in a late and unsuccessful attempt to get Stassen on the ballot). Personal contributions and expenses, particularly for travel, cost the candidate over $30,000; this figure includes trips to New Hampshire, Illinois, Indiana, and the San Francisco Convention.

Smith. An announcement by Senator Margaret Chase Smith, of Maine, that, while seeking the Republican presidential nomination in 1964, she would test whether one had to have a million dollars and an organization to go into a primary brought unsolicited contributions ranging from 50 cents to hundreds of dollars, many from sympathetic women; all were returned to the donors. Senator Smith's poor showing in the New Hampshire primary may have been due, in part, to her policy of not spending funds for purposes other than travel (which cost $250 in New Hampshire and $85 in Illinois—there, in contrast, she gathered 206,000 votes).

Admitted expenses of campaigns for candidates seeking the Republican presidential nomination broke down as follows: Goldwater, $5.5 million; Rockefeller, $3 million; Scranton, $827,000; Lodge, $100,000; Nixon, $71,000; Stassen, $70,000. The total came to $9.568 million. Goldwater and Rockefeller expenditures combined clearly exceeded those on behalf of Eisenhower and Taft in 1952—estimated at about $5 million combined.[23] In 1964, the Goldwater effort alone—for which figures are more complete than for that of Rockefeller—cost more than the combined Eisenhower and Taft preconvention campaigns of 1952, yet Goldwater was able to avoid costly campaigning in primaries in several major states such as Ohio, Pennsylvania, and Wisconsin. And the Goldwater and Rockefeller totals far exceeded expenses reported by the Kennedy prenomination campaign in 1960, which totaled $912,500.[24] Of course, the $4 million spent by Goldwater and Rockefeller in California account for much of the total.

Throughout the 1964 Republican campaigns, there were frequent charges of excessive spending. Some of the allegations concerning costs were extravagant, with Governor Rockefeller bearing the brunt of charges about high levels of spending, just as John Kennedy had in 1960. Throughout, the Rockefeller organization appeared ready to spend whatever seemed necessary. Since Rockefeller money came mainly from one source—the Rockefeller family—and Goldwater money came from many sources, obvious comparisons were drawn. During the period of gearing up in 1962, the expensive Rockefeller staff, even then at work in a large headquarters, was compared with the two-man Goldwater operation, then working out of a tiny, crowded office;[25] similarly, in 1963, it was noted that Goldwater traveled by himself on commercial airplanes while Rockefeller often traveled with a retinue of eight or ten.

The Preconvention Costs: The Primaries

The large amounts spent and the allegations of excessive spending point up the financial imperatives of serious contests for the presidential nomination; this was illustrated particularly well in three major primary states in 1964.

New Hampshire. New Hampshire holds the first primary, attracting early attention. The political consequences of the primary may be less important than the large sums spent indicate. If as much money per voter were spent in all the primary states, the totals would be astonishing. The New Hampshire primary of 1964 revealed much about the role of money. The two largest spenders, Goldwater and Rockefeller, came in second and third in the balloting, while the winner, Henry Cabot Lodge, did no campaigning whatsoever. Lodge won an amazing write-in victory, though his supporters spent less than a tenth of what his major opponents spent. Most of the money spent on behalf of Rockefeller and Goldwater came from outside the state and was sent in by or through the national headquarters of each candidate; some of the spending for each was charged to the national campaign in order to stay within New Hampshire's legal limits on amounts spent. Thus, campaign-fund reports, which, by official ruling, permitted pooling of expenses of candidate, committees, delegates, and alternate delegates up to a combined limit of $100,000, record that less was spent than the New Hampshire limit, while news reports indicate that substantially more was spent on behalf of each candidate.

Oregon. One slogan in Oregon went, "Don't let your vote be bought by Eastern money," which applied to Lodge as well as to Rockefeller. Governor Rockefeller responded that he "cared enough" to spend time and money enough to win—and he did spend about $490,000 to win in Oregon.

Rockefeller associates have admitted to expenditures in Oregon of just over $477,000. Governor Rockefeller was the only Republican candidate filing a personal-expenditure report in Oregon—showing almost $11,000 in personal expenses—which, if added to the $477,000 estimate, would bring Rockefeller expenses in Oregon to almost $490,000.

Although Goldwater did not campaign actively in Oregon, about $109,000 were reported spent on his behalf. The Goldwater for President Committee spent $88,500, of which $60,900 were transferred from the national parent committee and are included in the national Goldwater totals; the Oregon Draft Goldwater Committee reported spending $10,600; fourteen county-level and miscellaneous committees and individuals in Oregon reported spending a total of $9,965. There were, additionally, some individual out-of-state contributors who had been active in Goldwater financing—members of the Milliken and Kohler families, F. Gano Chance, Albert C. Wedemeyer, and others.

Even with such large expenditures, Rockefeller's victory was surprising. Lodge came in second, though the campaign on his behalf spent only $54,300—about 10 per cent of what Rockefeller had spent. Goldwater came in third without campaigning, and Nixon, for whom about $49,000 were spent, ran a close fourth. Senator Smith and Governor Scranton, who did not campaign and in whose behalf only small amounts were spent, trailed far behind.

California. The California primary was a battle royal, with both camps pitched for a last stand; at least $4 million were spent in "go-for-broke" efforts. Rockefeller and Lodge forces overtly—and perhaps other Republican opposition to Goldwater covertly—joined in the effort to stop Goldwater. Without a California victory, Goldwater's nomination was by no means certain. If Rockefeller had won the primary there, he probably still would not have received the nomination; yet, given control of the two largest delegations—New York and California—plus the organizational and financial assets he commanded, the New York Governor could have become a major force at San Francisco. Thus, the Republican nomination could well have gone to someone else had Rockefeller won in California, despite Goldwater's strong delegate support around the country.

With the exception of California, Goldwater supporters gained him the nomination by seizing state delegations, not by winning primaries. Although no mean accomplishment for the Goldwater enthusiasts, it is perhaps more significant as an indication of the weakness and vulnerability of many state party organizations. The organizational route Goldwater supporters followed is thought to be cheaper than the primary (media) route; yet the Goldwater costs were so high one must conclude that, in modern campaigning, there is no cheap route to the nomination.

The impressive Goldwater financial support—in California and elsewhere—though widespread in terms of past financial support for candidates of either party, may, nevertheless, have been limited to a relatively small portion of the population. The moderates may have given Rockefeller, Scranton, and Lodge less active financial support in part because as moderates they were, perhaps, less passionately concerned about the consequences of Democratic rule. Foreseeing an inevitable Johnson victory in November, some Republicans saw little reason to contribute money. As Lipset has said, "The Goldwater supporters gave their effort a degree of commitment which far outweighed the activities of their less fervently involved opponents."[26] Clearly, Goldwater supporters were able to occupy the field left open by the moderates.

Throughout 1964, the Rockefeller candidacy posed a problem for Republican moderates who desired to field a candidate against Goldwater. The consensus was that Rockefeller could not win the nomination, but many were willing to let him spend his money in opposition to Goldwater. Substantial sums of money would have had to be raised for any other moderate. Once Rockefeller announced, there was reason not to divide the field but to let him receive all of the moderate support. Later, coalitions were made; overt Lodge and Stassen support went to Rockefeller in the

California primary, after which Rockefeller and Lodge support went behind Scranton when he announced.

The Election Campaign

The finances of various national-level committees affiliated with the Republican Party are outlined in Table 3.

TABLE 3.

RECEIPTS AND EXPENDITURES—REPUBLICAN NATIONAL CAMPAIGN COMMITTEE, JANUARY 1–DECEMBER 31, 1964 (in Thousands of Dollars)

Committee	Gross Reported Receipts	Ad- justed Receiptsa	Gross Reported Disburse- ments	Total Trans- fers Out	Direct Expendi- turesb
National	$ 2,949	$ 2,949	$ 2,640	—	$ 2,640
National Finance Corporations	1,947	1,947	1,928	113	1,814
National Congressional	1,686	1,269	1,633	544	1,089
Congressional Boosters	190	190	141	141	—
Senatorial Campaign	465	430	480	258	223
Subtotal	7,237	$ 6,785	$ 6,822	$1,056	$ 5,766
Citizens for Goldwater-Miller	$ 2,957	$ 2,957	$ 2,648	$ 20	$ 2,627
Republican Campaign	2,057	2,052	2,048	6	2,042
Republican Television	2,790	2,690	2,697	8	2,690
National TV	2,516	2,516	2,009	5	2,004
5 miscellaneous campaignsc	784	761	759	24	737
Subtotal	$11,104	$10,976	$10,161	$ 63	$10,100
4 miscellaneous nonpartyd	$ 171	$ 171	$ 204	$ 44	$ 160
Totale	$18,512	$17,932	$17,187	$1,163	$16,026

a Adjusted for lateral transfers from national-level Republican, labor, and miscellaneous committee groupings included in the table.

b Direct expenditures were determined by subtracting all transfers of funds from gross disbursements.

c Brothers for Goldwater, Citizens' Campaign Committee for Goldwater-Miller, National Federation of Republican Women, Solid South Speaks for Goldwater Committee, Women Voters for Goldwater-Miller.

d Committee for the Election of Republican Candidates, Committee To Support Moderate Republicans, Committee for Forward-looking Republicans, Republican Citizens Committee of the United States.

e Minor discrepancies between items and totals are due to rounding.

The campaign was highly centralized, with most auxiliary committees well integrated with party committees. Most national campaign activity and financial operations centered in party headquarters. Both Goldwater and Miller were party men who valued party control highly. Both had been national-party committee leaders. Upon nomination, they announced their campaign would be operated centrally through the National Committee. Changes in staff were made rapidly, encompassing the Finance Division as well. One major exception to central control was the National TV for Goldwater-Miller Committee, located in Los Angeles, which operated with considerable independence of other party and Washington-based allied committees (see Chapter 1). Of course, the Republican nonparty committees operated by moderates were not part of the presidential campaign activity; these focused on assisting moderate Republicans, mostly candidates for Congress. In 1960, Republicans operated five national-level committees spending more than $500,000; in 1964, the number increased to seven.

The 1964 national Republican campaign operation attained a maximum of more than 600 employees. The vice-presidential campaign staff was more than twice the 1960 size. Republicans occupied space on each of seven floors of the building that permanently houses the National Committee, and other space in Washington was also rented. At a peak in the campaign, the Republican payroll reached $37,500 a week, compared with $23,500 for the Democrats.

Political spending can be conceived of as a function of availability of funds or of willingness to go into debt, and the financial realities of 1964 illustrate the relationships between financing and campaigning. The Republican National Committee entered 1964 with a deficit of $400,000. On July 31, when the Goldwater forces took over, there was still a deficit of $217,000; too little money had been contributed to the party just before the choice of a candidate. Yet, the general election campaign ended with a surplus.

In mid-September, a report—never confirmed, and later termed inaccurate—indicated that the Republican campaign might incur a deficit as large as $2 million.[27] In October, however, money started coming in faster, and, accordingly, spending for media was increased. For example, the Republicans had budgeted over $400,000 per week for spot television announcements; this was increased to $500,000 in each of the last four weeks before the election. These spots had to be paid for weeks in advance. Advance payments in September and early October were, in part, responsible for the Republican cry of lack of money and their fear of a deficit. Goldwater managers admitted spending over $500,000 more for media than was budgeted.

At the same time, the polls continued to be discouraging, and one report indicates that, ten days before the election, Goldwater knew he was beaten and took steps to trim costs.[28] Plans already being implemented for a telethon on election eve to cost $400,000 were scrapped, though some thought it was because Goldwater was not well suited to this format. Other reports claimed that certain nation-wide programs that would have featured the candidate were eliminated in favor of regional broadcasts in areas where it was thought Goldwater had the best chance of winning votes. On the Saturday before the election, Republicans broadcast a one-hour regional program on ninety stations in fourteen southern states, at a cost of $72,000, somewhat less than the cost of a nation-wide network broadcast. It was felt that broadcasts in the North would not help Goldwater, whereas those pinpointed in the South and in portions of the Midwest and Southwest might.

With the exception of media costs, Republican managers adhered as closely as possible to budget estimates, which had been tightly drawn.[29] The ethnic campaign unit was only one of several that were cut back when their spending exceeded budget estimates. There is contrary evidence of both cutbacks and increases, and, given the exigencies of a presidential campaign, both could be true. A Republican survey indicates that $2.8 million were received by national-level committees in the last six days of the campaign. In the final three days, income totaled $1.1 million. The combination of late money and some expenditure reductions, plus inability to spend so much so late even if desired, left a surplus at the end of the campaign.

After the election, a full comptroller's audit of Republican committee books was made by a major accounting firm. On learning of a surplus, Republican moderates had called for the audit, and Republicans claim this was the first completely verified national audit of most of a party's campaign funds for a single election. Republican expenditures are shown by expense category in Table 4, which presents the financial anatomy of a national campaign in detail rarely available to students of political finance. This breakdown includes expenses for the whole year for all committees, but, with the exception of the figures for the Republican National Committee, it consists almost exclusively of presidential-campaign expenses.

Campaign urgencies bring political expenditures for a variety of purposes, and several outstanding categories of expenses in 1964 are highlighted in the pages that follow.

Campaign Publicity. The American people were exposed to many millions of dollars' worth of advertising and publicity on behalf of the major-party candidates for president and vice-president. Both parties used advertising agencies to implement some, but not all, of their publicity budgets; the major advertising-agency functions related to political broadcasting, but agencies also prepared other types of materials. In 1964, the Democrats employed Doyle Dane Bernbach, Inc., and the Republicans hired Erwin Wasey, Ruthrauff & Ryan, Inc., a subsidiary of the Interpublic Group of Companies, Inc.

The Republican committees at the national level spent over $7.3 million on items identifiable as publicity. These included the following: television and radio advertisements (time and production costs), $5.6 million; printing and reproduction, $555,000; printed advertising, $530,000; promotion and campaign supplies, $380,000; motion pictures, $215,000; and outdoor displays, $100,000.

Political Broadcasting.[30] The "great debates" in 1960 were made possible by a temporary suspension of Section 315 of the Federal Communications Act. The President's Commission on Campaign Costs recommended suspension of this "equal-time" provision again in 1964.[31] Legislation to accomplish this passed

TABLE 4.

REPUBLICAN PRESIDENTIAL CAMPAIGN:
COST BY EXPENSE CLASSIFICATION, 1964[a]

Salaries	$1,586,672
Taxes	53,365
Rent	179,291
Insurance & Bonds	8,621
Advertising—Print	529,868
Outdoor Productions	102,525
Building Maintenance	74,753
Contributions To Committees	43,518
Employee Retirement	77,723
Executive Expenses	4,776
Furniture & Equipment—Purchase	60,200
Furniture & Equipment—Rental & Maintenance	76,596
Meetings & Conferences	62,657
Miscellaneous Expenses	73,437
Motion Pictures	125,889
National Committee Fellowship	8,708
News Services	37,446
Typographic Services	90,120
Postage & Express	955,827
Printing & Reproduction	555,252
Professional Services	357,210
Promotional & Campaign Supplies	380,757
TV & Radio—Production	1,066,484
TV & Radio—Time	4,542,151
Clerical Services	75,893
Surveys & Polls	165,416
Subscriptions & Publications	7,837
Supplies	333,250
Telephone	389,113
Telegraph	86,489
Travel Expenses	909,632
Air/Rail Charter	807,997
Mailing Lists	274,216
Mailing Services	141,816
Data Processing	155,349
Automobile Maintenance	1,505
Security	13,965
TOTAL	**$14,416,324**

[a] As of November 30, 1964, this table includes expenditures of the Republican National Committee, Republican National Finance Operations Committee, Republican Campaign Committee, Citizens for Goldwater-Miller, Citizens Campaign Committee for Goldwater-Miller, T.V. for Goldwater-Miller, National T.V. for Goldwater-Miller Committee, and Women Voters for Goldwater-Miller.

both houses of Congress in different forms, but a conference report was not adopted, and the suspension was never affected.
After some vacillation, it appeared to be high Democratic policy
to avoid suspension, probably for two reasons—to avoid last-
minute pressure on President Johnson to debate with Senator
Goldwater, and to deny the Republican candidate sustaining
time, thereby forcing him to pay for whatever broadcast time he
desired. (The Democrats, too, would have to pay for time, but, as
their candidate was the incumbent and, hence, able to secure
media coverage in his role as president as well as candidate, the
effect would be less severe.) The broadcasting industry has consistently linked suspension of Section 315 for the presidential
campaigns with the notion of debates between presidential candidates. President Johnson, apparently, did not want to debate with
Senator Goldwater; had suspension been voted, he would have
risked increased pressure to debate. As it was, Senator Goldwater
challenged the President to debate, offered to pay for the broadcast time, and also offered to film debates in advance in order to
obviate the possibility of any national-security leaks that might
occur in the heat of a debate.

Without suspension of the equal-time law, much less free time
was provided to the presidential and vice-presidential candidates
in 1964 than in 1960. Accordingly, most broadcast time had to be
bought, and it was much more costly than four years before.[32]
Total network and station charges (radio and television combined) for political broadcasting at all levels in primary and
general election periods in 1964 were $34.6 million. Of this total,
$12.8 million, or about 37 per cent, can be isolated as having been
spent in the presidential and vice-presidential contests. This
amounted to about 25 per cent of total radio dollars and 42 per
cent of total television dollars spent for all political broadcasts
in the nation. The Republicans out-spent the Democrats in the
presidential campaigns as follows: Republicans, $7.5 million;
Democrats, $5.1 million; other, $125,000. Of the Republican total,
more than $1.2 million was spent for broadcasts related to Re-
publican nomination campaigns for president.

Private Public Opinion Polls. A reliable estimate put 1964 political polling costs for all candidates and parties on all political

levels at $5 million.[33] Public opinion polling was relied upon heavily in 1960 by Senator Kennedy; Senator Goldwater's campaigners also used polls, spending more in 1964 than was spent on behalf of Richard Nixon in 1960. The large number of contenders for the Republican nomination put polling in the prenomination period at a higher cost than in Democratic prenomination contests in 1960. Various committees and supporters of Goldwater spent $152,000 for surveys by one polling organization alone, from June, 1963 to July, 1964.

In the general election period, the Republican National Committee spent $165,400 for surveys and polls, of which $136,000 were paid to one opinion-polling organization alone. Surveys for the Republican national campaign included "a panel study with four waves of interviewing among a national cross-section of voters, some trial-heat surveys in selected states, a measurement of the Goldwater campaign trip through Southern cities, a study of the Goldwater whistle-stop campaign in the Midwest, a measurement of the television campaign commercials of both the Democrats and the Republicans, and a number of special analyses."[34]

Sources of Funds

According to the Survey Research Center (SRC), 10 per cent of a national sample of adult Americans said they had contributed to some party or candidate in 1964; about another 1 per cent knew another member of their household had contributed. Paralleling the SRC finding of 11 per cent, a Gallup Poll indicates 12 per cent who either contributed or had a member of the family who did. Both surveys found about 6 per cent giving to the Republicans and 4 per cent to the Democrats, with less than 1 per cent contributing to both. While these figures are subject to possible sampling error, when matched with earlier samplings they tend to confirm that there has been a relatively stable level of contributing—roughly 10 per cent of adult Americans have contributed to a party or candidate in presidential election years since 1956. Translating these percentages into individuals who gave money at some level to some campaign, there were 3 million individual givers in 1952, 8 million in 1956, 10 million in 1960, and 12 million in 1964. The large increase in the number of national-level Republican contributors in 1964 is not readily evident in the findings. Of course, fewer than 1 million Republican contributors, while impressive in aggregate numbers, represent less than 1 per cent of the national adult population and, hence, may not readily appear in survey results. And there may have been some falloff in the numbers of Republican contributors at state and local levels, offsetting to some extent the large increase in Republican contributors at the national level. The SRC figures did show that 8 per cent of those polled were solicited by Republicans, while only 4 per cent were solicited by Democrats, and 3 per cent by both parties.

However, further analysis comparing 1964 and 1960 respondents in the SRC surveys shows that, in both election years, 19 per cent of Republican identifiers gave. Thus, despite the Republicans' minority status in vote getting, their superiority in contributing is clear: In aggregate numbers at all levels, there are about 5.7 million Republican contributors, compared with about 4.2 million Democratic contributors.

The number of national-level Republican contributions in 1964 can be stated with confidence, although there is some duplication because some contributors gave to more than one program. In sums under $100, direct-mail returns ran to 410,000, though about 30,000 of these were returned without a contribution. Television appeals by Ronald Reagan and Raymond Massey brought in 134,000 contributions of under $100 each; Dean Burch's appeals on television brought about 100,000 contributions of under $100 each; and a separate Citizens for Goldwater accounting shows 37,000 more small contributions. In all, approximately 651,000 contributions in sums under $100 were received, while, from all programs, there were 10,000 individual contributions of between $100 and $999, and 1,500 of $1,000 or more.

Republican successes in direct-mail solicitation were not without cost. During 1964, about $5.8 million were raised for party and citizens' programs through the mailing of over 15 million pieces of fund-raising literature. This represented an investment, in postage, printing, the purchase of mailing lists, and secretarial services, of more than $1 million. Most of the mailings were made early and sent via third-class mail, thus reducing the costs to about $65 per thousand pieces.

The Republican financial achievements of 1964 resulted partly from Goldwater's attraction and partly from a serious Republican effort, starting in 1962, to build a national sustaining fund made up from $10-a-year memberships. Introduced in March, 1962, the National Committee sustaining fund attracted 70,000 contributors in that year. In 1963, the gross receipts of the sustaining fund were $1.1 million, from more than 100,000 contributors. In the first six months of 1964, prior to the Republican Convention, $1 million were raised through this means. During some months, sustaining-fund income provided the bulk of money available to keep the national party operating. Amounts of contributions to the sustaining fund and other direct-mail campaigns consistently averaged more than $10.

After the Goldwater nomination, another $1.3 million were raised through sustaining-fund mailings, and the average amount of a contribution increased. Altogether, in 1964, $2.369 million were raised through the sustaining fund, approaching the $2.5 million goal that had been projected for the year regardless of who the presidential nominee was to be.

Table 5 shows the results of Republican direct-mail campaigns in 1964.

TABLE 5.

REPUBLICAN DIRECT-MAIL CAMPAIGNS, 1964

	Mailed	Returns	Dollars	Average Contributionb
Preconvention				
Sustaining fund	3,060,364	99,289	$1,029,075	$10.36
Postconvention				
Sustaining fund	2,145,000	89,288	1,340,265	16.68
Campaign				
Committee	3,768,000	83,160	1,598,800	21.36
TV Committee	323,138	30,485	561,419	20.46
Citizens Committee	5,980,840	108,082	1,244,156	12.79
Subtotal		311,015a		
Total	15,277,342	410,304	$5,773,715	

a Less 10 per cent returned with no contribution.

b Amounts in this column in the postconvention period were computed after corrections were made for the 10 per cent returns, noted in footnote above, not containing a contribution; a 10 per cent average correction was made for each figure in the "Returns" column in the postconvention period.

Considerable duplication was inevitable in such massive mailings, and many people—including many Democrats—received several appeals. But, the various mailings seeded the territory, so to speak, and built up momentum for contributions, many of which came in toward the end of the campaign. Television appeals may have helped to trigger mail responses by reinforcing written appeals for funds. Return envelopes included in mailings made it easy to contribute, and the combination of written and auditory appeals may have been irresistible for numerous Goldwater sympathizers. Nevertheless, the percentage response in 1964 was not as high as it had been for the Republican sustaining fund in 1962 or 1963, because the mailings were greater and the lists less selective.

The sustaining-fund and Goldwater mailing lists were bought from many sources including credit-card membership lists and lists sold by brokerage firms and by health and welfare organizations. The mailings even included the list of buyers of Kozak Auto Drywash cloths, which, surprisingly, proved very productive.

An important source of money was found in the accumulated lists of persons who had made a declaration of support of the National Draft Goldwater movement. Prenomination mailings asked for a contribution at the time of the mailing, another after Senator Goldwater publicly announced his candidacy for the nomination, and still another when he received the nomination. The pledge cards were milked for all they were worth. Unlike most presidential candidates, Senator Goldwater attracted many contributors—over 300,000—in the prenomination period, which served as a nucleus for support in the election campaign. Major sources of Republican funds in 1964 are set forth in Table 6.

To help generate last-minute income, a few mailings were made in late October and sent by first-class mail. In addition, about 80,000 telegrams were sent in the last ten days before the election to people who had already contributed, asking that they give more. Republican receipts throughout the year are shown in Table 7. The peak was reached in October; the funds received in November were concentrated in the first few days of the month (though some of the November contributions were actually the result of weekend mail from the last few days of October). The

TABLE 6.

REPUBLICAN NATIONAL AND CAMPAIGN INCOME BY
SOURCE OF FUNDS, 1964

Source	Amount[b]	Per Cent of Total Income
Direct mail	$ 5,815,100	32.4
State payments	2,710,100	15.1
Dinners	2,476,800	13.8
Associates[a]	2,171,700	12.1
Dean Burch TV appeal	1,274,300	7.1
TV Los Angeles	1,184,600	6.6
Special events	1,058,900	5.9
Miscellaneous	807,700	4.5
Raised directly by congressional committee	448,700	2.5
Total	$17,948,000	100.0

[a] Consisted of 1,500 contributors of $1,000 or more.
[b] Rounded to nearest $100.

TABLE 7.

REPUBLICAN NATIONAL AND CAMPAIGN MONTHLY RECEIPTS, 1964

Month	Receipts[a]	Per Cent of Total Receipts
January	$ 270,900	1.5
February	386,400	2.1
March	399,600	2.3
April	334,900	1.9
May	234,800	1.3
June	442,900	2.5
July	633,600	3.5
August	1,369,300	7.6
September	4,380,900	24.4
October	7,253,800	40.4
November	2,234,600	12.4
December	6,200	0.1
Total	$17,947,900	100.0

[a] Rounded to nearest $100.

figures in December tell much about the after effects of a losing
election; the month-to-month fluctuations tell much about the
difficulty of rationally planning expenditures in an election year

and reveal something about the operation of a national party and campaign in a system geared to scheduled elections but not to permanent party campaigning.

Of the states, California was the largest single dollar source for all national-level Republican committees in 1964, providing $2.1 million credited to the state in a Republican tabulation of state quota performance. New York provided $1.5 million. Next in order were: Illinois, $1.3 million; Pennsylvania and Ohio, $1 million each; and Texas, $880,000. (New York and Pennsylvania provided excellent mail responses to the national drive for funds.)

There was much discussion of increased Republican financial support in the West and South and a drop in contributions from the East. One indicator is national credit given to states for contributions from all sources originating in those states. While quotas may have increased since 1960, and significant dollar amounts may not be involved in certain smaller states, Republicans found their national quota-performance record for 1964, compared with 1960, as follows:

- Eight southern states increased their percentage, but Florida, North Carolina, and Tennessee decreased theirs.
- California increased its quota performance from 78 per cent, in 1960, to 118 per cent, in 1964, but New York's decreased from 132 per cent to 62 per cent.
- Of some large states, Illinois, Ohio, Pennsylvania, Michigan, and Minnesota decreased, while Indiana, Oklahoma, and Wisconsin increased.
- Of ten New England and Middle Atlantic states, seven decreased, with only Maine, Vermont, and New Jersey showing small increases.
- Of eleven Pacific and mountain states, every one increased its percentage, though Oregon's and Washington's were up only slightly; increases in Arizona's, Idaho's, Montana's, and New Mexico's were sizable; Nevada's rose from 42 per cent of its 1960 quota to 262 per cent of its 1964 quota.
- For all states, the District of Columbia, Puerto Rico, and the Virgin Islands, the Republican quota-performance record in 1964 was 105 per cent, compared with 113 per cent in 1960.[35]

These quota results were sufficiently variable to warrant a search for other means of measuring shifts in sources of Republican funds according to region. Accordingly, a count was made of numbers of contributions (not contributors) and total amounts, in sums of $500 or more, contributed to clearly identifiable national-level presidential-campaign committees; the end in view was to compare Goldwater's financial strength, state by state, with that of Nixon in 1960. The regional results, drawn from the state analysis are shown in Table 8.[36]

TABLE 8.

NUMBERS AND AMOUNTS OF CAMPAIGN CONTRIBUTIONS
BY REGION, 1960 AND 1964

Region	1964		1960	
	Contri- butions	Amount	Contri- butions	Amount
New England	204	$ 288,500	171	$ 206,000
Middle Atlantic	552	763,500	1,024	1,304,300
Border	239	255,300	184	201,300
South	433	485,700	314	331,100
Midwest	721	844,700	592	714,600
Mountain	140	171,600	32	25,500
Pacific	257	307,700	254	273,000
Total	2,546	$3,117,000	2,571	$3,056,000

This compilation shows Goldwater ahead of Nixon in six of seven regions, and in thirty-five of fifty states. Nixon ran ahead of Goldwater in California, Nixon's home state, even though, throughout 1964, it was reported that Goldwater was receiving unusual financial support in southern California. In the District of Columbia, Nixon ran ahead. In Texas, Arizona, New Mexico, and neighboring states in the Southwest—where Goldwater's financial support also was reported to be heavy—he led Nixon in contributions of $500 or more, but not by substantially greater margins than in many midwestern states. Pennsylvania and Illinois were almost standoffs, while Nixon did much better in New York and Goldwater did much better in Ohio. In total numbers of contributions and in total amounts contributed, however, the two were almost even. Goldwater financial strength among large contributors was distributed more generally in all areas except the Middle Atlantic states. Even there, Goldwater attracted more funds in New Jersey and Pennsylvania; his big dropoff came in New York and Delaware. Nixon's decided advantage had been in New York, the District of Columbia, Michigan, and California. The conclusion must follow that, except for the last-named states, Goldwater's financial strength was not as concentrated as many supposed. The main shift in over-all Republican financial support occurred in sums under $500. The aggregate of these small sums was so great that much of this money had to come from sources untapped by Nixon in 1960 or Eisenhower in the 1950's.

While some Republican contributing was fragmented and polarized between national-level (Goldwater) and state-level (moderate) committees, the Republican national leadership in 1964 solicited the states more energetically and more deeply through direct-mail drives, phone blitzes, and other means than in other recent campaign years. Normally, contributors in metropolitan areas and certain states are asked to give to the United Republican Finance committees (URFC's), whence funds are distributed, approximately, on a basis of equal thirds to the national, state, and county levels. In 1964, the URFC's were, in some states, unable to appeal to some regular contributors. The New York URFC raised $600,000 less than in 1960. Goldwater supporters tended to give directly to the national campaign in Washington to avoid giving to the campaigns of moderates such as Kenneth Keating, Hugh Scott, Charles Percy, and Robert A. Taft, Jr. Moderate Republicans were equally averse to giving to the URFC's, portions of funds from which would be shared with the Goldwater campaign. In fact, the New York and Pennsylvania URFC's, and perhaps other moderate-oriented URFC's, sent practically no funds to Washington after Goldwater's nomination.

A reliable survey of Republican state committees showed deficits in eleven key states far in excess of normal indebtedness.[37] While, in fairness, it should be pointed out that some of the states went into the campaign in debt,[38] and some spent unusually large amounts on state-wide campaigns to offset the seemingly lost presidential contest, most managers attributed the problem of slight state finances to the Goldwater candidacy—both because it drew off funds directly to Washington and because it lacked appeal to some regular Republican contributors.

The third major source of funds—after direct mailings and state payments—was the fund-raising dinner. In 1964, Barry Goldwater attended, before his nomination, dinners at which at least $1.6 million were raised, and afterwards, others at which at least $2.6 million were raised.[39] Other Republican leaders whose personal appearances in 1964 benefited the GOP were: Dwight Eisenhower, $1.1 million; Richard Nixon, $1.6 million; and William Miller, at least $237,000. Republicans twice used closed-circuit television to hold dinners simultaneously in different cities during single nights, but the circuits were considerably smaller than in 1960, when the same device was used in support of Nixon. The combined total of simultaneous dinners in 1964 was about 40, compared with a total of 119 such dinners in 1960. Republicans claim to have received, in 1964, for the combined national-party campaign committees, about $2.5 million (or 14 per cent of their income) in net proceeds from dinners. In 1964, Republicans made one innovation—at some functions, they honored credit cards.

One additional source of funds needs to be broached, given the highly emotional impact it had on the 1964 campaign. This is the right wing.

The Right Wing. Democrats and others[40] were not reluctant to link right-wing support to the Goldwater candidacy or to point to examples of ultraconservatives capturing control of Republican Party organizations. Even before his nomination, Senator Goldwater was moved to declare it a myth that the right wing's "big money" was coming his way.[41] Clearly, some well-known financial supporters of organizations usually classified as right wing were active supporters of Senator Goldwater in both the pre- and postnomination periods. As an index, a list of individuals identified as important sources of right-wing funds[42] was matched against the file of party contributors who had given $500 or more. In 1964, of forty-three individual donors on the right-wing list, twenty-three had given to the Republican Party (a total of $114,893), and seventeen had given to miscellaneous organizations (a total of $24,928). The number of overlapping donors—that is, those who contributed both to the party and to miscellaneous organizations—was thirteen. There were no contributors to the

Democratic Party. With two exceptions (totaling $2,015), all "miscellaneous" contributions went to the right-wing organization Americans for Constitutional Action. But many of the Republican contributions went to national-level Republican Party committees early in 1964, *before* Goldwater was nominated, and several went to Republican congressional committees, including the Republican Congressional Boosters Club. Thus, though substantial funds did reach the Goldwater campaign from right-wing supporters, there is no conclusive evidence to uphold the contention that they were supporters of Goldwater rather than of the party, or that they had moved in, after his nomination, to dominate the party.

Similarly, it has been argued that the great outpouring of contributions to the Goldwater campaigns emanated, in large part, from a relatively small base of ultraconservative enthusiasts.[43] Clearly, some elements of the far right worked, for the first time, for the candidate of the Republican Party rather than for a third-party effort and their output had an important bearing on the funding of the major-party campaigns. For example, political pamphleteering reached new dimensions with the sale of large numbers of "hate books," so called because of their tendency toward a virulent one-sided presentation; various claims about the amounts of orders and sales were made for four books in particular,[44] and a careful survey indicates that at least 17 million copies of these four books alone were ordered and distributed.[45] While prices ranged as high as $1 each, some were sold at 35 cents, and many were given away. These mass-produced books were published at a cost of about 20 cents each by companies established especially for the purpose, with printing and binding contracted to trade publishers. Thus, a minimum of $3.4 million[46] was spent on these items alone,[47] while some political committees raised campaign funds by selling the books at higher prices.

In any case, the Goldwater campaign did not seem to draw off any considerable amount of money from right-wing organizations. Careful studies indicate that at least $14 million[48] are spent annually on right-wing activities, and some estimates range to as much as $30 million a year. Since much of this income is from membership dues, purchases of literature, and corporate support, the basic income of such organizations tends to be stable and appears not to have been greatly affected by the Goldwater candidacy. The 1964 experience led to the initiation of new ultraconservative bids for recruits and money, in part within the two-party framework and focused upon selected campaigns for Congress in the future.[49] But, right-wing splinter groups continued to draw off some support that otherwise might have been channeled through the party.

The Aftermath

The aftermath of an election reveals the strength and resiliency of each party. After the 1964 election, considerable attention focused on the financial conditions of the two major parties. Republican moderates protested the existence of a surplus after so many party candidates had been defeated—some, perhaps, for lack of money. There were charges that the Goldwater faction, in control of the national campaign, had not supplied the senatorial and congressional campaign committees with promised funds and had secreted funds to ensure its continued control of the party machinery.[50]

In rebuttal, National Chairman Dean Burch replied that too much of the contributed money had come in too late in the campaign to permit spending to achieve a reasonable impact. He said it was not his function to get rid of money just for the sole purpose of ending up even. Senator Thruston B. Morton, chairman of the Republican Senate Campaign Committee, came to his defense, as did Congressman Bob Wilson, chairman of the Congressional Campaign Committee. Both indicated there had been no lack of cooperation between the National Committee and the congressional campaign committees.[51]

Various published stories indicate that the Republican surplus amounted to from $.5 million to $1.8 million. The cash held by the National Committee and the senatorial and congressional committees, as of January 1, 1965, totaled $457,000. The treasurer of the Republican National Finance Committee claimed a year-end surplus of $.5 million, no doubt a rounding out of the actual figure. Official reports, filed in January, 1965, indicated about $1.4 million more income than outgo.

The various figures are misleading unless one recognizes that part of the Republican surplus included funds raised by the National TV for Goldwater-Miller Committee and the Citizens for Goldwater-Miller. When, in January, 1965, an amended official filing indicated that $600,000 more had been spent than had been originally reported, dispute developed as to how much the TV-committee surplus actually was. This still left that committee with a surplus of $.5 million. While controversy raged over whether Dean Burch would continue as Republican national chairman, there were reports the Goldwater faction was utilizing the TV-committee surplus as a lever to help retain Burch. Apparently, calls had been made to some state finance leaders suggesting that the surplus might not be available for national purposes if Burch were forced out of office. A meeting of the Executive Committee of the RNFC, on December 19, 1964, supported the Burch leadership. Out of that meeting came reports that one committee member had been delegated to seek the support of large contributors for the retention of Burch. Burch himself later wrote members of the National Committee that repudiation of him could mean the loss of some of the Republican financial base.[52] To some, publication of the stories of Republican surpluses seemed to have been timed to help the Goldwater forces retain control of the National Committee. The controversy was terminated by Burch's agreement to step down; Ray Bliss assumed the chairmanship, and Burch accepted $8,200 in severance pay. The National Committee never received the TV-committee funds; Barry Goldwater urged that the money be returned to donors, but, apparently, it was not. Goldwater then accepted $50,000 from the national party to help pay for office facilities and a staff to answer his correspondence. The surplus held by the Citizens for Goldwater, amounting to more than $200,000, was never turned over to the Republican Party; during 1965, a few disbursements were made by this committee: $8,000 to Tom Van Sickle, who ran successfully as the conservative faction's candidate for the presidency of the Young Republican National Federation; $5,000 to Friends of Senator John Tower of Texas, up for re-election in 1966; $5,000 to the by-election campaign of U.S. Congressman Albert W. Watson of South Carolina, who had switched from the Democratic to the Republican Party and who won re-election. The Citizens Committee also reported $23,000 in contributions in 1965. Finally, it was announced that more than $200,000 in funds would be used to help conservative Republicans seeking re-election to Congress in 1966.[53]

In his final report, Burch called for a $250,000 increase in the research budget; additional amounts, beyond those already adopted, to finance the Republican Coordinating Committee; an additional $100,000 to staff ten special task forces; a $100,000 public opinion survey to test national issues and to profile the motivations of Republican workers; increases in spending for public relations and for a field staff to assist local committees in voter registration, fund raising, and other activities. He also suggested that volunteer contributions be sought in a "buy a brick" campaign to construct a permanent headquarters for the Republican Party in Washington. The Burch proposals were ambitious, and some were partially adopted; in part or in whole, they would contribute to the nationalizing and institutionalizing of party politics—now also evident in aspects of Democratic operations and, perhaps, a portent of the future.

For 1965, a bare-bones minimum budget of $2.7 million was adopted by the Republican National Committee, but a larger national victory budget of $4.7 million was projected if funds were available. Actually, $4.2 million were raised by national-level party committees—an increase of $1.5 million over the amount raised by the Republicans in 1961.[54] This was accomplished despite Dean Burch's relinquishing of control. The Republican sustaining fund was projected at $1.2 million for 1965, and $1.7 million were received; about 3.8 million fund-raising appeals were mailed (at a cost of $425,000), and about 140,000 individuals responded with sums under $100.

Upon assuming the chairmanship, Ray Bliss introduced strict economy measures, going beyond those Burch had initiated after the election. Bliss also reorganized, and tightened control over, some national party activities such as the Young Republican National Federation. The national party gave little direct monetary aid, but other units gave assistance to Republicans running in 1965 for state and local offices. Congressman Watson received $5,000 in Booster Club funds and $5000 in Congressional Cam-

paign Committee payments; additionally, Washington supplied
polling services and paid the salary of a Watson field worker,
which, together, amounted to $10,000, though this money was
not given to Watson directly. Congressman Prentiss Walker
received $2,500 from the Congressional Campaign Committee for
legal expenses in meeting the Mississippi Freedom Democratic
Party's effort to unseat him and others.

After the November, 1965, elections, in which Republicans saw
some signs of revival in New York, Philadelphia, Louisville, and
other cities, Ray Bliss announced intensified efforts in the big
cities and budgeted funds for 1966 to finance the urban offensive.
These efforts, encouraged by surveys finding the Democrats losing
some support in northern urban areas,[55] came at the same time
that the Democrats were cutting back their urban, registration,
and labor staffs.

In the aftermath of the 1964 election, the Republicans went
for months without a national finance chairman. J. William
Middendorf remained treasurer, signifying continuity in the
broad-based finance effort.[56] Even Bliss had difficulty finding a
finance chairman; he offered the position to several who turned
it down, until, reluctantly, Lucius D. Clay accepted. At the
same time, C. Langhorne Washburn replaced Frank Kovac as
finance director.[57]

Bliss and Clay sought to centralize control of Republican fund-
raising and to win back some lost contributors. Clay had difficulty
with Goldwater-oriented committees, and he also found it hard
to convince key congressional leaders that unified fund-raising
would bring in as much money, and that the National Committee
could ensure the financing of the congressional campaign committees. For example, before Clay assumed office, the Congressional Campaign Committee made a desperate plea for funds to
prevent drastic staff reductions; though $60,000 came in within
a few weeks, this kind of stop-gap financing and duplication of
effort was roundly criticized. The Republican Congressional
Boosters Club, a separate unit patterned on the Democrats' President's Club, sought 2,000 members, to pay a membership fee of
$1,000 each, with the funds earmarked for marginal candidates
for Congress in 1966; its funds were not available for Congressional Campaign Committee expenses. The Boosters Club pre-

sented a particularly trying problem in duplication of effort because it succeeded in attracting only $600,000 of its $2 million goal for 1966 campaigns.

In early 1966, the Republicans decided to organize eleven regional finance networks to finance national and state committees, and began to combine Booster Club and general-party appeals to large contributors. The Republican impulse to unify fund-raising campaigns was beginning to reassert itself after breaking down with the advent of the Goldwater and right-wing splinter movements.

The Financial Future

With the Democrats strongly in power, Democratic ability to obtain funds would seem to be greatly enhanced. Yet, despite significant financial support from certain Republicans in 1964, the Democrats still raised and spent less than did the Republicans at the national level in 1964. Campaigning is especially expensive for the challenger, and fund-raising is normally difficult for a party largely out of power. Yet, even in the face of heavy electoral losses, the Republicans were, in some ways, in better financial shape after the 1964 campaign than they were after the 1960 campaign. In the adverse circumstances of the intervening years, their ability to raise funds had been demonstrated and their bases had been broadened remarkably. The National Committee was not saddled with a deficit. The large number of contributors in 1964 gave the party a larger potential contributing constituency than ever before. Some observers contend that the outpouring of Republican money in 1964 was basically a result of the conservative movement in this country, rather than an outgrowth of a broadly based desire to help the Republican Party; accordingly, it was argued that contributions came from a relatively small base of active and enthusiastic conservatives. But, clearly, the National Committee had built a solid list of sustaining members before the Goldwater candidacy; and, undoubtedly, it continued to attract some of his followers. Mail solicitations sent to 1964 contributors, along with some on new lists, continued to bring highly satisfactory results; national-level party receipts continued at record levels, thanks to the direct-mail drive for smaller contributors.

Of equal importance is the relative decline in Republican dependence upon large contributors. Most evidence indicates that Republican contributions in sums of $500 and over—largely from contributors of $10,000 or more, from members of twelve prominent families, from leaders of thirteen selected groups—have notably decreased at the national level since 1956.[58] Some maintain that at least part of this lost money is now being given to candidates and committees, particularly in the South, that are not required to file official reports with the Clerk of the House. Some maintain that conservative and right-wing movements have drawn off funds, though, clearly, much of their financial support has always been, and will remain, outside the two-party channels.

Republicans need large sums to compete with the Democrats, who now control the presidency and both houses of Congress. It will be costly for Republicans nationally to agree on how to re-shape their image and then to do it. In the 1965 budget, money was provided for revitalizing the party. At that time, it was agreed to finance a Republican Coordinating Committee, which would serve as a new policy arm. Unified fund-raising through the Republican National Finance Committee broke down in 1964. Multiple solicitation took place because the polarization of conservative Republicans (behind Goldwater) and moderate Republicans (behind certain state and local candidates) magnified the importance of the soliciting agency, and funds were not as effectively raised or shared as is normal through united finance committees. This diversity carried over into 1965, when many Republican agencies competed for funds. The Republican Associates (a National Committee program) and the Congressional Boosters Club both sought large contributions; the congressional and senatorial campaign committees each planned to sponsor separate fund-raising events in 1965, until the congressional group agreed to cancel theirs. The National Committee's sustaining fund was only one of several that sought small sums. By early 1966, some semblance of financial unity appeared possible, but only after heroic efforts on the parts of Ray Bliss and Lucius Clay.

Following the 1964 election defeat, the political spectrum was dotted with organizations of all shades and varieties—factional and nonparty—affecting Republican financing. Competitively, all sought funds; some pointed their efforts toward promoting conservatism or moderation within the Republican Party; some sought to influence independently the nomination and election processes. Most focused immediately on the 1966 elections. As noted, several of the Goldwater citizens' committees were reorganized into new committees with new foci (but with old money raised during the 1964 campaign). Some Republicans preferred to support financially the nine moderate organizations loosely grouped in the Council of Republican Organizations, each with its own membership, program, and fund-raising. A new American Conservative Union was formed,[59] the Americans for Constitutional Action beefed up their fund-raising, the John Birch Society announced new goals.[60]

By May, 1965, the Republican Party leadership complained that competing splinter groups were diluting the sources of party income.[61] Even after that, Barry Goldwater announced support for the establishment of a Free Society Association (FSA), purportedly organized for conservative educational purposes and not for political activities that would compete with the Republican Party. Goldwater personally solicited funds for the FSA. Some conservative groups seem to have formed to exploit the momentum and lists of contributors gathered in the Goldwater campaign.

By 1966, however, national party fund-raising had improved and the threat of conservative splintering receded. Yet, the Republicans will need continued vigilance to control the diffusion of energy and money and to channel diverse efforts into meaningful political action. With Democratic dominance in Washington and in many of the statehouses, it would seem that the challengers will need as much time and money as they can get to project themselves and their views. Republicans will need to campaign continuously to reach a competitive position worthy of a two-party system. If competition increases, and continuous campaigning—patterned on politics in other democracies—comes into vogue, political costs could get even higher.

II

.

The
Party
in
Defeat:
The
Rebuilding

EDITORS' INTRODUCTION

Winning public office by mobilizing electoral majorities is the primary function of the party-in-the-electorate. Once in office, those who wear the party label, however lightly, form still another component of the party system, the party-in-the-government. These elected party members not only operate through institutions separate from nongovernmental party machinery but also develop skills and modes of operation appropriate to their responsibility for the exercise of governmental power. Not infrequently, they respond to governmental problems in ways that appear to bear only a tenuous connection to the pronouncements and promises of the campaign. Indeed, there are those who suggest that it is analytically useful to differentiate presidential from congressional parties, and both of these from the electoral party and the permanent, nongovernmental party organization. Yet, despite very real differences in structure and modes of operation, the various elements of the party system remain functionally interrelated; a change in one will produce change in the others.

Change is almost certain to follow a devastating defeat, as survivors undertake the task of reconstructing their party. It is scarcely surprising that Robert L. Peabody should conclude, in his analysis of the Ford-Halleck contest, that the Goldwater nomi-

nation and election results created more internal dissension in the
Republican Party than any event since the split between the Taft
and Roosevelt wings in 1912. In fact, Republican members of
the House of Representatives showed dissatisfaction with their
leadership well before 1964. Yet, the Goldwater defeat and the
net loss of thirty-eight congressional seats created the psychological climate for revolt. It is this revolt that Professor Peabody describes as he focuses on the minority-leadership contest of 1965,
which resulted in the defeat of House Minority Leader Charles
Halleck.

Another casualty of the Goldwater campaign and the 1964
election debacle was Dean Burch, chairman of the Republican
National Committee. The national chairman presides over an organization that appears to be neatly arranged in the best pyrami-
dal design, with clear lines of authority and responsibility flowing
from the top down through the hierarchy. In reality, a national
party organization is merely a confederation of state and local
parties. Whatever cohesiveness it has derives largely from its primary objective, which is to win the presidency. In those years
when the party has a reasonably good chance of winning that
office, the national organization may display a high degree of cohesiveness. When, however, there appears to be little chance for
victory, state party organizations may, in effect, secede from the
national party apparatus and concentrate almost exclusively on
state and local races.

Under these circumstances, the role of the party chairman is
difficult, to say the least, and his prospects for the future—if he
wants to remain as chairman—are less than bright. For, although
he is elected by the National Committee, he is really, in presidential years, the designee of the presidential nominee. When that
nominee loses decisively, the party chairman will be among those
most likely to bear the brunt of the dissatisfaction with the outcome.

Dean Burch was the personal choice of Senator Goldwater for
Republican national chairman. He was formally appointed to the
post by the Republican National Committee, meeting in San
Francisco, in July, 1964. Six months later, in January, 1965, the
National Committee voted to replace Burch with Ray Bliss. As

John Bibby and Robert Huckshorn make clear, it was not that Burch was disliked personally but that he symbolized the outcome of the preceding national election. Professors Bibby and Huckshorn provide a descriptive analysis of the attempt of Chairman Bliss to rebuild the Republican Party in the aftermath of the Goldwater campaign, drawing from their analysis generalizations relating to the impact of decisive defeat and divisive factionalism upon the national organization of the out-party.

Rebuilding is also the subject of the final chapter of this volume, in which Bernard Cosman and Robert Huckshorn analyze the Goldwater phenomenon, relating it to the party's present situation and future prospects. Making no attempt to predict the future direction the Republican Party will take, the authors do, nonetheless, indicate the regions where success is most likely to lie.

5

.

THE SURVIVORS: THE 1965 HOUSE MINORITY LEADERSHIP CONTEST[1]

.

ROBERT L. PEABODY

On the morning of January 4, 1965, the House Republican Conference met in the Ways and Means Committee hearing room, in the Longworth House Office Building, to select a Republican candidate for Speaker of the U.S. House of Representatives for the Eighty-ninth Congress. The outcome of the speakership contest, to be held two hours later on the House floor, was already a foregone conclusion. Thus, the 140 Republican representatives-elect were actually meeting to choose their minority leader for the next two years. Since December 19, 1964, the challenger, Conference Chairman Gerald R. Ford, Jr. of Michigan, had been engaged in an open fight to overthrow the incumbent minority leader for the past six years, Charles A. Halleck of Indiana. Halleck had counteracted the efforts of the Ford supporters with a lower-keyed campaign of his own to obtain votes from among the

One version of this piece was published by the Eagleton Institute of Politics under the title *The Ford-Halleck Minority Leadership Contest, 1965* (New York: McGraw-Hill, 1966). Used by permission of the Eagleton Institute.

120 returning congressmen and 20 freshmen who had survived the November, 1964, election.

This contest, at least on the surface, was not one of ideological contrasts. Both candidates had equally conservative voting records, but these records masked rather sharp differences in age, image, and the kind of strategy each felt the minority party should adopt in the months ahead. Ford, at fifty-one, sandy-haired, with an athlete's trim build, the symbol of a new generation of young, articulate, executive-type politicians, urged the promotion of a "fighting, forward-looking party seeking responsible and constructive solutions to national problems." Halleck, at sixty-four, an old pro, with thirty years of service in the House, red-faced and heavy-jowled, campaigned on a "record of solidarity in support of Party principles" and the Republicans' nearly unanimous opposition to the "costly, unwise, and unnecessary proposals" put forward by Democratic administrations.

Ford won by a secret-ballot vote of 73 to 67. After the balloting, Halleck, who took his defeat hard, but with courage and good grace, moved to make Ford's election unanimous.

Both ideological and regional differences were involved in the contest for conference chairman that took place immediately before the Ford-Halleck vote. In December, Representative Melvin Laird of Wisconsin had announced his candidacy; a midwestern conservative, Laird had aroused the enmity of the eastern moderates and liberals by his firm and unbending management of the Republican Party platform prior to Senator Goldwater's nomination, in July, 1964. On the Sunday evening before the House Republican Conference, the Wednesday Club—a group of about twenty young, moderate-to-liberal Republican congressmen—had met and agreed to challenge Laird with a candidate of their own, New Jersey Representative Peter H. B. Frelinghuysen, Jr. Though Laird won the chairmanship, 77 to 62, the surprising strength of Frelinghuysen's vote was strong enough to push him forward as a candidate to unify the party in a subsequent—and unsuccessful—challenge to the incumbent whip.

During the next months, the new minority leader was to undergo a series of challenges to his leadership—including a contest over minority personnel; a second defeat of Frelinghuysen, Ford's choice to replace Les Arends of Illinois as party whip; a failure to win a seat for one of his principal supporters, Charles Goodell of New York, on the important Ways and Means Committee; and another challenge to Goodell as Ford's first choice for Policy Committee chairman, to replace the resigning Chairman John Byrnes of Wisconsin. Ford, Laird, and Arends subsequently resolved this last challenge by creating a Committee on Planning and Research, under the Republican Conference, and appointing Goodell as its chairman. On February 23, 1965, the day this appointment was approved, the Republican Conference elected John Rhodes of Arizona to the chairmanship of the Republican Policy Committee, without opposition.

Halleck, the defeated minority leader, dropped from the top position in the Republican Party hierarchy to eighth-ranking minority member on the Committee on Public Works.[2] Joe Martin, defeated six years earlier by Halleck in a bitter, behind-the-scenes struggle and now eighty years old, had remained in the House to vote against Halleck and for Ford. Ironically, both Martin and Halleck had been victims of election disasters, for which neither could be held directly responsible, but which, nevertheless, served as catalysts for revolution.

The Seeds of Discontent: 1959–64

The seeds of unrest existed long before the election disaster of 1964. Dissatisfaction with Halleck's leadership went back at least to the 1959 revolt; it came into the open at the beginning of the Eighty-eighth Congress, when Ford defeated Charles B. Hoeven of Iowa in a secret-ballot vote for conference chairman, and the agitation for leadership change continued to grow during the long and arduous legislative sessions of 1963 and 1964.

The 1959 revolt against Joe Martin began with a different objective—getting the ailing Minority Leader to appoint someone other than himself as chairman of the dormant Policy Committee. Martin, underestimating the extent of the challenge, did not seriously consider this possible compromise until it was too late. The junior insurgents, led by Bob Wilson of California, settled on Halleck, who had been majority leader in the Eightieth and Eighty-third congresses, as the heir apparent, even though he was not an overwhelming first choice. The insurgents thought the contest was all but over when, by a vote of 96 to 50, they won the right to make use of a secret ballot. But many members who favored a secret ballot ended up, nevertheless, by voting for the incumbent. On the first ballot, Halleck received 73 votes and Martin 72, but neither candidate had a majority, because one ballot was illegible. Halleck emerged the winner on the second ballot by a vote of 74 to 70, with two members, presumably Halleck and Martin, voting present. While Halleck's election gave House Republicans more aggressive leadership, most of those advocating the change did not interpret it as a complete victory. For the time being, these younger members, among them Thomas B. Curtis of Missouri, Ford, and Laird, satisfied themselves with a revitalized Policy Committee under a separate chairman, John W. Byrnes of Wisconsin.[3]

House Republicans had suffered a net loss of forty-seven seats in the 1958 election, just before Martin's defeat. Under Halleck's leadership, Republicans reaped the benefits of a net gain of twenty seats in 1960, as John F. Kennedy ran behind three-fourths of the Democratic House candidates in his close victory over Richard M. Nixon. In 1962, the traditional pattern of mid-term gains for the minority party were not realized. House Republicans picked up only two additional seats, increasing their membership in the 435-member House from 174 to 176 representatives.

On January 2, 1963, just before the opening of the Eighty-eighth Congress, two junior members—Robert P. Griffin of Michigan (first elected in 1956), and Charles E. Goodell of New York (first elected in a special election, May 26, 1959)—met for lunch. What began as a discussion of forthcoming legislation in their House Education and Labor Committee shifted to matters of Republican Party organization. Before that luncheon was over, it had been transformed into a planning session for a challenge to the established leadership. After considering and rejecting contests against either Halleck or Arends, Griffin and Goodell launched a weekend campaign aimed at capturing the Republican Conference chairmanship. With the active support of most of the House members elected since 1958, and the tacit approval of many of the same activists who had helped Halleck defeat Martin in 1959, the young-Turk candidate, the forty-nine-year-old Ford, defeated the sixty-seven-year-old incumbent conference chairman, Charles Hoeven, by a secret-ballot vote of 86 to 78. As Hoeven left the 1963 Conference, he described himself as the "scapegoat and fall-guy" of an effort by younger Republicans to take over the leadership. "I was picked as the lamb for the slaughter. This should serve as notice to Mr. Arends and Mr. Halleck that something is brewing."[4] Two years later, the Iowa Republican's predictions were to prove quite accurate.

By 1964, at least four developments in House Republican Party organization had given younger members a more active role in policymaking. The House Republican Policy Committee was operating under a separate chairman, John Byrnes, and with a wider base of membership. The House Republican Conference had a new chairman, Jerry Ford, and presumably would meet more often and work more closely with the Policy Committee. A Subcommittee on Special Projects, under the chairmanship of Arizona Representative John Rhodes, was beginning to develop longer-range policy through a series of task forces. Since 1961, at Halleck's suggestion, the Committee on Committees subcommittee charged with making committee assignments had included class representatives—including a spokesman for the freshman class. Despite these developments, the continued domination of these organizations by senior members and the continuing frustrations of minority status led to further unrest and dissatisfaction among the more junior members who made up well over a majority of the House Republican Party.

With majority status comes not only control of the House but also the benefits that accrue from drafting and passing legislation conforming to personal and party philosophy. On rare occasions, a member of the minority party can take advantage of a situation that requires bipartisan action so as to play a major and constructive role in the legislative process. Thus, Griffin, as ranking minority member of the Education and Labor subcommittee, which dealt with labor-law reform, became a cosponsor (with Halleck's support) of what was to become the Landrum-Griffin Act of 1959. Similarly, Goodell, with even less seniority than Griffin, was able to rework the proposals set forth by the Curtis task force on "Employment in a Dynamic American Economy" into Republican amendments, which became the basis of the Manpower Development and Retraining Act of 1962. A number of young House Republicans—among them John V. Lindsay of New York; Clark MacGregor of Minnesota; and Charles McC. Mathias, Jr. of Maryland—joined ranking Judiciary Committee minority member William M. McCulloch in shaping what was to become the Civil Rights Act of 1964—again, with Halleck's cooperation.

In the main, however, the minority's victories had come not from drafting constructive alternatives or modifying the administration's proposals but from the defeat of the majority party's legislation. It was at this endeavor that Halleck was particularly adept. He had served with the astute leader of the southern Democratic conservatives Howard W. Smith, of Virginia, on the Committee on Rules in the early 1940's. He knew most of the senior conservative southern Democrats on a first-name basis. He had gone hunting or fishing with many of them and shared the bourbon, branch water, and conviviality of many a Rayburn "Board of Education" gathering.[5] Halleck's ability to rally Republicans in opposition to the Kennedy-Johnson programs was impressive. He summed up his own record as minority leader in this December 21, 1964, statement:

> In my first two years, being the last two years of the Eisenhower Administration, practically all of his proposals were enacted into law, although we were much in the minority. During the past four years of the Kennedy-Johnson Administration, most of the constructive legislation bears a very definite Republican imprint. Many costly, unwise and unnecessary proposals were either defeated or abandoned by virtue of almost solid Republican opposition.[6]

But these efforts to secure unanimity had their costs. They were particularly distasteful to members of the Wednesday Club; both by conviction and by the kinds of constituencies they represented, these men were most likely to bear the brunt of efforts to secure near unanimity on issues that became tests of party loyalty. Two comments from members of this group illustrate this concern:

> Halleck wasn't a bad leader. The trouble was that when he was pushed, he submitted to a push from the right, rather than from the left. There has been too much negativism in the leadership, too much emphasis on saying "No" to everything. . . . We need to look for

constructive alternatives, and be there first with some alternatives; not just listen to H. R. Gross [of Iowa] and vote "No."

We owe a great debt to Halleck. He's given us good leadership for the better part of six years. I still think he's the most capable leader we have. Our biggest complaint was that he didn't lead—he'd be absent or disinterested in what was going on on a day-to-day basis. And his attitude was apt to be "let's beat them just for the victory," not carefully choosing when to hold the line. And then it was likely to be a Pyrrhic victory—just being proud that we had lost only 2 or 3 Republicans. I'm tired of always painting ourselves into a corner. I don't like being there all the time.

Throughout the long and trying first session of the Eighty-eighth Congress, Halleck was under attack from both the left and the right. Conservatives—among them Richard Poff of Virginia, William Cramer of Florida, James Utt of California, and George Meader and August Johansen of Michigan—criticized Halleck for lending his support to the bipartisan coalition implementing civil rights legislation. On the day the civil rights bill was reported out of the House Judiciary Committee, a black furled umbrella, symbol of appeasement, was placed on the Minority Leader's table on the floor of the House. Halleck recouped some ground with conservatives on other issues, for example, his support of Illinois Representative Paul Findley's amendment restricting the sale of wheat to Russia, in December, 1963. But, by making this and other issues tests of party loyalty, he further antagonized the more liberal wing of the party. As one senior House Republican summed up the squeeze that Halleck continually faced: "A floor leader makes enemies. Halpern and Lindsay of New York—they are criticizing him for not moving fast enough. And on the other hand, Doc Hall and what's his name from Iowa—they are after him for moving too fast. So, he accumulates enemies no matter what he does." If Halleck was more susceptible to a "push from the right," it was as much because of his own beliefs and the nature of his rural and small-town Indiana district as because of his recognition that the substantial base of the House Republican Party was, and would remain, more conservative than moderate-to-liberal in its orientations.

Halleck's six-year reign as minority leader was subject to another kind of limitation, which his predecessor had been able to overcome in part. During Martin's tenure, the Republican Party had achieved majority status both in the Eightieth Congress (1947–48) and in the first two years of the Eisenhower Administration (1953–54). The limited patronage available to a minority leader had been augmented both by service under a Republican administration and by Martin's friendship with Speaker Rayburn. But, a minority leader, compared to the Speaker and the majority leader, inevitably suffers from having fewer choice committee assignments to dispense to promising newcomers and party regulars; he has fewer positions on prestige boards and commissions with which to reward his friends and placate his enemies. Since the rewards are fewer and the competition usually keener, he often ends up pleasing only one member or one state delegation, at the cost of antagonizing several.[7]

The kinds of irritations and personal animosities generated by conflicts over committee assignments or policy differences on legislation were, if anything, complicated still further by Halleck's temperament. He was a leader, not afraid to lead even if it meant stepping on other people's toes. By his own definition, he ran a "damn tough shop." He was at his best on the floor of the House engaged in debate with his Democratic counterparts. His ability to make the quick retort, the caustic comment, while it won him admiration and respect when directed at the other side, did not endear him to his colleagues when this same testiness and abrasiveness were left unmodified in party councils. As a close supporter summed up Halleck's leadership styles:

> His opponents were saying that Charlie had marshalled the Republicans too sternly. . . . They were saying that he was too effective, too harsh a disciplinarian. The label "drill sergeant" was used. I think that argument back-fired. A leader, to be successful, has got to keep his flock in line. If you are going to be a leader, you have got to lead. It's as simple as that.

The unrest and dissatisfaction with minority status, and the personal irritations stemming from frustrated seeking of committee assignments and differences over policy, were heightened, in

1964, by the pressures that inevitably mount in an election year. The rancorous contest for the Republican presidential nomination further increased frictions between the liberal and conservative wings of the GOP. In early July, the week preceding the Republican National Convention, liberals complained that a platform was being drawn up that would be "rammed down our throats." Republican Platform Chairman Laird, together with his two principal assistants, Representatives Glenard Lipscomb of California, and Charles Goodell of New York, worked effectively together to bring about a platform upon which the leading contender, Senator Goldwater and his eventual running mate could campaign. At the same time, Laird and his associates tried to avoid planks that would needlessly irritate liberals or drive them out of the party. Civil rights, control of nuclear policy, and the issue of extremism were focal points of conflict.

Halleck, who, in 1940, had promoted the candidacy of Wendell Willkie, and who had helped to secure the nomination of Governor Thomas E. Dewey, in 1948 (only to be rejected by Dewey as a vice-presidential candidate), played a relatively minor role in the 1964 Republican Convention. He joined former Senator William Knowland, Clare Boothe Luce, and Senator John G. Tower of Texas, in seconding Senate Minority Leader Everett M. Dirksen's speech nominating Goldwater. Ford, who received some attention as a possible vice-presidential nominee, supported his own state's favorite-son candidate, Governor George Romney, and emerged relatively unscathed from the 1964 Convention.

Congress, under continuing pressure from President Johnson, remained in session until October 3, 1964. As tempers became more unruly and members champed to get back to their districts in order to campaign, personal animosities flared within parties and across party lines. Halleck, put on notice that his leadership was under scrutiny, at least since Ford's 1963 defeat of Hoeven, was probably more irritable and quick to react with anger to the demands placed upon him by his colleagues. One Ford supporter discoursed on the causes of friction that led to the challenge to Halleck's leadership:

It had been a long, hot summer, as long as any I can remember. There were several sources of irritation which crystallized around Halleck.

If I had to put it in one word, and this is a great oversimplification, [the word] would be arrogance. Not a case of being stuck on himself, not that, but rather a detachment, seemingly purposively—he wouldn't consult with others. It seemed as if he saw himself as the fountainhead of wisdom. He became a little impatient and short-tempered. . . .

I think a contest would have come, sooner or later, even if we had won. Sure, the elections were clearly a factor, not a motivating factor, but a convenient excuse.

Election Post-mortem

On November 3, 1964, President Johnson led the Democratic Party to its greatest national election victory since 1936. The impact of Senator Goldwater's candidacy was particularly disastrous for Republican House candidates. The Democrats picked up forty-eight seats previously held by Republicans. Republican candidates won only ten seats previously held by Democrats, for a net loss of thirty-eight seats.

Conservative House Republican incumbents, identified by low federal-role-support scores in the Eighty-eighth Congress, were particularly hard hit (Fig. 1). Of the forty Republican incumbents who ran for re-election and were defeated, twenty-eight (or 70 per cent) had voted seven times or fewer for a larger federal role in eighteen key roll-call votes selected by *Congressional Quarterly* in 1963 and 1964. Twenty of these defeated incumbents had been among the sixty-two Republican representatives who had endorsed Senator Goldwater's candidacy prior to the 1964 Republican Convention.[8] In contrast, only a scattering of liberal House Republicans, including one Wednesday Club member, Abner Sibal of Connecticut, were defeated. Figure 1 also demonstrates the predominantly conservative base of the House Republican Party.

While Republicans averaged seven votes or fewer on these eighteen selected votes, House Democrats averaged thirteen votes or more in favor of maintaining or increasing the federal government's role in our society. The leadership of the House Republican Party has generally come from the right-center of the party, as the voting records of Halleck, Arends, Laird, and Ford clearly

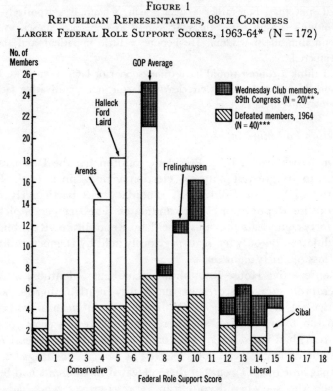

FIGURE 1
REPUBLICAN REPRESENTATIVES, 88TH CONGRESS
LARGER FEDERAL ROLE SUPPORT SCORES, 1963-64* (N = 172)

SOURCES:

*Congressional Quarterly Weekly Report, XXII (October 23, 1964)
pp. 2549-2560. Based on number of times a Republican Representative
took a position in support of a larger federal role in the 88th Congress
on 18 roll call votes selected by Congressional Quarterly. The voting
records of six members with incomplete scores are omitted.

**Washington Post, November 7, 1964, p. A-4; Paul Duke and Stanley
Meisler, "Republicans After the Debacle: 1. The Frustrated Moderates,"
The Reporter, February 11, 1965, pp. 26-28. One Wednesday Club
member, Abner Sibal of Connecticut, was defeated.

***Based on the 40 incumbent Republican members who ran for re-
election on November 3, 1964 and were defeated. Congressional
Quarterly Weekly Report, XXII (November 7, 1964), pp. 2662-2663.

illustrate. All four voted against a larger federal role on all but four or five of these eighteen votes; two of the exceptions were votes for the first and final passage of the Civil Rights Act of 1964. The most conservative voting records in terms of this index are held by John M. Ashbrook of Ohio, and two defeated candidates for re-election, Bruce Alger of Texas and Ralph F. Beerman of Nebraska. None of these members cast a vote among the eighteen that could be interpreted as support for a larger federal role. At the other extreme, Seymour Halpern of New York voted in favor of maintaining existing programs or increasing the federal role on seventeen of the eighteen votes. The voting records of Wednesday Club members ranged from the moderate scores (seven out of eighteen) of Howard Robison (New York), Herman T. Schneebell (Pennsylvania), and Robert Ellsworth and Garner Shriver (Kansas), to the liberal voting record of John V. Lindsay (fifteen out of eighteen).

What is more significant in terms of the Halleck-Ford contest is that a substantial proportion of the forty defeated Republican incumbents were older and more senior members; hence, they were more likely to support the established leadership. Nineteen of the forty had served ten or more years in Congress; in this group were such senior members as Benjamin Jensen of Iowa and Walter Horan of Washington—the ranking minority members of the Appropriations Committee, with thirteen and eleven terms in Congress, respectively. New York, the hardest-hit Republican delegation in Congress, lost six senior members including Katharine St. George, second-ranking on the Rules Committee; Walter Riehlman, ranking minority member of the Committee on Government Operations; and J. Ernest Wharton, second-ranking Republican on the Committee on Interior and Insular Affairs. These losses, coupled with the retirement of such senior members as Clarence Kilburn, Harold Ostertag, and the Republican vice-presidential candidate, William Miller, drastically reduced the strength of the New York delegation within the party hierarchy. At the same time, it radically improved the opportunities for revolt against Halleck. As one of Halleck's supporters assessed the impact of the 1964 election: "There was a general feeling of dismay at the results. If the election had gone the other way, no

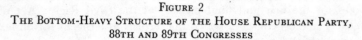

FIGURE 2

THE BOTTOM-HEAVY STRUCTURE OF THE HOUSE REPUBLICAN PARTY,
88TH AND 89TH CONGRESSES

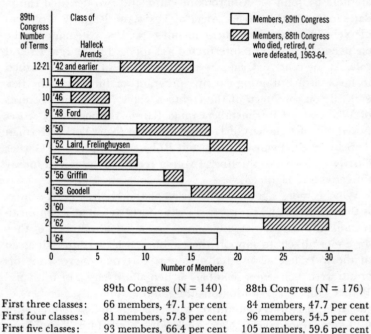

	89th Congress (N = 140)	88th Congress (N = 176)
First three classes:	66 members, 47.1 per cent	84 members, 47.7 per cent
First four classes:	81 members, 57.8 per cent	96 members, 54.5 per cent
First five classes:	93 members, 66.4 per cent	105 members, 59.6 per cent

Sources: *Congressional Quarterly Weekly Report,* **XXI** (January 4, 1963), pp. 20-21; **XXIII** (January 1, 1965), p. 24.

doubt Charlie would have remained. . . . Many of the people defeated would have been Halleck supporters. In general, the more seasoned members of the House favored Halleck. It was the newer and less seasoned members who turned basically to Ford." And as Halleck himself summed it up, "Many of my most stalwart friends lost out."

Figure 2 illustrates this bottom-heavy structure of the House Republican Party in the Eighty-ninth Congress. It also illustrates the relatively heavy losses suffered among the more senior ranks of the party as a result of deaths, retirements, and the heavy election losses of 1964: For example, of the fifteen House Republicans in the Eighty-eighth Congress first elected in 1942 or earlier, four were defeated for re-election, three had retired, and one had died. Only seven of these members remained at the opening of the Eighty-ninth Congress—among them, Martin, Arends, and Halleck. The relatively large number of new members, compared to the decimated ranks of senior members, had resulted in a substantial majority of the party, almost 58 per cent, having been elected in 1958 and subsequent elections. The first five classes (members elected in 1956 and subsequent years) made up two-thirds of the total House Republican Party membership in 1965. It was this fertile ground for revolt that led younger activists to contemplate seriously the possibility of a leadership change after the election disaster.

The December, 1964 Conference

Open speculation about a direct challenge to Halleck's leadership at the opening of the Eighty-ninth Congress apparently dates from a story that first appeared in the Scripps-Howard newspaper chain on October 28, 1964, six days before the election.[9] As Marshall McNeil surveyed the scene: "The candidate of the 'rebels' is Rep. Melvin Laird (R., Wis.), a rising star on the GOP side of the House." Among Laird's backers, McNeil listed his two close associates on the Republican Platform Committee, Goodell and Lipscomb, and conservative New York Representative Steven B. Derounian (subsequently upset by the Johnson landslide). The same day that the Scripps-Howard story appeared, Ford was campaigning for Halleck and the Republican ticket in Warsaw,

Indiana. In response to a reporter's inquiry, Ford issued a press statement reiterating his support of Halleck and praising House Republican leadership as "constructive and effective." Ford concluded that "no case thus far has been made for a change in either our principles or leadership."[10]

In the aftermath of election disaster, while Goldwater called for rebuilding the Republican Party along conservative principles and urged consideration of a realignment of the national parties, GOP liberals and moderates were challenging his control over the party organization. Republican National Chairman Dean Burch, a young Arizonan hand-picked by Goldwater, became the focus and the symbol of this struggle.

While the fight for control of the national party organization continued, a number of junior Republican congressmen—among them Griffin and Goodell—were assessing the implications of the November election for their own legislative leadership. As members returned to Washington and met for lunch, talked by telephone, rehashed the election at social gatherings, and pondered the directions party policy should take, it was inevitable that Halleck's leadership, and possible challengers to it, would be discussed. As one congressman summed up the state of affairs in November: "If you took a general poll right after the election, I think that most of the Republican members would have been ready for a change. The whole thing was sort of chaotic after that period. Sentiment for a change subsided and then got to a point where there didn't seem to be much of a consensus at all."

Ford had flown back to Washington the day after the election in order to put himself into isolation to fulfill two prior publishing commitments. He had promised to write an article for the January issue of *Fortune* analyzing the state of the Republican Party. He had also agreed to collaborate on a book on the Warren Commission. Both drafts were due by late November. As a matter of routine, with Halleck's assent, he had sent out a call for a Republican Conference to be held on the morning of January 4, the day the new Congress would convene. While working in his office, Ford talked with an occasional member and received several telephone calls that raised the general question of leadership change. He also discussed party affairs and the leadership question, in a general and preliminary way, with several close friends including Representatives Laird and Griffin. As of early November (and, indeed, as late as the December 16 Conference), he did not consider himself to be an active contestant for the position of minority leader.

During this same period, the Wednesday Club held several meetings to discuss ways to "rebuild the party in the tradition of Lincoln" and to expand its membership so as to be able to play a more effective role in the coming Congress. In the main, the Wednesday Club had adopted a "wait-and-see" attitude on the question of leadership change. Attitudes ranged from those of members who feared a Laird-Ford conspiracy to those of several who leaned toward Ford; a few advocated running one of their own members as a third candidate, should a leadership fight take place.[11]

In the meantime, a number of Republican representatives who felt more strongly about the need for a change had been meeting informally or holding telephone conversations. One of these members was Donald Rumsfeld of Illinois, first elected to Congress in 1962. Rumsfeld had previously served on the staffs of two congressmen, including an interval on Griffin's staff in 1959. Dismayed by the election results and unhappy with the future prospects of the Republican Party's becoming the majority party without more constructive leadership, Rumsfeld telephoned a respected senior colleague, Missouri Representative Thomas B. Curtis, the week after the election. Curtis, second-ranking on the Ways and Means Committee, ranking member of the Joint Economic Committee, and long an intellectual gadfly of the House Republican Party, was already engaged in writing what had become almost a biennial letter to his House colleagues. As in the past, the letter dealt with problems of minority staffing, needs for long-range policy research, and the general state of the House Republican Party. Spurred on by several Republicans, Curtis sent, on November 18, a remarkable eight-page, single-spaced typewritten letter to all of his colleagues.[12] Curtis began his letter as follows:

> Like most of the rest of you, I suppose, I have been reading in the newspapers what is supposed to be going on in respect to the Republican leadership in the coming Congress.

Frankly, I am a little tired of behind the scenes maneuverings when it comes to establishing Party machinery and policies which deeply concern all 140 Republican Congressmen and should concern our entire Party.

Why not have these matters out in the open so all 140 of us can get our two bits worth in? I received a notice from Gerry [*sic*] Ford with Charlie Halleck's blessing that, on January 4, 1965, we will meet in Republican caucus. Well, that is entirely too late to get moving, unless again it is the plan for a few self-appointed members of our waning group to make the decisions for the rest of us ahead of time in the hopes they can get the majority of us to go along.

Let's get our leadership established on one basic premise, if no other, that major decisions on Party organization and policy matters be made on as broad a base as possible. It may take a little more time and a bit more patience, but the net result will be, I am certain, a better organization, better policies, and better politics. In order to do this, I suggest that we have a Party caucus within the next two or three weeks. . . .

Curtis then proceeded to outline, in detail, some of the changes in minority staffing, House rules, and the Republican House organization that he felt warranted the calling of a Republican Conference in mid-December. As he stated toward the end of his letter:

Yes, I am dissatisfied with our leadership in the House, not necessarily our leaders, however. . . . I'm not arguing for a change of leaders, but I am arguing for a change in the techniques of leadership. Regrettably, what happened after 1958 was a mere change of leaders, with only a few minor changes in the techniques of leadership.

In Washington, D.C., Griffin and Goodell reacted to the Curtis letter in the same way. Together, and in conversations with other members, they had discussed the desirability of holding a mid-December meeting as a testing ground for the leadership. It also seemed to them appropriate to use the meeting as a means of capitalizing on essentially dead news space to promote Republican alternatives to the Johnson Administration proposals on such subjects as Medicare and federal aid to education. Finally, like Curtis, they felt a genuine need to meet to consider and plan Republican alternatives to the substantial House rules changes that would be put forward by the House Democratic leadership under pressure from the reform-oriented Democratic Study Group. As they later recalled, "the Curtis letter opened up possibilities."

On November 25, the day before Thanksgiving, five young moderate conservatives met in Griffin's office with Curtis, who had flown in from St. Louis just for this meeting. The group included —in addition to Griffin, Goodell, and Curtis—Albert H. Quie of Minnesota and Donald Rumsfeld and John Anderson of Illinois.[13] In addition to the independent and highly respected Curtis, there was at least one representative present from each of the classes elected in 1956 and subsequent elections, save for the freshman class of 1964. In agreement on the need for a mid-December meeting, they made plans to generate the requests from fifty of the party's House members that were necessary to call a conference. Among other proposals for party organizational change, they discussed one with far-reaching implications: that members in top leadership positions not hold ranking minority positions on legislative committees at the same time. If this were to be adopted, three of the top four leaders—Arends, Ford, and Byrnes—would have to choose between their leadership positions and their ranking minority memberships on Armed Services, Appropriations, and Ways and Means, respectively.[14]

Over the Thanksgiving holidays, Ford flew with his wife to Puerto Rico for a vacation. While he had discussed the leadership question with several GOP House members, his attitude, as he was later to recall it, "was one of keeping at arm's distance." Just before Ford flew back to Washington for one day, December 1, he and Griffin discussed by telephone the calling of a conference. By this time, Ford had heard from a "substantial number" of House Republicans, either by letter, by telephone, or in face-to-face conversation. Most of them had reacted favorably to the Curtis proposal. Ford took one letter calling for a December 16 conference to the Minority Leader. Knowing full well that the calling of a conference was within Ford's discretion, Halleck gave his reluctant endorsement. Neither man felt sufficiently concerned about a possible contest to cancel out-of-town vacation plans. On December 2, Ford flew to California to fulfill several speaking engagements and to enjoy three days of golf while vacationing in Palm Springs. Halleck flew back to Lake Wales, Florida.

On December 10, dismayed that the leadership had not yet circulated a conference agenda, Curtis sent out a five-page proposal of his own. That same day, Ford returned to Washington and discussed the conference agenda with Griffin and Goodell.

Friday, December 11, was a full day for Ford. In the morning, he met with Representative Laird, a good friend and close associate on the Defense Subcommittee of the House Committee on Appropriations. He also conferred with Governor Romney, in town to meet with the Michigan delegation. Ford lunched with the three other principal leaders of the House Republican Party—Halleck, Arends, and Byrnes, the Policy Committee chairman. The subject was the conference agenda. At the end of the lunch, as Ford later recalled,

> Mr. Halleck went around the room and asked the various members if they planned to run again for the leadership. Mr. Arends said, "Yes," he planned to run for Whip. John Byrnes said that while he agreed in principle with the suggestion that the ranking member of a committee should step down and not hold a leadership position at the same time, he thought that with that exception, he would probably be a candidate, again, for Policy Committee Chairman.
>
> Then Charlie asked me what my plans were. I said, "I don't intend to run again for Conference Chairman, but I can't tell you if I'm going to be a candidate for the leadership or not. I haven't made up my mind. There are some people who are promoting me and talking to me about it. But I will say this. If I decide to be a candidate I will tell you before I go ahead." This was the first time, I think, he felt that I was seriously considering running. It was a little tense.

The calling of the House Republican Conference was widely interpreted in the press as both a warning to Halleck and a preliminary victory for the younger members. By the time the Conference convened, on Wednesday, December 16, it was being described as a testing ground for Halleck's strength. One hundred and nineteen Republicans were present for the morning session, including sixteen of the twenty newly elected members and eighteen "lame-duck" members of the Eighty-eighth Congress. Attendance dropped off rather sharply for the afternoon session.

By the time the Conference finally broke up, about 5:00 P.M., less than fifty members remained on the floor. The Republican Conference had not generated the pyrotechnics that many newspapermen and even some members had expected. It had largely concerned itself with forthcoming legislative issues, House rules changes, and Republican Party organization—matters not calculated to bring on a clash of personalities, at least not out in the open.

One of its most important actions was the creation of an eleven-member Committee on Organizational Structure, chaired by Quie, and including Byrnes and Curtis among its members. After the Republican Conference adjourned, another, much smaller meeting got under way in the office of Representative Goodell. From the point of view of most of the members who gathered in Goodell's office, the Conference had more than lived up to expectations. Said one:

> The Conference was a great success. For seven hours we met. There was good discussion and good ideas [were] put forth. About 30 to 40 members participated—only one guy was negative. Whenever anybody would propose something, Charlie would get up and he would try to say why he wasn't at fault. No one was trying to pin the tail on Charlie. At that meeting he could have picked up the ball and run with it. . . . Charlie was at bat, but he struck out.

And another:

> Ford was no shining light at the Conference, but most of us realized the difficult and delicate restraint with which he played his role. It enhanced his image. By the same token, Charlie Halleck's efforts to be dynamic fizzled. The result was it put guts into Goodell and Griffin and others of us who played a part.

The Challengers

Insurgents who wish to challenge an incumbent House leader face four interrelated problems: (1) Is a contest justified? (2) Can they win? (3) What *single* candidate can they coalesce behind? (4) How do they secure commitments or otherwise adopt a strategy that will discourage other strong potential candidates from entering the race? Thus, the broad problems faced by House Republican activists in 1964, if not the particular details, were quite similar to those confronting Republican members concerned about Martin's leadership in 1958. They were also related to the problems encountered by Democratic House members who considered a challenge to Majority Leader John McCormack, the heir apparent to the speakership, upon Rayburn's death in 1961.

In 1964, the first question—whether a challenge to Halleck was justified—was quickly resolved. Most of the fifteen Republican House members who gathered in Goodell's office the evening of the December 16 Conference readily agreed that Halleck had not assumed positive leadership; instead, he had reacted negatively or merely tolerated their proposals for change. These younger members, frustrated by continued minority status and dismayed by the election results of 1964, were looking for something more than "business as usual." Given their restricted number, they were convinced that their appeal had to be directed to a wider audience than just the House itself. As one of the more junior members summed up the reasons for going after Halleck: "The decision to run was made on the grounds that certain things had to be done. It was not made on the conviction that victory was possible, that Ford could win."

But, no matter how strong the grievances, real or imagined, as a more seasoned insurgent put it, "you don't go, unless you think you can win." Running a campaign against an incumbent leader is replete with hazards. It would inevitably generate antagonisms that would be long-lasting and potentially damaging to the minority party's chances of becoming a majority party. If their challenge were unsuccessful, the incumbent would have a great deal to say about the way in which future benefits, particularly committee assignments, would be handed out. Many of the young Turks were still at a career stage where they were giving serious consideration to a transfer to a more prestigious committee. Almost all were ambitious enough to want to play a more important role in party organization and policy determination.

But, if the risks were high, the rewards of winning would also be high. They would, they felt, have taken a long step forward toward the achievement of their eventual goal—majority status. They would have built up a sense of obligation on the part of the man they had helped put into office. They would be in a position to play an active role in the decisions he would subsequently make.

In the main, these were conservative Republicans, albeit a younger generation of "pragmatic" conservatives. They were united in the need for new and vigorous leadership, although they disagreed among themselves as to which of several candidates was best equipped to project this more constructive, positive, forward-looking image. While their broad base was moderate conservative, they ranged in philosophical outlook from far right to unorthodox liberal. They represented districts from California to Massachusetts. The characteristics, if any, that distinguished them from other House Republicans were summed up by one of the key participants:

> We picked activists and those who could stand the heat. When you hold one of these [meetings], pretty soon the word gets around. Halleck knew who was there. We didn't want those who would be embarrassed if Halleck found out—those who have a particular legislative interest and just want to pursue it or those who need Halleck's support to get the committee assignment they require.

Above all, they had among them a range and diversity of outlook that would enable them to make a reasonably accurate estimate of the strengths and weaknesses of any of the possible opposing candidates.

Only two potential challengers—the forty-two-year-old Laird, first elected to the House in 1952, and the fifty-one-year-old Ford, first elected in 1948—were seriously considered. Laird had been tapped for the important Appropriations Committee as a freshman; Ford had made the Committee in his second term and had gone on to become the principal Republican spokesman on defense appropriations. Laird had specialized in health matters and Department of Health, Education and Welfare appropriations as well as defense. Both had impressive records of party service. Ford had served as chairman of the Republican Conference since 1963. Both were key members of the Republican Policy Committee. Laird, in addition, was a member of the Republican Congressional Campaign Committee. Beginning in 1952, he had helped

put together the Republican Party platform, serving as vice-
chairman of the Platform Committee in 1960, as chairman of the
Joint Committee on Republican Principles in 1962, and as chairman of the Platform Committee in 1964.

In terms of television presence and potential for making more
effective use of the press, both candidates were considered superior to Halleck. Each of the potential challengers had other
strengths, which were at the same time, perhaps, their greatest
liabilities. The forthright and likable Ford was respected by his
colleagues. Yet, some of them felt he lacked initiative and had
failed to exploit the potential of the Republican Conference. As
two members explained the problem:

> There is a problem with any leadership position—a lack of time,
> the pressure of just so much to do and so little time to do it.
>
> That was the problem with Jerry, last year. He took over the Con-
> ference from Hoeven and everybody had high hopes, but Jerry spent
> a lot of his time on Appropriations. He's a dedicated technician. The
> Defense Subcommittee took up most of his time. He did a hell of a
> job on that committee working from 10:00 in the morning until 5:00
> at night, or later. And then Johnson put him on the Warren Com-
> mission and that was important, but time-consuming. He just couldn't
> do all that and as a result, the Conference suffered. He tried to
> recognize it, to take this dead body—not a dead body, but an in-
> effective body—and make it work, but he was spread too thin.

> Laird has some characteristics which make him better suited for the
> Conference Chairman than Ford. He's not afraid to step on people's
> toes, to push people. Ford was too good-natured, too affable.

Laird, on the other hand, was considered both more vigorous as
a leader and more controversial as a candidate, particularly
among the Wednesday Club members. Two comments illustrate
the play of these factors in the final choice of Ford over Laird.
The first comes from a strong Laird lieutenant:

> From my point of view, Mel Laird has the most prospects for leader-
> ship. He has the knowledge; he listens to other people, and he makes
> decisions. . . .
>
> I don't think resentment from San Francisco amounted to much.
> . . . If Laird had decided to go, the Wednesday group was not

enough to block him from winning. That's not the point at all. The reason Laird did not go was that he was convinced that it was not the time to have a major upheaval.

The second is from a key Ford supporter:

I felt strongly all along that Ford was the only one who had a chance to win. There wasn't any other person seriously considered other than Mel Laird. Criticism of Mel came mainly from the convention, his role as platform chairman. That criticism hasn't affected me. I just read the liberals, the Wednesday group, as pretty solidly opposed. If you split up the moderates and conservatives between Halleck and Laird, and the Wednesday group voted solidly for Halleck, that would be decisive. . . .

Laird is more controversial. He's more dynamic. He's got more leadership. At the same time, he's irritated and antagonized some people, made enemies along the line. Ford has not. I don't know how you measure these things. It's a feeling, a reading you get. There were fewer people mad at Ford and some people who were quite opposed to Laird. You end with the conclusion that Ford could command more support than anybody else. The members respect him and they like him.

Ford emerged as the stronger candidate, if not the more aggressive leader. His position as chairman of the Conference gave him an initial advantage. His age and his sixteen years of congressional service (compared with Laird's twelve) took some of the sting away from a "youth versus age" issue, which might have driven some of the more senior members, who were critical of the incumbent, back into the Halleck camp. If Laird possessed more inherent political acumen, he had also antagonized more members than Ford. As another conservative colleague commented, "Laird had several strikes against him, and not just with the Wednesday crowd. . . . Mel is damned able; he's ambitious, and that's not necessarily a fault; but he's also a maneuverer—and a lot of people have this feeling."

The most critical problem of all was keeping the number of challengers restricted to a single candidate. Here, the group that met in Goodell's office was, in a sense, only ratifying an agreement at which Ford and Laird had tentatively arrived before the Conference: Should one of them decide to enter the race, the other would not run. Laird went even further: On December 10 and 11, during the week before the Conference, he suggested to newspapermen that a contest might take place and that Ford was the likely choice.

Ford did not want to run unless he had a good chance of winning. At the same time, he recognized that it might be now or never. The 1964 election defeats provided more impetus for change than would probable mid-term gains in 1966. His position as conference chairman was a more likely springboard than the ranking minority position on Appropriations, and he felt he could not effectively discharge the demanding obligations of both positions in the Eighty-ninth Congress.

Laird's opportunities to seek higher office were more restricted than Ford's. Both Laird and Halleck were more closely identified with the Goldwater candidacy than was Ford—Laird because of his role as platform chairman, Halleck as a result of his seconding speech. A further complication faced by Laird was the presence of another member of the Wisconsin delegation, John Byrnes, in one of the top four leadership positions.[15] Byrnes, sympathetic to the Quie Committee proposals, was seriously considering resigning from his chairmanship of the Republican Policy Committee in order to devote his full-time efforts to Ways and Means. But until Byrnes submitted his resignation or let it be known that he was willing to step down, Laird's freedom to seek higher office was further limited. Finally, and probably most important, Laird recognized an obligation to side with Ford should the latter seek the opportunity to run. They were good friends. Both belonged to the influential Chowder and Marching Society. They had developed a mutual trust and admiration through long association on the Appropriations Committee and a parallel devotion to Republican Party principles. A close associate of both men reviewed the situation in mid-December: "The newspapers have been wrong about this thing. If we decide to go, the difficulty won't be in deciding between Laird and Ford. It will be up to them. . . . Once the decision is made, both are big men. They are good personal friends. They both have a great deal of admiration for each other. They will see that it does not become a three-man race."

After the Wednesday-evening meeting, Griffin tried unsuccessfully to reach Ford at home. The next morning, Griffin, Goodell, and Quie met with Ford to report the consensus of the meeting—that there should be a challenge, that Ford was the first choice of most of the participants, and that preliminary assessments seem to indicate that Ford had a good chance of winning. Ford withheld a final decision until he could discuss his plans with his family that evening. However, the young Turks were sufficiently encouraged by Ford's response to hold a second and smaller meeting that afternoon with other Republican House members in order to take further readings. In the meantime, Ford conferred with several friends who were high-ranking officials of national business associations and was not discouraged by their reactions. He later recalled the reasons that convinced him that he should run: "I think it was the fact that some very good people felt I should be a candidate and that there should be a contest for the Minority Leadership. I finally concluded that these people ought to have an opportunity for a vote."[16]

Insurgent Strategy

Perhaps the key decision in a campaign against an incumbent leader is the choice of an opposing candidate. Once that choice is made, subsequent decisions on strategy and tactics are heavily influenced by it. For example, the Ford supporters really had no choice as to whether the campaign would be conducted out in the open or, as in 1959, behind the scenes. Even before the December 16 Conference, Ford had advised Halleck that, if he decided to run, he would notify him in advance. In any event, press reaction to the Conference made an open contest almost mandatory. Television and newspaper accounts had so dampened the idea of a contest, that Ford's supporters felt they had to move rapidly in order to generate momentum for a challenge. Other key decisions such as the timing of the announcement, the content of the campaign, the decision to run independent of other contests, the kinds of individual commitments that were sought, and the degree of emphasis on "outside" versus "inside" influence were all affected by the personality of the challenger and his working relationships with his principal supporters.

On Friday, December 18, Ford went ahead with a planned

meeting of the incumbent minority members of the Appropriations Committee in his office. One of these members stayed behind to discuss the problem of leadership change; this was Silvio Conte of Massachusetts, an outspoken Wednesday Club member. Ford and Conte were still talking when a small delegation headed by Griffin, Goodell, and Quie arrived to get Ford's answer. Together with Donald Rumsfeld and Robert Ellsworth, this group formed the nucleus of the Ford campaign organization. Ellsworth, one of the more conservative members of the Wednesday Club, had gone to Ford on his own immediately following the election. They had held several conversations about party leadership before Ellsworth had been invited by Griffin to attend the smaller Thursday-afternoon meeting. In the two weeks that followed, Quie became less involved in the Ford campaign in order to concentrate on the *ad hoc* committee on organization. Conte became less active as the need to keep the Ford campaign divorced from the Wednesday Club became more acute. In addition to this organizational core, as many as thirty additional members were to play a crucial role in the Ford campaign, working primarily with their state, regional, or class delegations.

By the morning of Friday, December 18, it was assumed that the campaign was on. No debate ever took place as to whether Ford should run or not. Other Republican House members joined the group, and the key questions became those of when and how Ford should announce his candidacy. Some members urged withholding the announcement until Monday, December 21, in order to obtain maximum television exposure. Others argued for holding a press conference as early as possible, even though this would bring the incumbent Minority Leader back from his Florida vacation that much sooner. These members argued that it was imperative to seize the initiative and to get Ford on the telephone calling other members as soon and as often as possible. Persuaded as much by pressure from newspapermen as by any logical arguments, Ford scheduled a press conference for Saturday, December 19, at 11:00 A.M. After several unsuccessful attempts to reach Halleck by telephone in Florida, Ford ended up notifying him by telegram. On Saturday morning, Ford sent a telegram to the balance of his colleagues:

Today I am announcing my candidacy for the Minority leadership of
the House. During the next two years our performance as Republican
Congressmen will have a great impact on the future of our party.
I am convinced that our House Republican talent, energy and dedication can and must be utilized fully if we as a party are to better
represent and promote the best hopes of the American people and if
we are to become a majority Party. I hope I have your support. I look
forward to a personal visit with you in the near future.

My best wishes for a happy holiday season.

JERRY FORD

More than one member, and certainly Minority Leader Halleck,
would find his holiday season cut short.

Ford formally launched his campaign at a press conference held
in the hearing rooms of the Committee on Veterans Affairs, across
from his third-floor office, in the Cannon House Office Building.
After noting that the Republican Party had controlled the White
House and Congress simultaneously for only two years out of the
past thirty-three, Ford called for "new ideas, new spirit, and new
leadership."

We have within our Republican ranks a great wealth of talent,
energy, and dedication. When properly channeled and utilized to
the fullest, this talent will promote and communicate the image of
a fighting, forward-looking party seeking responsible and constructive
solutions to national problems.

By finding ways to better utilize these impressive talents through
new techniques and bold leadership, by a willingness to try new ideas,
by leading rather than simply reacting, and we can and we must develop the respect and the support of the American people.

In the question period following, Ford promised to make 60-
minute ballplayers out of all 140 members of the House Republican Party. The *Washington Sunday Star* featured a three-column
Associated Press wirephoto of the University of Michigan's most
valuable player in 1934—football center Gerald R. Ford, Jr.
Except for his receding hairline, Ford did not look much the
worse for wear in 1964. During the question period, Ford made it
clear that his campaign was in no way related to the movement to
replace Dean Burch as Republican national chairman. When

asked if Mr. Laird had indicated his views about the contest for minority leader, Ford replied, "My candidacy is on my own. I am not a part of any slate or ticket. There will be a vacancy for the House Republican Conference Chairman in January. Anyone of the 140 members can be a candidate at that time, Mr. Laird included." Ford and his supporters had considered, but abandoned, the idea of running a slate headed by Ford and Laird. They had concluded that any such slate would run the risk of antagonizing other influential members who would not be a part of the slate but who might otherwise support Ford running independently. Above all, Ford wanted to run a campaign that would not be ideological in nature and that would appeal to both the conservative and the liberal wings of the party. If, for example, Ford had suggested a Wednesday Club candidate for either whip or Policy Committee chairman, he would have run the risk of losing the support of those House members who felt an obligation to the incumbents or of those southern House members who resented the role played by the liberals in the civil rights fight. Ford also feared that, if he ran in tandem with Laird, the Wednesday Club members, who were still resentful of Laird's role as Platform Committee chairman in San Francisco, would be further alienated. While relatively unimportant in the House in terms of numbers, the Wednesday Club members had ties with the national press and with governors such as Rockefeller and Scranton that could not be discounted. In the final analysis, it was as much the difficulty of putting together such a slate as it was the problem of maintaining party harmony afterward that led Ford to his decision to run independent of any other candidate.

. The main thrust of the Ford campaign was based upon obtaining as many solid commitments to his candidacy as possible as early as possible. It was hoped that he then would be able to hand on or increase his majority up through the day of the vote, January 4. His supporters were aware that Halleck's forces had estimated that they would win by twenty votes in 1959, only to barely edge Martin by four votes on a second ballot. The Ford strategy called for the candidate and his supporters to contact as many members as possible by telephone and in person before Halleck could return and begin his counterattack. Because many members were in their home districts or on vacations, one of the first steps taken by Ford's supporters was the preparation of a master list indicating the current location and telephone number of each member. Before the campaign was over, three updated lists had been prepared. Thirty to thirty-five of the House members used information taken from these lists to urge their colleagues to vote for Ford.

Vote counting is an intricate process. At his press conference, Ford properly avoided giving a premature answer to the question of just how many members were committed to his candidacy. Given the tendency for each side to overestimate its strength—particularly true of the incumbent side—only the most cautious interpretation of what constitutes a commitment is justified under conditions of a secret-ballot vote. At the beginning, both sides operate with imperfect information:

> You start with the boys you know are with you. Those are the ones you know best. Then, you take the boys who you know are with Halleck. You talk with other members and you build up the lists on both sides. At the beginning the bulk are in the middle and those are the ones you concentrate on. You go down the lists with other members, members who know them, who are in the same delegation, those who know who is mad at Halleck and who is close to Ford. You find out who are the people who are likely to be influential with the members.
>
> Without counting the new members, I would say as of now that Ford has a 3 to 1 ratio of those who are definitely for Ford or Halleck. Of course, we know our own side better; we don't know those who are definitely for Halleck. And if they are, if Ford calls, they won't tell him. So the ratio could be 3 to 2 or 3 to 3 or even 3 to 4 for Halleck. The big group right now is in the middle—the undecided. Leaving out the new members, it's god-damn close.

The twenty freshman members presented a particularly difficult problem for the insurgents. Too much was at stake in the way of committee assignments to ask these incoming members to make a formal commitment. However, a number of contacts were made to inform these members as to the nature of Ford's challenge and to obtain a sense of how they were leaning. In the final analysis, the freshmen were heavily dependent upon the advice given to them by senior members from their region or state. For example, several senior southern members close to Ford played a particularly crucial role in securing a sympathetic response from among the nine new Republican members from southern and border states.

From the beginning, the Ford forces emphasized an inside strategy.[17] That is to say, the bulk of their time and effort was concentrated on member-to-member contacts. But they did not neglect outside, or indirect, pressures. They had worked until midnight Friday night and for several hours on Saturday morning, drafting Ford's press release and preparing Ford for the kinds of questions he might face at the press conference. They hoped to capitalize on front-page Sunday headlines as evidence of how Ford's favorable image would help the Republican cause in the months ahead. Other indirect pressures were utilized when and where they were thought to be effective, but the main thrust of this part of the Ford campaign was to neutralize the efforts of outsiders. National party leaders, interest-group representatives, state and local party officials and fund raisers who might otherwise have been active in Halleck's behalf were told that this was an internal affair, a decision that should be left to House members. The word was passed that "Jerry was a sound guy, that he had a good chance of winning, and it would be a good thing not to be active against Ford." Ford's position on the Defense Appropriations Subcommittee and his contacts with the Michigan automotive industry, U.S. Steel, the National Association of Manufacturers, the Chamber of Commerce, and other national business leaders stood him in good stead. As one House member commented, "It was mostly Jerry's reputation—he had sold himself over the years." Ford also made a point of calling national political leaders, including Goldwater, Miller, Nixon, and a number of important governors, as soon as he announced. Ford's supporters felt that it was particularly important that his efforts to oust Halleck not be associated in any way with movements either to remove or to keep Dean Burch as national chairman.

As the campaign entered its second and final week, Ford flew to Michigan to join his family in a planned skiing vacation over the Christmas holidays. Ford's supporters were convinced they had the votes to win, but they began to worry, more and more, about how to maintain their lead. If anything, the absence of a vigorous counterattack from the Halleck camp made them all the more uneasy. Griffin, Goodell, and Rumsfeld began to reach out for ways to keep the momentum of the campaign alive. Outside strategies began to occupy more of their time. Every related column and newspaper story was scrutinized for its implications and the kinds of reactions it might engender among the various factions of the party. Reprints of Ford's January *Fortune* article —"What Can Save the G.O.P.?"—were mailed to as many members as possible, despite the advice of one Ford supporter, who feared the moderate tone of the article might lead to right-wing defections. In the hope of generating a bandwagon effect, vote estimates were released to the Associated Press and United Press wire services on Thursday, December 31, five days before the vote. That day, the wire services carried stories containing the following breakdown: solid for Ford, 61; leaning toward Ford, 20; unknown sentiments, 29; solid for Halleck, 25; leaning toward Halleck, 5. Halleck aides responded by announcing their own total of 85 votes committed or leaning to Halleck, but, unlike the Ford supporters, they did not offer a breakdown of votes.[18]

Ford flew back from Michigan on Saturday, January 2. On Sunday, his supporters learned of a mid-day meeting of ten or twelve members, mainly conservatives, to which Halleck had been invited. Three members who had been active in Ford's behalf were among those who attended. By mid-afternoon, the "solid" count for Ford began to drop. Counterefforts by Halleck and his supporters were beginning to cut into the Ford lead.

Incumbent Response

Charles Halleck had flown back from Lake Wales, Florida, the day after Ford's December 19 announcement, upset and irritated by the challenge but confident that he could campaign and win on his record. He had several times been disappointed in his quest for higher national office, but he had never lost an election. Five consecutive times, the citizens of the Jasper-Newton circuit, in Indiana, had elected him prosecuting attorney—his first success coming in 1924, shortly after his graduation from the Indiana

University Law School. In 1935, he had entered a special election and won the first of sixteen campaigns for election to the U.S. House of Representatives. With the behind-the-scenes support of presidential aspirant Thomas E. Dewey, Halleck had emerged as majority leader at the beginning of the Eightieth Congress (1947–48).[19] He had been re-elected majority leader for the Eighty-third Congress (1953–54) without opposition. As incumbent minority leader from 1959 to 1964, Halleck had a number of assets working for him. Chief among these were his demonstrated record as a party leader; his position at the center of communications for House Republicans; his past and present influence over committee assignments and other appointments; credits built up from past favors rendered to members, particularly campaign and fund-raising speeches; strong ties with party officials outside the House and with interest-group representatives; good contacts with the national press, particularly syndicated columnists; and a general resistance to change on the part of many Republican House members.

Halleck's initial steps were calculated to bring these advantages into play. His first decision was to campaign on his record as minority leader under Eisenhower and, particularly, on his record of successful opposition to the Kennedy-Johnson programs. On Monday, December 21, he held a press conference. The text of a statement, which had been sent to all House Republicans, was released to the press. It began:

> I expect to continue as Republican Minority Leader in the House of Representatives and will do all that I properly and reasonably can to that end. In this endeavor I sincerely hope for the support of my friends.
>
> After all, the decision is for the Republican Members of the House to make. In making that decision I would assume that my record as Minority Leader over the past six years would be an important consideration. . . .

After summarizing a number of organizational changes he had helped to implement, Halleck stressed the Republican record of solidarity in support of party principles:

> On vote after vote Republicans from North, South, East and West— from urban and rural areas—have stood shoulder to shoulder on issues

of vital importance to America. On six major issues over the past two years, our roll call votes averaged 162 to 3, an amazing example of teamwork. A study of Republican votes in the House from January 1961 to mid-1964 shows that where we had a policy position, the Republicans averaged 150 to 14 on 51 House roll calls.

With our numbers reduced it is more important than ever that we continue this sort of teamwork.

This would be my purpose as Republican Leader.

As the party's principal legislative floor leader for eighteen years, Halleck was in a position to know more about what kinds of influences moved men and about their strengths and weaknesses than any other Republican in the House.

Halleck spent most of that first week activating the communication network that had been so effective in the past. His first calls were to personal friends including members of the Indiana delegation and Les Arends, the minority whip. Other House members such as James Utt, Bob Wilson, John Rhodes, and Paul Findley phoned or dropped by Halleck's office to offer assistance. Later, Halleck expanded his contacts to include the "deans" of large state delegations and other House members whom he had rendered favors in the past. He seldom asked for an outright commitment. When he talked to freshman House members, he inquired about their committee preferences but made few, if any, outright promises. A close associate commented on the reasons for Halleck's approach:

> Charlie feels that you cannot seek a commitment for yourself without committing yourself to repay that commitment. If you get a commitment there would be some obligation, and maybe the leader wouldn't be able to live up to his side of the agreement. . . .
>
> As a leader you must be careful what you promise and to whom. It's damn practical politics not to overcommit yourself—not promise something you can't follow through on. You don't know if you can keep your promises.

Halleck did not appear to capitalize fully on his credits outstanding. If "he had money in the bank," as one close associate put it, "he wasn't able to cash in." In part, this was because Halleck was reluctant to ask others to help him. In part, his problem was complicated by the fact that many of his most loyal supporters had been defeated. He was aware that the contest would be decided by secret ballot, a precedent established in his own victory over Martin. Thus, commitments would be difficult to enforce. Toward the end of the campaign, Halleck began to press more strongly the claims he had accumulated over the years.

From the beginning, Halleck's strategy in terms of inside versus outside influence had been mixed. Probably no challenger could match Halleck's ties with state and local party leaders, ties that fund-raising dinners and appearances had helped to strengthen. Halleck's contacts with interest-group representatives, enhanced by favors rendered on legislation over the years, were equally pervasive. A Ford supporter commented:

> We knew that Charlie would make use of lobbyists. He knows most of them. A lot owe their positions in the companies they represent to their close associations with Halleck. So he has many contacts and many good friends, among them. . . . And, of course, Halleck has done favors in the past for others. So these people have a vested interest in maintaining Halleck in the position of Minority Leader.

While some lobbyists would hesitate to interfere with an internal matter like a vote on party leadership, most would proceed, but with caution so as not to antagonize whoever might win. In some cases, newspaper publishers and financial contributors in a member's home district made veiled and more direct inquiries about how the member intended to vote, and this generated more resentment than support for Halleck. Again, the secret ballot would, largely, render such pressures ineffective.

Halleck's national press support had, if anything, probably been hurt by his performances at the joint Republican congressional press conferences. Almost any man would have been overshadowed by the mellifluous Senate minority leader, Everett M. Dirksen. Quickly dubbed the "Ev and Charlie show," the straightman, Halleck, more often than not, got only a profile shot in subsequent television news programs. However, the contacts with newspapermen Halleck had cultivated over the years were an undeniable asset. For example, during December, a number of national columnists, including William S. White, Arthur Krock, Richard Wilson, and Raymond Moley, wrote columns sympathetic to Halleck and critical of efforts being made to depose him.[20] Editorial comment was generally supportive of Halleck.

Even the liberally inclined *New York Times* warned against the dangers of playing musical chairs with the leadership.

A final advantage possessed by any incumbent leader—one that proved particularly effective in Halleck's case as the contest drew to a close—is a general resistance to change. House, and, particularly, the senior, Republicans had become familiar with the ways in which Halleck operated. Any new leader would bring about a change in these working arrangements. If the new relationship might be an improvement, it was as likely as not to be less satisfactory. A number of the proposals being discussed by the Quie Committee, including those aimed at limiting the number of positions that could be held by ranking minority members, were threatening to some senior members; others—such as the second-ranking members on the Appropriations and Armed Services committees—stood to gain. Probably no member could look forward to the vote, and the bitterness it would probably engender, without mixed feelings. These cross-pressures helped to generate further support for the status quo.

Halleck faced a series of complications as the campaign entered the final week. His efforts to reconvert House members committed to Ford were inhibited by the Christmas and the New Year's holidays. Most of his supporters—and they were far fewer than those working for Ford—did not begin making telephone contacts until after Christmas. Over the weekend preceding the January 4 vote, as House members began to reassemble in Washington, D.C., both sides launched final intensive drives to capture wavering members.

Laird Announces

While the pace of the Halleck-Ford contest had been intensifying, several House members close to Representative Laird had been quietly, but effectively, engaged in a low-keyed operation to line up votes for their candidate for conference chairman. Laird made no formal announcement until December 29, the Tuesday after Christmas.[21] However, Glenard Lipscomb, a close friend and long-time associate on the Appropriations Committee, had circulated a letter on December 22, 1964, urging support for Laird. His letter read in part:

With Jerry Ford having announced that he will seek the position of Minority Leader in the 89th Congress, we will need to give attention to the task of filling the position of Chairman of the Republican Conference.

I strongly believe that Mel Laird has the ability and experience to make him a very effective Chairman of the Conference and hope you feel the same.

We are all aware of Mel's fine record in the House and as a member of the Appropriations Committee. In addition, he has served the Party brilliantly in positions of highest responsibility. His service as Chairman of the Committee on Republican Principles and Policies in 1962 and as Chairman of the Platform Committee for the 1964 Convention are two outstanding examples. . . .

Several other able young conservatives, among them Robert Michel of Illinois, first elected in 1956, and James Battin of Montana, first elected in 1960, joined Lipscomb in rounding up votes for Laird's candidacy. All were in agreement that his campaign should be kept separate from the Ford-Halleck contest.

Laird's announcement for conference chairman was like a red flag to East Coast liberals. It reinforced their belief that Ford and Laird were linked in a conservative conspiracy to take over the party leadership—a leadership team they feared Laird would dominate. Furthermore, they believed the conference chairmanship possessed much greater potential for innovation than either the Policy Committee chairmanship or the position of House whip—a view shared by the Laird supporters.

Later that week, the new dean of the New York Republican delegation, Paul A. Fino, announced his support of Halleck's leadership and his own candidacy for conference chairman. Laird supporters estimated that almost any liberal eastern candidate would receive as many as fifty votes. As a result of other developments, including the lack of unanimous support within the New York delegation, Fino's campaign got no further than a brief discussion at the breakfast caucus the New York delegation held on the morning of the Conference.

On the Sunday evening preceding the vote, Wednesday Club members, meeting at the Washington, D.C., home of New York Representative Ogden Reid, decided to field a last-minute candidate of their own against Laird. After considering several possibilities, they finally settled on Peter H. B. Frelinghuysen, one of the few moderate members in their ranks who had seniority equivalent to Laird's. Probably only a scattering of Republican House members outside the Wednesday Club were aware that, after the November, 1964, election, Frelinghuysen had accepted an invitation to join the Club.

Down to the Wire

In the hectic atmosphere of the final weekend, the fears of the Ford supporters that their campaign would peak too early began to materialize. The swing of votes back toward Halleck continued at a faster pace through Sunday afternoon. Earlier that day, Halleck had met with a group made up, in the main, of midwestern conservatives; this group put forth its demands about the kinds of leadership changes it would like to see if Halleck were retained. Among this group were several members who had worked actively for Ford. Griffin, Goodell, and Rumsfeld, the key counters for Ford, had been keeping their estimates as conservative as possible, changing members from solid to leaning, or leaning toward Ford to leaning toward Halleck, as more information came in. By 4:00 P.M., Sunday, their count had dropped to fifty-six solid votes for Ford. As they later commented, in reference to the arguments that were winning votes for Halleck, "These Republicans liked Charlie and they respected him. He's been a hardworking Republican. He's spoken in many of their districts. Many of these felt they had a personal obligation to Charlie Halleck. Almost every Republican in the House is indebted to him in some way."

The challengers intensified their efforts. Ford, who at one point was considering going home for dinner, stayed on to continue his telephoning until 11:00 P.M. By 6:00 P.M., the tide toward Halleck appeared to have ebbed. Several of the members who had been considered doubtful called in with reassurances or dropped by Ford's House office to report on new converts.

Attention now shifted to keeping wavering large-state delegations in line. Members of the Pennsylvania delegation, which caucused at 6:00 P.M., were reassured that no decisions had as yet been made about House minority employees; they were upset because of rumors that one of their patronage appointees was in danger of demotion. The Ohio delegation was also a center of intense activity; one of Halleck's chief supporters in that delegation was arguing, "Why blame Halleck for the election outcome?" and seemed to be making some inroads among other Ohio members who had previously been leaning toward Ford. Telephone calls were made to shore up support in these and other key delegations.

Throughout the final drive, every effort was made to prevent the Ford campaign from being labeled either proconservative or proliberal. In order to avoid alienating the liberals, Ford refused to meet with the conservatives who had earlier approached Halleck. When, on Sunday evening, the Wednesday Club met to evaluate its position, one Ford campaigner commented, "God help us if they endorse Ford as a bloc—we'll lose conservatives all over the place." Calls were made to several sympathetic club members to prevent such a possibility from being realized.

A whole range of last-minute concerns kept the Ford supporters working until midnight. A respected senior member of a wavering large-state delegation was approached about nominating Ford. In part because of his past relations with Halleck and in part because of the unrest within his delegation, he declined the opportunity. Ford turned to Michigan Representative Elford A. Cederberg, who had nominated him for conference chairman in 1963. When Ford left, about 11:00 P.M., he took home with him a copy of the opening day's *Congressional Record* from 1963. If he won, he would have little time to familiarize himself with procedures or to prepare his introduction of the Speaker-elect.

The Halleck supporters worked neither as intensively nor as late. When they went home, however, most believed that their final weekend efforts had been successful. Their Sunday-evening count, while not as "hard" as the Ford estimates, showed over eighty members committed or leaning to the incumbent Minority Leader. Several of his close supporters were not as optimistic: "I thought we had a fifty-fifty chance. . . . I will say this. I think there was probably a greater reluctance to level with Charlie than with Ford." And another recalled, "On the Sunday before the vote, I knew it was going to be close. I thought we would win by about two votes."

The Ford supporters spent Sunday evening going over the conference agenda and discussing various contingencies that might arise from last-minute maneuvers by the Halleck forces. Ground rules had been worked out by Clarence Brown, ranking member of the Rules Committee, and agreed to by both sides. Plans were made to counteract any changes such as an attempt to do away with the secret-ballot agreement or to postpone the vote on the minority leadership. As the small group of Ford supporters broke up its meeting, at midnight, some ten hours before the vote, its members were cautiously optimistic. Their final estimate read: solid for Ford, 67; leaning toward Ford, 22; undecided, 7; solid for Halleck, 36; leaning toward Halleck, 8. They reminded each other that Halleck was supposed to have at least a twenty-vote edge going into the Conference in 1959, and that Martin had been confident that he, Martin, was going to win, too. But they reasoned that neither side in 1959 had engaged in anything like the organizational effort that they had undertaken in the past two weeks. In making the comparison to 1963, they felt much more confident. Again, that contest had been a far more spontaneous, short-term effort. Except for some preconference telephoning by Ford and endorsements at state-delegation breakfast meetings the following morning, the challengers had done about all they could do to ensure Ford's success.

The January, 1965 Conference

The first Republican Conference of the Eighty-ninth Congress was gaveled to order promptly at 9:30 A.M. on Monday, January 4, 1965; wielding the gavel was the outgoing conference chairman, Gerald R. Ford, Jr. Since Ford was a candidate for higher office, he turned the gavel over to the past vice-chairman William Cramer of Florida, who was subsequently elected temporary chairman of the Conference by acclamation. Representative Richard Poff of Virginia was elected temporary secretary, and the first roll was called to ascertain a quorum.[22] The next order of business was to adopt the rules, including provisions for secret-ballot elections for contested offices. Both Halleck and Ford had agreed to this provision, in advance, following the precedent set in the Martin-Halleck contest of 1959 and ratified in the Ford-Hoeven contest in 1963. They had also agreed to limit the nominating speeches to a single speech for each candidate. The Ford forces suffered several anxious moments brought on by comment made during the Illinois delegation's breakfast caucus that Arends, who had fought for an open ballot for Martin in 1959, might make a similar appeal this time. However, Clarence Brown offered the rules resolution as agreed upon, and it passed without dissent.

The next item on the agenda was the election of a permanent conference chairman. Glenard Lipscomb nominated Laird. Frelinghuysen, who had not been put forward as a candidate until 8:00 the previous evening, had not arranged for someone to nominate him until he had talked with fellow New Jersey Representative William T. Cahill on the way to the Conference that morning. Frelinghuysen was, perhaps, as surprised as anyone by the strength of his showing: 62 votes against 77 cast for Laird. He had reaped the benefit of what anti-Laird sentiment existed, together with most of the East Coast regional vote. In addition, it appeared that a late Sunday evening telephone call to Halleck by John Lindsay had generated a scattering of votes from among Halleck's supporters for the Wednesday Club candidate.[23] Some of these Halleck people felt that Laird had worked for Ford, or even pushed him into the campaign. (Lindsay, Bradford Morse of Massachusetts, and several other liberals, apprehensive about Laird and believing that Halleck was no more conservative than Ford, were to respond by casting their votes for Halleck for minority leader.) The stage was set for the climax of the campaigns waged by Ford and Halleck.

Ford was nominated by Cederberg, Halleck by Indiana Representative Ross Adair. Both nominators took the highroad in their nominating speeches, saying little about the opposition and talking mainly of the virtues of their respective candidates. The mechanisms of the vote were simple. No formal roll was called. The congressmen merely wrote the name of one or the other candidate on white slips that had been provided and dropped their ballots into a closed box placed on a table sitting in front of Representative Catherine May of Washington, the chief teller. To the consternation of Mrs. May and her fellow congressmen, no matter how many times they counted the ballots, the tally came out 72 votes for Ford, 68 for Halleck, and one ballot marked "present." This totaled 141 votes, one more than the full quorum of Republican representatives. In order to prevent any possible charge of misconduct, newly elected conference Chairman Laird ordered a second roll call. This time, members brought forward their ballots as their names were called alphabetically. Despite some last-minute efforts to change the outcome, the lines held firm, and Ford was elected the new minority leader by a vote of 73 to 67. The former incumbent moved to make the vote unanimous. In the few minutes remaining before the new Congress convened, its Republican members re-elected John Byrnes Policy Committee chairman. They also listened to a brief explanation from Brown on the Republican position on proposed changes in House rules.

Approximately a half-hour later, on the House floor, all the Republicans joined ranks to vote for Ford for speaker of the House of Representatives of the Eighty-ninth Congress. To no one's surprise, his Democratic opponent, John W. McCormack of Massachusetts, was overwhelmingly re-elected. Ford was to find himself a minority leader in more ways than this, even within his own ranks, in the months ahead.

Why did Ford win and Halleck lose? As with all close leadership contests, a great range of factors combined to decide the outcome. Halleck's own cryptic explanation masks as much as it reveals. "It's the only election I've ever lost," Halleck said, "and it was because I got myself involved in a beauty contest." Much more was at stake than contrasts in age and physical appearance, as the respective statements of the two candidates on December 19 and December 21 clearly demonstrate. While ideology, in terms of their voting records, was not directly at issue, the activists were able to convince a majority of their colleagues that Ford would project a more positive image to the nation and work toward more constructive alternative programs within the House of Representatives.

Personal factors—"the mysteries of how men interact with one another, of what leads people into enmity, jealousy, friendship"—played an important part in the outcome.[24] Some Republican House members were so dominated by strong friendship, a long-held grudge, or intense personal ambition that they made up their minds early for one of the two candidates and were not to be budged. The vast majority of the members approached the vote with considerable ambivalence. A key Ford lieutenant commented, "Most members were trying to make an assessment on the merits of the two candidates and most were torn between [them]. They were, themselves, in conflict. They were moving in different directions, struggling to decide which way to go. These were guys really trying to think about what was best for the party, not just what was best for themselves." And a Halleck supporter echoed these remarks: "I doubt if any person who voted did not have mixed feelings at the time." Since close leadership contests inevitably involve a high degree of personal indecision, the search for an underlying rationale for change and the ability to seize the initiative and maintain the momentum of the campaign become all the more important.

The necessary, but not sufficient, cause for revolt was the Republican election disaster of November, 1964. The Goldwater defeat, together with the net loss of thirty-eight Republican House seats, created the psychological climate within which revolt flourished. Some of the same pressures that eventually led Dean Burch to tender his resignation as Republican national chairman, in mid-January, 1965, were at work in the overthrow of Halleck. The Goldwater nomination and the election results created more internal dissension and unrest in the Republican Party than any event since the split between the Taft and Roosevelt wings of the party, in 1912, which led to Wilson's election. But Halleck, unlike Burch, was not primarily a scapegoat. The seeds of dissatisfaction with Halleck extended back to bitterness engendered by his defeat of Martin in 1959. This irritation and unrest were compounded by the continuing frustrations of the minority status of the party. Agitation for change, only temporarily quieted by Ford's defeat of Hoeven in 1963, intensified throughout the long and trying sessions of the Eighty-eighth Congress. Halleck could not be blamed directly for the election debacle, but it provided an excuse for promoting a revolt that had long been fermenting. But it was not so much the psychological climate created as the kinds of House Republicans who were defeated that ultimately made a change in leadership possible. The activists, led by Griffin and Goodell, would not have challenged Halleck's leadership unless they had thought they stood a good chance of winning. In the main, it was the more senior and conservative House members who were defeated. It was these same kinds of members who subsequently rallied behind Halleck in his contest with Ford. Without the heavy election losses of 1964, it is extremely unlikely that a challenge would have been initiated, though the continued frustrations of minority status and increasing dissatisfaction with Halleck's leadership probably made an eventual challenge inevitable.

By late November, however, sentiment in favor of a leadership change had largely abated. Only a scattering of the Republican House members had returned to Washington. Many had gone south for vacations or were out of the country. While a few members were still debating ways to improve party leadership, perhaps the majority of the members had, by this time, decided to go along with Halleck and Arends for at least another two years. It was at this point that the Curtis letter was circulated to the membership. As a key participant later recalled, "It was like throwing a match into some tinder that was dry." The Republican Conference in mid-December was called for purposes other than leadership change. Its most important consequence, however, was to put Halleck on trial and bring back to Washington a widely diversified group of younger activists, convinced that the first step toward achieving majority status was to obtain new and more vigorous leadership. Of the two most likely challengers, Ford and Laird, the former emerged as the candidate with the best chance of winning. By dint of superior organization and hard campaigning, the young Turks were able to establish an early lead, which was reduced but never relinquished. Ford was successful because 30–35 members worked actively in his behalf to obtain commitments from a majority of the 140 Republican representatives-elect.

Halleck's counterattack was a classic illustration of "too little and too late." His first decision was to campaign on his record. From the beginning, he underestimated the strength of his opposition. He did most of his own telephoning. He had far fewer members working actively in his behalf. He seldom asked for commitments, and he failed to press home the natural advantages accruing to the incumbent. Not until the last days of the campaign did he begin to go all out in calling in the obligations owed to him for past favors rendered. As a close associate reviewed the Halleck campaign: "Ours was a low-key operation. The other side was cranked-up. Halleck felt he had made his record as best he could, and if that wasn't good enough, O.K. It was not a great production over here. There were no panic buttons pushed as far as he was concerned." Halleck did not even make full use of the potential influence he could exercise on committee assignments, particularly with freshmen. While the Ford supporters were able to contact every member at least once, a number of Republicans never heard from the Halleck camp—including at least two freshmen. One of these commented:

> One thing that impressed me about the Ford people were the statistics. They apparently had the votes to back them up. Halleck was claiming he had eighty-five votes, but he hadn't even bothered to contact me. If Halleck was that much out of touch with his troops, he wasn't doing a good job as far as being a leader. Frankly, this had as much to do with my vote as anything. That impressed me very unfavorably.

Halleck himself concluded, "The vote was 73 to 67. I didn't go all out. I could have put a lot of heat on in a lot of places, and I think changed the outcome. It was my decision to campaign on my record."

Despite Halleck's slow start and his tendency to "go it alone," the tide was turning in his favor in the final stages of the campaign. The many advantages possessed by an incumbent began to have their effect. An observation by one member, who was listed as "solid" by the Ford supporters until just before the vote, is revealing: "A lot of people just didn't know how they were going to vote up until the end. . . . I waited myself until the morning of the vote to make up my mind. I finally decided to vote for Halleck. There were so many reasons to vote for Ford, but not enough reasons to vote against Halleck." And a member of the Indiana delegation commented:

Charlie was better known. He came into the districts; he met the party workers. He was one of the best campaign fund-raisers there was. I'm sure this bothered a lot of people who had made commitments to vote against Charlie. Their consciences hurt them, because they had been the people who had said, "Gee, Charlie, I'm having a fund-raising dinner in my district. Will you come and help me?" And Charlie would say, "Well, I'm tied up and awfully busy, but I'll come out and do it for you anyway." And out he'd come. This helped us particularly as the lines began to narrow, as we began to know where people stood. I think it began to affect the outcome. If we had had a few more days here on the spot, Charlie could not have been tipped.

The secret ballot prevents any definitive assessment of the final vote. It is possible, however, to reconstruct from newspaper accounts and interviews a reasonably accurate estimate of the breakdown of votes by state delegations. Halleck's chief sources of strength came from his own Indiana delegation, a substantial majority of the Illinois delegation (headed by Arends), and near standoffs in the large California and Ohio delegations. Halleck probably retained a majority of Ohio's fifteen votes; Ford won a somewhat higher proportion of California's fourteen votes. In addition to these votes, Ford's winning coalition was composed of his own Michigan delegation, the preponderance of votes in New York, Pennsylvania, New Jersey, and the New England states, and an unexpectedly high proportion of southern Republican votes. When a shift of four votes will make a difference in the outcome, all votes are crucial. However, Ford's ability to enlist the support of several senior southern Republicans in his behalf was one of the most important factors in his victory. In addition, Ford held an edge in most of the middle-sized state delegations such as those of Wisconsin, Kansas, Minnesota, and New Jersey. With the possible exceptions of the last two, no medium-to-large state delegation—save those of the candidates' own states—lined up solidly for either member. Many of the smaller state delegations split their votes as well. In terms of ideological support, Ford received a substantial majority of the Wednesday Club members' votes, more than held his own with the moderate conservatives, and picked up most of the South and a scattering of hard-core conservatives elsewhere. Halleck, in contrast, did somewhat better among the most conservative members outside the South, almost held his own with the moderates, and picked up as many as six to eight liberal votes. Ideology was not directly at issue, but differences in outlook were reflected in the "young Turk versus old guard" division that developed. In the final analysis, it was the bottom-heavy structure of the House Republican Party that made victory possible for Ford. The bulk of his support, and certainly the organizational nucleus of his campaign, came from members elected since 1956.

Whether Halleck could have reversed the outcome if he had gone all out, or if the had put on "a lot of heat in a lot of places," is, of course, a moot question. It does seem probable that, if the campaign had continued for a week into the session, or if the secret ballot had not been used, Halleck would have retained his position. But these are academic speculations. For want of a reversal of four votes on the morning of January 4, 1965, Halleck's long career of party leadership in the House of Representatives was ended.

6

.

.

OUT-PARTY STRATEGY: REPUBLICAN NATIONAL COMMITTEE REBUILDING POLITICS, 1964–66

.

JOHN F. BIBBY AND ROBERT J. HUCKSHORN

When a political party suffers a crushing electoral defeat, a defeat so severe as to raise questions about its capacity to function as a viable alternative to the dominant party, how does it react and how does it attempt to regain its vitality? What strategies is it likely to follow? What types of leaders will it choose? What institutional mechanisms for rebuilding are available to a defeated minority party?

These questions have obvious relevance for the post-1964 Republican Party. The defeat administered in 1964 was so severe that one acute observer suggested that the United States no longer had a two-party system, but, rather, a "one-and-one-half" party system.[1] The questions of how the recovery drive of the party would be directed and who would direct it became salient intra-party concerns almost immediately after the election, as various elements of the party vied for positions of influence. There was, for example, an intense leadership struggle among House Republicans (see Chapter 5),[2] and, from the GOP governors, an assertion of their intention to play a prominent role in national party politics. Because the Republican National Committee's operations are national in scope and, therefore, affect the activities of Republican governors, senators, representatives, state chairmen, and state legislators, the question of who would control the Committee became critical in the months following the election; whoever gained such control could be expected to play a decisive role in determining the route the GOP would take on what it hoped would be the way back to power.

Specifically, the National Committee controversy revolved around whether Dean Burch of Arizona, Senator Barry Goldwater's designee as national chairman, would be retained. The manner in which this question was resolved had symbolic and ideological implications for the various elements of the party, as well as direct relevance for the actual strategies the party would pursue.

In spite of the importance that was attached to the National Committee leadership struggle, many seasoned observers and knowledgeable scholars have found national committees to be severely limited in power; their functioning has, in fact, been characterized as "politics without power."[3] Nevertheless, some national committees have been more important than others, and some chairmen have made a greater impact than others. The character and operations of either national committee depend largely on three factors: (1) the chairman and his style of leadership, (2) whether the party is in control of the White House, and (3) the internal conditions of the party.

A national chairman can, if he wishes, dominate his committee, because it is unwieldly in size[4] and composed of members scattered throughout the nation; it meets infrequently (usually twice a year) and usually ratifies the initiatives of the chairman and the executive committee. Even if he is part-time, as most Republican chairmen have been, his very presence in Washington and at the headquarters usually assures him of the loyalty of the staff and the acquiescence of the members. In short, the chairman of the party can direct the operations of the national committee and can, in fact, put his personal stamp on it if he so desires.

The character of the national committee is also shaped by its position vis-à-vis the White House. If a party controls the presidency, it has a central focus and it has more resources, including those of the executive branch, available for the task of electing fellow partisans. In such circumstances, the national committee is apt to become relatively unimportant and fellow partisans within the administration are apt to shoulder important party responsibilities.[5] Lacking the resources and benefits that go along with winning the White House, and often badly split internally, the out party desperately needs a national party organization to direct its intended recapture of major offices. Hence, the national committee of the out party is normally of more significance than that of the in party.

National committee activities and policies will also be influenced by the internal condition of the party. For example, if the party is severely divided ideologically and if relations between various party organs are strained, national committee influence is apt to suffer. Similarly, the committee's capacity to effect its goals will be hampered if its treasury is depleted.

Since political leadership of a national committee involves the complex interrelationships of political circumstances and personal leadership styles, an analysis of the Republican National Committee's post-1964 role in party affairs must take into account both the situation in which the GOP found itself after the election and the personality and leadership style of its national chairman at the time.

The Post-1964 State of the GOP

The Electoral Problem. The calamitous consequences of the 1964 election left the GOP in its weakest position since the Roosevelt landslide of 1936 (Fig. 1). The erosion of Republican strength was not just a 1964 phenomenon. Rather, the party's descent could actually be traced from 1952 (Fig. 2). These losses were but symptoms of a basic Republican problem: the diminishing percentage of Republican identifiers among the electorate. Despite

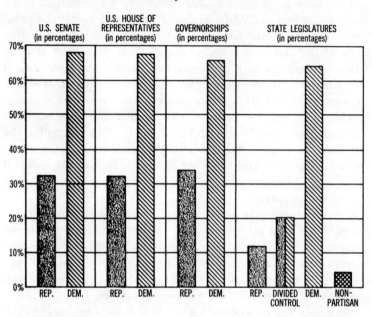

FIGURE 1
PARTISAN CONTROL OF MAJOR ELECTIVE OFFICES IN 1965

the lopsided Eisenhower victories in the 1950's, the Republican percentage of the electorate had fallen from 38 per cent, in 1940, to 27 per cent, in 1965, whereas the Democratic percentage had risen from 42 per cent to 50 per cent during the same period (Fig. 3). Without question, the basic strategic problem for every GOP chairman during this period had been the minority position of the party itself. The 1964 results had reinforced that position, and speculation was widespread that the party might not survive.

Intraparty Conflict. The wounds inflicted by Republicans upon their own kind during the preconvention period were festering sores after the San Francisco Convention. The Convention had failed to meet one of its primary responsibilities—that of supplying a basis for compromise among the party's competing groups. Furthermore, the intensely partisan atmosphere of the campaign that followed intensified the disunity of the party. Renewed intraparty warfare broke out immediately after the election, as

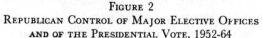

FIGURE 2
REPUBLICAN CONTROL OF MAJOR ELECTIVE OFFICES
AND OF THE PRESIDENTIAL VOTE, 1952-64

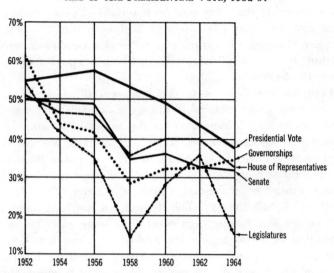

contesting factions hurled recriminations at each other.[6] Some pro-Goldwater forces deeply resented the reluctance of some moderates to support the presidential ticket. The moderates and

FIGURE 3
PARTY IDENTIFICATION OF THE U.S. ELECTORATE, 1940-65

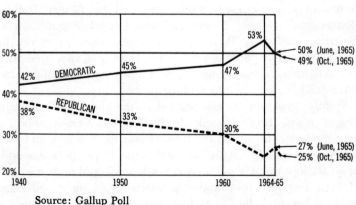

Source: Gallup Poll

liberals, for their part, accused the Goldwater organization of caring little for the party, wishing only to preside over its ruins.[7] The Goldwater supporters themselves were torn by dissension, some believing that they had been unfairly treated during the campaign and that the campaign had been ineptly managed. Stephen Shadegg, a long-time aide to Senator Goldwater, wrote a scathing indictment of the campaign, which was published shortly after the election.[8]

Complicating these unity problems was the lack of an acknowledged leader who could draw the divided party together. The House Republicans were in the throes of a campaign to unseat their leader—Charles Halleck of Indiana. Senator Goldwater was no longer in office and, in any case, was in no position to unite the warring factions of the GOP. Former President Eisenhower, though maintaining his interest in party affairs, was not inclined to enter the fray. The Republican National Committee was at low ebb, having been blamed by some party leaders for managing or mismanaging the Goldwater campaign. Separate extraparty groups were sprouting across the country, threatening to draw manpower and money resources away from established party organizations.

This proliferation of independent Republican "splinter groups" was one public manifestation of the party's lack of internal cohesion. Three major conservative groups formed within a short time after the election: The Free Society Association, led by Senator Goldwater and his campaign manager, Denison Kitchel; the American Conservative Union, organized by former Indiana Congressman Donald Bruce; and the United Republicans of America, headed by Wainwright Dawson. These were not intended to be mere paper organizations. By setting, and attempting to reach, financial goals amounting to more than $3 million, they threatened the very lifeblood of the party.

Splinter groups were not limited to the right; moderate and liberal groups also developed. Charles Taft and a group of prominent moderates organized the Republicans for Progress, and leading Negroes established the National Negro Republican Assembly in an attempt to carve out a greater role for Republican members of their race. To coordinate the activities of these and other moderate groups, the Council of Republican Organizations was set up; it chose former Minnesota Governor Elmer Anderson as its chairman.

Republican officeholders also were restive. The Republican governors made plans to open a Washington headquarters for the newly established Republican Governors' Association. To be patterned after the National Republican Congressional Committee, it included all seventeen GOP chief executives. The governors planned to set up a policy committee and a campaign committee and hoped to maintain independence from other established party groups. The proposal to establish a separate headquarters for the governors brought into the open many of the underlying antagonisms within the party. Senator Goldwater accused the governors of seeking to establish yet another "splinter group [to] represent the views of a special faction of the Party" and suggested that Republicans must look to the congressional leadership for guidance.[9] Governor Robert E. Smylie of Idaho, chairman of the Governors' Association, promptly replied that the Goldwater comment was based on erroneous information. He also stated that the governors believed they could play a role in national politics and be of assistance to the national chairman in the task of saving the two-party system.

In the summer of 1966, at the Portland, Oregon meeting of the National Legislative Conference, a new Republican State Legislators' Association was organized. Comprising Republican members of the state legislatures throughout the nation, the new group endorsed the establishment of a State Legislative Campaign Committee, which was to focus attention on legislative races, exchange information and personnel, conduct workshops, and cooperate with interest groups. The state legislators were sensitive to the vulnerability of their group to the vagaries of national politics as demonstrated by the loss of nearly 500 state legislative seats in the 1964 election.[10]

Party Finances. Unlike most parties that have suffered a severe loss in an election, the Republican National Committee ended the 1964 campaign without a deficit. Yet, even with a small surplus, the financial position of the party was weak. For example, not all of the unexpended funds raised during the 1964 campaign were controlled by the National Committee. The Citizens for

Goldwater organization still held over $200,000, which it would not release to the Committee. The money was used, instead, to support conservative causes—for example, Representative Albert Watson's special election campaign in South Carolina, Kansas State Senator Thomas Van Sickle's election as chairman of the National Republican Federation, and the election of Senator John Tower of Texas. The existence of this money was significant, since it meant that powerful groups within the Republican Party had the resources to act independently if they so chose.[11]

As in the case of any party that has suffered a severe defeat, Republican leaders found it difficult to raise money in the months immediately following the campaign. Fund-raising efforts were further hampered by Ralph Cordiner's resignation as chairman of the Republican National Finance Committee after the election. With the office of chairman vacant, fund-raising was left in the hands of the Finance Committee's executive director, Frank Kovac, the principal fund-raiser for the Draft Goldwater movement. For a number of years, each political party has used a united fund-raising approach. This calls for a separate hierarchy of finance committees and means that money must be raised from various levels of the party. Money coming from state and local governments is credited to a preassigned quota established by the national finance committee of the party. By 1965, unified fund-raising had broken down in the Republican Party, and state committees, for the most part, had ceased to meet their quotas to the National Committee. Consequently, the Republican National Committee, and the national Republican Congressional and Senatorial Committees were raising their money to a significant degree independently of the Finance Committee.

Ray C. Bliss Assumes the Chairmanship

The question of who would lead the Republican National Committee was settled at the January, 1965, meeting of the Committee, in Chicago. There, a combination of old-line GOP leaders and moderates installed Ray C. Bliss of Ohio as national chairman and forced the resignation of Dean Burch.[12]

The process of recruitment and the conditions surrounding the assumption of a leadership post of necessity influence and limit later behavior; this was certainly true of the circumstances surrounding Ray Bliss's election as national chairman. Bliss did not seek the office, but, because of the wide respect he had earned through the years as a skilled professional and a successful and nonideological leader of the party in Ohio, he was as noncontroversial a candidate for Dean Burch's position as it was possible to find. He was not ideologically identified with any segment of the party; nor was he considered overly ambitious, having declined several past opportunities to become national chairman.

The pro-Dean Burch forces elected not to contest Bliss's election and risk embarrassment and defeat.[13] Bliss thus became a unity candidate and was unanimously elected, without a clear mandate from any particular segment of the party. His supporters could point to no clear-cut victory in his election. Rather, Bliss, by virtue of his unanimous election and the fact that Burch was permitted to serve for three months after the Bliss election, was dependent upon the good will of all segments of the party. His election did not signal a clear intraparty victory for any faction. Rather, it was but another round in the continuing fight for control of the GOP.

In assessing a new party leader, one must go beyond the political conditions that led to his election. His personality, style of leadership, and background are all important to an understanding of the leadership role he plays. Bliss is a quiet, almost shy, man who does not enjoy public speaking or the spotlight of publicity. He is an intense perfectionist, capable of extended periods of concentration and attention to detail. His standards and expectations for himself and his staff are high, and he insists that the programs initiated by his office be fully and carefully executed. His consuming interest is politics. He is totally immersed in political life, and this has left him little time for outside interests or hobbies. Bliss places a high priority on personal integrity and honesty in politics. He considers himself a straight shooter who levels with political associates and does not promise things he cannot deliver. As a political professional and an expert in organization, he attaches great importance to party loyalty. He also exercises great care to protect the organization of which he is a part from real or potential opponents—without or within the party. He knows that a miscalculation or mistake on the part of a major party leader can have reverberations throughout the party structure. Consequently, he exercises great care in making decisions.

Although he is the president of a successful Akron insurance company, most of his adult life has been devoted to politics. His political involvement has been almost exclusively in nonpublic, organizational activities. Indeed, until he assumed the chairmanship of the National Committee, he was relatively unknown outside of Ohio and GOP leadership circles. His list of party offices, however, is impressive. He was chairman of the Ohio State Central and Executive Committee for sixteen years, a member of the Republican National Committee since 1952, a delegate to four national conventions, a county chairman for twenty-two years, chairman of the Republican State Chairman's Association from its inception in 1963, and a precinct committeeman since 1932.

The Bliss style of leadership, as demonstrated in Ohio, stressed strong party organization, recruitment of attractive candidates, unified fund-raising, a high degree of personal staff loyalty, and a commitment not to ideology but to winning elections. In a handbook of practical politics, he described his orientation in the following manner:

> In modern American politics, the primary role of a state chairman . . . is to build a party organization. . . . Whether his party wins or loses an election, a state chairman should build and maintain an effective year-around organization. . . . A political organization must be a continuous thing. It must always be an alive, alert and aggressive operation. . . . Organization is a major key to success in politics on any level—county, state, or national. ·

His conception of a state chairman's role was as follows:

> At some time nearly every state chairman must make a basic decision as to whether he will be an office or be a speaking chairman, traveling over the state day in and day out making public appearances. There are both types. I have chosen to be primarily an office chairman.[14]

Almost everyone would agree that Bliss is not an ideologue. He looks at issues in terms of their strategic significance and not as matters about which to become dogmatic. Unlike most state party chairmen, he insisted upon being a full-time paid state chairman, reflecting his belief that a party organization should be run as a professional enterprise. His success in unifying the Ohio Republican Party and in establishing an efficient, successful state organization served to increase the respect with which he was held by Republican professionals.

The new Chairman quickly moved to establish the "Bliss" pattern of leadership of the Republican National Committee.[15] Whereas most of his predecessors had served on a voluntary basis as part-time chairmen, Bliss insisted that the chairmanship be paid as a full-time post.[16] He served as his own executive director, a post most previous part-time chairmen had created and to which they had delegated vast authority because of their extended absences from the national headquarters. Whereas William E. Miller, national chairman from 1961 to 1964, used the chairmanship as a platform for constantly attacking the Democratic Party and its leadership, Bliss continued his established pattern of operating as an office chairman rather than as a speaking chairman. This role was more difficult to maintain in Washington than it had been in Ohio, because the demands upon a national chairman are different from those upon a state chairman. The press corps expects public statements from a party chairman. In addition, state and national leaders constantly ask him to appear and speak in their states, and most hope that the speech will be a rousing call to party battle. Bliss, however, shunned such pressure and purposely avoided involvement in issue controversies, believing that activity in this area would only fragment the party further. He attempted to work with all factions in the party and to favor none. He believed that the greatest healers of wounds are impartiality and fairness and that these attributes should be exemplified by the national chairman and his National Committee staff.

With a chairman whose skills and interests are primarily organizational, and with a party seriously divided, financially weakened, and, in many areas, organizationally defective, it is not surprising that the activities of the National Committee during the Bliss era have revolved mainly around the interrelated problems of party unity, finance, and organization.

The Struggle for Unity

One of the initial problems any national chairman must face is
that of establishing a satisfactory relationship with his party's
congressional leaders—in the case of the out party, the national
committee's principal intraparty rivals for leadership. Establishing an independent position for the national committee is apt to
be difficult for a national chairman who comes from the ranks of
Congress but who is not a member of his party's congressional
leadership. Such a national chairman is apt to find himself constantly involved in role-conflict situations. However, Bliss did not
enter the national chairmanship under such limiting circumstances. Rather, he was a powerful and respected figure within the
party in his own right and independent of congressional alliances.

With the Republican congressional leadership, Bliss initiated
regular participation in the Wednesday-afternoon meetings of
the joint House-Senate Republican leadership. He thus became
the first national chairman to be a formal member of the joint
leadership and he was to serve as presiding officer at the Wednesday sessions. These meetings provide an opportunity to discuss
matters of common concern and to plan the weekly press conferences of the congressional leaders, Senator Everett M. Dirksen
and Congressman Gerald R. Ford. The meetings have not been
without their sensitive moments, but no open rifts have developed; by the spring of 1966, the National Committee's research
and public relations divisions were closely involved in planning
the content and staging of the weekly leadership press conferences. Even so, although Bliss has been a ranking participant in
all joint leadership gatherings, he has avoided making appearances at the press conferences, in keeping with his view that the
people "on the Hill" should make the policy statements.

Some have criticized the Chairman for his reluctance to become
involved in substantive issues, arguing that to fail to do so is to
cause drift within the party.[17] By adopting such a course, a national chairman could probably strengthen the position of certain
elements within his party, but he would have little power to in-
duce intraparty agreement with his policy statements. And, if fur-
thering party unity is a prime objective, policy statements by a

national chairman can hinder its achievement. Policy pronouncements by a national chairman frequently have the effect of putting other party leaders (particularly congressional leaders) in the uncomfortable position of having to state publicly the extent of their agreement or disagreement with their national chairman. Thus, far from providing direction to a party, a speaking chairman's policy statements may stimulate formation of an array of party-leadership positions on particular issues. In addition, issue statements by a national chairman may serve to further widen the breach between elements of the party—something a minority party can seldom afford.

At the staff level, periodic meetings of research and public relations staffs from the National Committee, the Senatorial and Congressional Committees, the House Conference, and the House and Senate Policy Committees have been held. These meetings, while not free from rivalry, have had some success in eliminating duplication of effort in research and have facilitated coordinated public relations and research work.

Bliss has also developed amiable relationships with the Republican governors. Indeed, the governors have, for the most part, been his consistent supporters within the party. He agreed to help finance their new Washington headquarters on the seventh floor of the Cafritz Building (where the Republican National Committee is quartered), and the various printing, mailing, duplicating, and communications facilities of the National Committee were made available to the Governors' Association. These activities brought sharp criticism from conservatives who viewed the Governors' Association, equipped with a Washington office and staff, as an important counterforce within the party. While there remains considerable uneasiness between the conservative forces and the Governors' Association, the latter's headquarters has not been particularly active and has not posed the threat that some feared—or hoped—it might.

To offer a tangible demonstration of his conception of the National Committee as a service agency for the entire party, Bliss has invited party leaders, regardless of their viewpoint, to visit the national headquarters and to address the staff. Among those who have accepted the invitation has been former Senator Goldwater, as well as Governors Smylie (Idaho), Love (Colorado), Chafee (Rhode Island), Volpe (Massachusetts), and Reed (Maine). Ronald Reagan, during his gubernatorial campaign in California, also visited headquarters and addressed the staff.

The basic approach to the unity problem, however, has been to stress the role of the National Committee in helping state and local Republican leaders to develop organizations capable of recruiting attractive candidates and conducting successful campaigns. The basic vehicle for this purpose has been a series of workshop meetings whose emphasis has been on technique—the "nuts and bolts" of politics; at these workshops, ideology has been forgotten—at least temporarily—in the quest for the means to win.

It is the Republican Coordinating Committee, however, that probably stands out as the most significant achievement within the party in the post-1964 era. This advisory group, composed of the top echelon of the Republican leadership, has been meeting approximately every three months since its inception early in 1965 and, by December, 1966, had issued eighteen position papers on major issues.

Out-party advisory committees are by no means new. The Republican Coordinating Committee had a series of predecessors: The Advisory Committee on Policies and Platforms, in 1919; the Republican Program Committee, 1938–40; the Postwar Advisory Council, which met at Mackinac Island, in 1943; and the Republican Citizens' Committee's Critical Issues Council, led by Dr. Milton Eisenhower, in 1964.[18] Such advisory bodies have normally faced hostility and a lack of cooperation from congressional leaders and other regular party leaders. For example, one national committeeman was quoted by the United Press as saying that the abortive National Republican Citizens' Committee of the 1960's could "drop dead."[19] These organizations are often viewed as disruptive to normal party activities and, particularly to the congressional leaders, as threats. Consequently, the contributions of the advisory committees in both parties have been limited.

The first public indication of the agitation within the party for a top-level policy advisory committee came in the "Declaration of Denver," issued by the Republican Governors' Association on

December 5, 1964. In this declaration, the governors called for an "all-inclusive intra-party conference in the spring of 1965 . . . to . . . restate . . . basic principles and develop positive Republican solutions to current problems." The governors also asked for the creation of an executive committee that would be representative of the major segments of the party and would express "party policy positions and programs promptly and constructively during the interval between national conventions and meetings of the National Committee."[20] The governors, however, lacking a national base from which to operate, found it difficult to implement their own suggestions. The initiative for what eventually became the Republican Coordinating Committee came instead from the congressional leadership. Congressman Ford and Senator Dirksen first announced plans for the Committee at their weekly news conference of January 11, 1965. In making the announcement, Dirksen emphasized that the Republicans in Congress would continue to state party policy while they consulted with other party leaders. He noted that two basic facts had been kept in mind in framing the Republican Coordinating Committee. These were

> First, that the only elected Republican officials of federal establishment are the 32 Republican members of the United States Senate and the 140 members of the House of Representatives. Obviously and beyond dispute they will guide Republican policy at the national level, in the absence of a Republican president and vice-president, by the record they write in Congress. It is their responsibility.
>
> Second, that an additional repository of advice and counsel on party policy exists in former presidents and nominees for president, in our present elected governors, in the members of the Republican National Committee, and the state chairmen of our several states, and of course, in active Republican advocates at all other levels of the party structure. Their wisdom must be channeled into party policy formation.[21]

Congressman Ford then outlined the organization and functions of the Coordinating Committee. It would, he said, "continuously examine party policy and party operations [and] establish task forces for the study and examination of major national problems and issues."[22] The Committee, as Ford and Dirksen envisioned it (Fig. 4), would include former President Eisenhower, the four living former presidential candidates (Landon, Dewey, Nixon, and Goldwater), five representatives of the Republican Governors' Association, eleven congressional leaders, and the chairman of the National Committee, making a total of twenty-two members. The congressional leaders brought their plan to the Republican National Committee and asked that it be supported and financed. They made clear, however, that a high-level party advisory committee was going to be created whether or not it was supported by the National Committee members. With the plan envisioning places on the committee for the eleven GOP congressional leaders, the congressional viewpoint on all party matters was certain to be well represented.

The governors, who were on record as favoring an advisory committee of this type, agreed to support the Coordinating Committee, as did former President Eisenhower and the former GOP presidential nominees. Internal pressures had built up, however, for an increase in membership to include representatives of the Republican National Committee. Consequently, five members of the National Committee were appointed to the Coordinating Committee.[23] Though this apportionment of representatives tended to dilute congressional strength, the intraparty prestige of the congressional leaders, plus their familiarity with national issues, virtually guaranteed that the congressional contingent would be a powerful force in all committee deliberations.[24] Chairman Burch and incoming Chairman Bliss gave their support to the revised plan, and the National Committee agreed to finance and staff the group.

The Committee met for the first time in Washington on March 10, 1965, and adopted a statement of purpose:

> The Republican Coordinating Committee was created (1) to broaden the advisory base on national party policy; (2) to set up task forces to study and make recommendations for dealing with the problems that confront the people of our nation; and (3) to stimulate communication among the members of the party and others in developing a common approach to the nation's problems.[25]

The most remarkable aspect of the Coordinating Committee's record has been its ability to survive and gain intraparty accept-

FIGURE 4
REPUBLICAN COORDINATING COMMITTEE AS ORIGINALLY PROPOSED

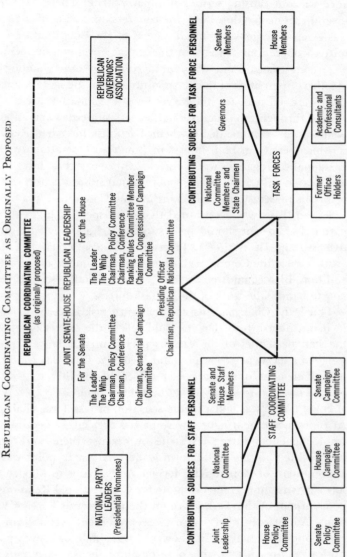

ance without causing serious intraparty strife. There have been several reasons for this. First, the congressional wing of the party was given a major voice in all aspects of the Coordinating Committee's operations. Twelve of the original twenty-nine members were congressmen, and they could count on others among the membership to support them. Appointments to the six task forces[26] that were created to study specific subject-matter areas were cleared through the congressional leaders—indeed, some appointments were recommended by them. Each task force had Republican members from both houses of Congress. Operationally, congressional prerogatives were protected, since each task force paper was cleared with appropriate congressional subject-matter experts before being sent to the full Coordinating Committee.

Second, Bliss was determined that this aspect of his tenure as national chairman should be a success. He, and his administrative assistant, Dr. Arthur L. Peterson (who also served as staff coordinator for the Committee), devoted much time to the effort. In addition, Bliss committed the budgetary and staff resources necessary to handle the work of the six task forces.

Third, the Chairman insisted that each task force be balanced in its membership so that it would reflect the expert opinion of the staff personnel of the various party units. Balance was also sought in terms of geography and ideology. Bliss was concerned that all elements of the party be represented and that none should be in a position to say they had been excluded.

Fourth, care was taken in the selection of task force chairmen. At times, prominent figures were passed over either because they would engender intraparty strife or because there were other, more skilled but less well-known leaders. A case in point was the appointment of Robert Hill, former Ambassador to Mexico and former Assistant Secretary of State for Congressional Relations, to be chairman of the Task Force on the Conduct of Foreign Relations. Admittedly, there were more prominent Republican foreign-policy spokesmen. Hill, however, was a man of proved political leadership skills, capable of reconciling diverse viewpoints and willing to work. He later demonstrated his skill by steering a controversial paper on Latin America through shoals of gubernatorial and congressional disagreement.[27]

The format for the meetings of the Coordinating Committee also has worked against intraparty bickering. Each participant has a chance, prior to a meeting, to suggest revisions in papers, and, once all his peers are present, the committee member does not wish to appear as a person willing to disrupt party harmony. The presence of GOP senior statesmen, like former President Eisenhower and former New York Governor Thomas E. Dewey, also discourages internal conflicts. Support among this elite leader group is an important commodity for all present. No one wants to lose standing. The wrong comment during a meeting, or to the waiting Washington press corps, could discredit and undo the work of all; to make such a comment would be to risk social and political ostracism. One prominent member, for example, temporarily damaged his position when, on a touchy issue, he departed from the agreed-upon script in his statements to the press. There is, then, a powerful drive toward agreement and conciliation within the Coordinating Committee. This is seen most clearly in the now well-established group norm of adopting all statements of policy unanimously.

By January, 1967, after two years of operation, the Coordinating Committee had held eight meetings and issued a series of papers and short statements that had generally received favorable and somewhat extensive press coverage. No splits that would destroy the Committee were in sight, and critics had been consistently outnumbered by those seeking to cooperate with Bliss in making the Committee succeed.

The Struggle for Funds

Traditionally, the Republicans have a reputation for fund-raising that is more systematic and better coordinated than that of the Democrats.[28] The National Committee's vehicle to this end has been the Republican National Finance Committee; this unit is an affiliate of the National Committee, and its chairman is appointed by the national chairman. The Finance Committee is responsible for raising funds for the party's principal campaign organizations—the National Committee and the national Republican Congressional and Senatorial Committees. Each of these organizations submits its budget to the Finance Committee and asks that unit to raise the requested funds. This centralized system of fund-raising was most effective when the GOP controlled the White House and large numbers of people were anxious to be identified with the party. After 1961, however, there was a tendency for each of the three campaign committees to raise most of its money separately.

Bliss believes strongly in the necessity for unified party fundraising. The centralization of fund-raising in Ohio had been an important source of his strength within the state party. His highest priority, upon becoming national chairman, was to strengthen the party's financial organization, which had deteriorated in the postelection period. After a thorough screening of many candidates, a respected figure in business and public life, General Lucius D. Clay, was appointed as chairman of the Finance Committee. The Bliss-Clay job of unifying fund-raising was, however, inherently difficult because the GOP was the out-party and had just suffered a devastating defeat. The party lacked the centralizing influence of the White House, and, at the same time, the national Republican Congressional and Senatorial Committees were independently seeking financial assistance for their respective operations. Bliss and Clay were forced to move slowly. They expanded the highly successful direct-mail sustaining program, which had been inaugurated in 1962 to encourage small contributions ($10 annually) and, in 1965, had raised $1.7 million.[29] In addition, they obtained a sizable number of $1,000 contributions in the second half of 1965. They were also able to merge administration of the Congressional Committee's $1,000-giver program (the Congressional Boosters) with that of the National Committee's own $1,000-contributor program (the Republican Associates).

Even so, the Congressional and Senatorial Committees have continued to raise large amounts of money independently. For example, in February, 1966, a $500-a-plate dinner honoring Senator Thruston Morton, of Kentucky, raised approximately $520,000 for the Republican National Senatorial Committee. That was $60,000 more than that committee's projected campaign budget. The surplus was turned over to the Congressional Campaign Committee.

While GOP fund-raising has not yet been completely unified, it is on a firmer basis than it was in April, 1965. One indication that the national GOP fund-raising effort had become stronger was the apparent inability of some of the splinter groups to meet their projected budgets in 1965 and 1966. The American Conservative Union, for instance, was reported in April, 1966, to have only $25,000 on hand and to have raised only $218,000 of its 1965 goal of $400,000.[30] The Free Society Association also failed to meet its membership and fund-raising objectives in 1965 and 1966.

Toward a More Effective Political Organization

Because of his commitment to organizational politics, Ray Bliss devoted much of his first year in office to reorganizing and strengthening the National Committee's operations. At the same time, he undertook to build new and better state organizations and strengthen city and county political units.

Bliss actually began working on organizational problems the night after his election. Subsequent events such as the creation of the Republican Coordinating Committee forced him to devote much time and effort to organizational problems. The Coordinating Committee, for instance, required an expanded National Committee Research Division, because, with Bliss's support, the Division had become a secretariat to the Coordinating Committee; much of the basic research and the drafting of position papers was done in the Research Division of the National Committee and each of the Coordinating Committee's task forces had at least one member of the Research Division staff assigned to it.

Since 1965, there has been a major increase in the number of research studies done for national and state GOP leaders; in addition, the Division has continued to perform its traditional function as a national Republican reference service.

Approximately 500 requests for information are received each month from congressmen, senators, governors, state legislators, party leaders, students, and the general public. It has always been difficult to recruit a public relations staff and maintain it in political headquarters. Resignations after the 1964 election made it necessary to recruit almost an entire new staff. By the fall of 1965, this had been done, and Bliss had a well-coordinated working Public Relations Division.

There were few changes in the campaign divisions of the National Committee. The most significant change, however, was in the Minorities Division, which has traditionally directed its activities toward gaining support among Negro voters. When Bliss took over the National Committee, the Minorities Division was virtually inoperative. His initial response to the problem was to hold a closed meeting with Negro Republican leaders, in the fall of 1965, to discuss what course of action to follow. In February, 1966, Bliss and the newly organized Negro Advisory Committee met again, to explore further what could be done to strengthen party support among the Negro populace. At the meeting, it was agreed that the National Committee's minorities program desperately needed to be upgraded by the appointment of a special assistant to the Chairman to work full time in the minorities field. The new special assistant was to be assisted by a public relations specialist and a research person. Bliss appointed a three-man subcommittee of the Negro Advisory Committee to screen applicants for the special assistant's post and asked that the full Committee recommend a person for the position. To thus delegate decision-making authority to a group over which he had no control was most unusual for Bliss, who normally maintains tight control over organizational activities.

This approach was considered essential; participants believed that, if the GOP were to win Negro support, it would have to demonstrate from the outset that it was seeking Negro opinion, not merely using selected Negro leaders. Advisory Committee members noted that when they had served on similar committees in the past, the decisions had often been made prior to the meetings and Negro participation was only window dressing.

In April, Bliss announced that the Advisory Committee had unanimously recommended Clarence L. Townes, Jr., executive assistant to the Republican State Chairman of Virginia, to be special assistant to the National Chairman. In addition, the staff of the Minorities Division was expanded for the first time in several years.

Preparing for the 1966 Campaign

By late 1965, the National Committee had been organizationally strengthened. Most of the needed staff additions and replacements had been recruited, and necessary reorganizations had taken place, bringing the headquarters closer to what Bliss thought an optimal status. Staff morale had improved over what it had been in the uneasy days of the interregnum. Revenues were flowing into the treasury with increased regularity and volume. Intraparty sniping, from both the left and the right, had diminished in volume and intensity. With the diminution of the criticism that had drained off considerable staff time and energy, and with the improved organizational structure, it was possible to begin a series of programs geared to assisting and strengthening state and local organizations.

As Ohio state chairman, Bliss had used workshop sessions for party workers and state legislators; as head of the Republican State Chairmen's Advisory Committee, he had organized workshops on campaign techniques for state chairmen. He now extended this format to the Republican National Committee. The first such workshop session, in Kansas City, brought together state and local research personnel. Bliss invited each state committee to send representatives to the conference, which was planned and sponsored by the National Committee's Research Division. The three-day session was staffed by leading research personnel from the National Committee, from the staffs of the congressional leaders, from the Governors' Association, and from selected state organizations—such as those of Michigan and New York—that had well-developed professional research organizations.

The response to the meeting was beyond all expectations, with representatives from twenty-three states attending. The most important accomplishment was to convince many that the Republican Party could not flourish, or perhaps even survive, without extensive professional research efforts. This interest in research resulted in the National Committee's sponsoring a second conference, held in Chicago in early 1966. The Chicago meeting was called to deal with the techniques of modern political research—polling, electronic data processing, aggregate vote analysis, campaign scheduling, and so forth. Again, this meeting was well attended by state and local GOP leaders. Such men represent the basic constituency of the National Committee, whose operations are geared primarily to serving state needs; in contrast, the national Republican Congressional and Senatorial Committees have a more restricted constituency.

A third research conference, intended to aid congressional,

senatorial, and gubernatorial campaign staffs, was held in September, 1966; 160 political-research personnel from thirty-nine states attended.[31]

Another effort of this type was designed to train campaign managers. The National Committee's Political Education Division administered four regional seminars for campaign managers. These were cosponsored by the Congressional and Senatorial Committees. The impetus for the seminars was the critical shortage of skilled campaign-managerial personnel within the Republican Party. Each of the seminars was held in a setting devoid of the convention-like atmosphere that often surrounds political gatherings. Participants were carefully screened, required to pay their own expenses, and given an intensive course in practical politics by experts selected by the Senatorial and Congressional Committees. In all, over 400 people attended the seminars; the Republican National Committee paid the bill.

Closely related to the management seminars was the hiring of four regional field men to serve as direct liaison between the Washington headquarters and candidate organizations operating during the 1966 elections in the fifty states. These were the first off-year elections in which the National Committee extended its services to include such field operations, although, in the past, the Republican Congressional Committee had made use of field men.

In recent years, the success of Republican efforts in the big cities has been minimal. In 1960, Richard Nixon's record in the large cities caused concern among Republicans. Of forty cities with populations exceeding 300,000, the Republican ticket carried only fourteen, whereas twenty-six were carried by Kennedy. With the exception of Omaha, Columbus, and Indianapolis, all of the cities carried by the GOP were in the West and South. The cities carried by the Democrats were in the large pivotal states east of the Mississippi, where Democratic pluralities increased by over 2 million votes between 1956 and 1960.[32]

Bliss, who had gained considerable national attention after the 1960 election with his committee study of the Republican prospects in the big cities, was particularly anxious to improve Republican chances in those areas. Consequently, in late December of 1965, he called one of his rare press conferences. Speaking to members of the Washington press corps, Bliss announced that, in late January, he would call a meeting of Republican chairmen in seventeen of the nation's largest cities. He stressed that the party had been losing elections consistently because of its failure to penetrate urban areas and he noted that he had been the principal author of the 1961 *Report on Big City Politics,* which had outlined a scheme of organization for Republicans in urban America.[33] The January meeting, Bliss said, would be the first step toward implementing the recommendations in this earlier report. The arrangements for the meeting and the attendant publicity were handled largely by A. B. ("AB") Hermann, a long-time National Committee staff member who now serves under Bliss as a special assistant. Hermann had learned his politics in the rough urban politics of New Jersey and, therefore, had a strong interest in Republican activity relating to labor and minority groups. The nonideological format that Bliss and Hermann worked out for the meetings stressed the techniques successful Republicans had used to win in areas where Democrats normally could expect huge majorities, for example, New York, Philadelphia, and Louisville. Experts in headquarters operations, campaign management, labor, Negro interests, and nationality groups also participated.

The interest in the first big-city meeting was so great that three additional meetings were scheduled: one in Washington for large cities east of the Mississippi, one in Denver for cities of the West, and another Washington meeting for GOP leaders from key suburban areas. Over 100 additional city and county chairmen participated in the second, third, and fourth sessions. A big-city field man was assigned to Hermann's office, and a special mailing list was set up for big-city chairmen; neither of these steps had ever before been taken. Hermann's office also was placed in charge of a program to send functional experts specializing in such fields as precinct organizations, minority groups, and labor into the big cities to assist local leaders.[34]

A program of this type points up the difficulties caused by the decentralization that characterizes the American party system. In implementing the big-city program, it was always necessary to obtain the approval of a state chairman before a city or county chairman from his state could be invited to a meeting. Some chairmen were more cooperative than others. Next, the urban leaders had to accept the National Committee's invitations; since they could not be required to attend and were expected to pay their own expenses, this was not always a simple matter. Furthermore, in every case, the National Committee had to work with the duly constituted local organizations, regardless of how effective those organizations were or of how willing they were to try new methods. Nevertheless, where vital and responsive local leadership existed, the big-city sessions had an impact.

The Republican National Committee was not, however, in a position to make certain that the recommendations presented at the meetings would be carried out. There was no existing mechanism to ensure that adequate GOP organizations would be activated in participating cities. The National Committee held no sanctions over local leaders and was restricted to attempting to spur interest through intraparty communication and by offering the services of its field men and its roster of campaign experts. Even these could only be used when requested by state and local Republican organizations. The success of the program ultimately rested not with the National Committee, which had initiated it, but with the state and local party organizations that participated in it.

Another pre-1966 campaign workshop session, this one attended by state public relations personnel, was held in Washington, in April of 1966. Like the others, this meeting featured presentations by Republican public relations experts from all sections of the country. The session also served to alert state public relations men to the services available from the various Washington-based Republican campaign committees.

As a part of its 1966 campaign drive, the National Committee sponsored a series of "Countdown '66" workshops for state-wide and congressional-district party workers. These workshops concentrated on the traditional party functions of registering party voters and getting out the vote. Bliss personally participated in most of the state-wide meetings. The Republican National Committee estimated that 20,000 party workers participated in these sessions.[35]

Each of these meetings was a "how to do it" session devoid of ideological content. They reflected a conviction on the part of the National Chairman that the cornerstones of political victories are neither purges nor excoriations of the opposition but, rather, "good candidates, good financing, and good organization."[36] This conception of national party leadership was not without its critics from the right and the left and among the party pros. But the results of the 1966 elections tended to make criticisms moot and they certainly strengthened Bliss's position as chairman of the National Committee.

Few attempts have been made to apply modern organizational theory to the American political parties. It would be presumptuous to attempt such an application on the basis of a brief account of the travail of one party over a relatively short period of time. Nevertheless, certain conclusions are suggested by this study. The following generalizations deal with the role of the national committee in party organization, the recruitment and role conception of an out-party chairman, the development of an out-party position, and the financing of out-party operations.

The National Committee

The out-party national committee, even with its limited powers, is the only established mechanism available to coordinate the activities of the party and to set the tone for its rehabilitation during its minority years.

The national committee of the out-party lacks the resources necessary to influence directly the ideological tone of the party.

The national committee of the out-party, when faced with serious intraparty cleavages, will tend to emphasize organizational rather than issue-policy aspects of party activities.

The out-party's national committee and its leaders can influence party leaders more readily in terms of campaign and organizational matters than in terms of ideology.

Out-party congressional leaders will pre-empt the role of policy spokesmen during the minority years of the party, and the Congressional and Senatorial Campaign Committees will zealously guard these prerogatives of the congressional leadership.

State governors, lacking a national base of operations, a familiarity with national issues comparable to that of congressional leaders, and a nation-wide fund-raising mechanism, are not likely to constitute a powerful counterforce either to the national committee or to the congressional leadership.

After a serious defeat, while organizational mechanisms are in disrepair, splinter groups will emerge to fill the voids left by an ineffective party organization. Such groups seldom have official party sanction and they tend to collapse, or at least deteriorate, as the regular organization regains its strength and stamina.

The National Chairman

A national chairman who has led his party during an election campaign that has ended with a serious defeat cannot normally expect to remain in his post.

A party, racked with severe internal dissension among competing ideological forces, will likely turn to a nonideological candidate to replace the incumbent national chairman.

A chairman elected with some support from each ideological faction within the party and having no clear mandate will be restricted in his activities until he has demonstrated his leadership ability and developed support within the national committee. Such a nonideological chairman will, almost inevitably, develop the unification of the party as the major theme of his tenure.

Two types of leadership patterns are possible in the national chairmanship of an out-party: that of the "speaking," or issue-oriented chairman or that of the "office," or organization-oriented chairman. Full-time, paid chairmen can be expected to be office chairmen; similarly, nonideological, unity-oriented chairmen can be expected to be office chairmen.

The Party Voice

Lacking a party spokesman—in the person of a president or an issue-oriented chairman—out-parties tend to create, under national committee auspices, extraorganizational policy-formulating groups composed of prominent party leaders representing various party factions.

Extraorganizational policy-making groups can gain acceptance only if the congressional leadership's prerogatives as policy spokesmen are protected. If such protection is not guaranteed, the congressional leadership will assume an important, and perhaps dominant, role in party policy-making.

Fund-raising

Unified fund-raising is extremely difficult for an out-party because its national committee lacks the prestige and support of a president with whom potential contributors wish to identify.

Other party groups, such as congressmen, senators, and governors, will seek to assure themselves of adequate financial assistance by independently approaching established party contributors.

An out-party's national committee is forced to rely more heavily on small-scale contributor programs as large contributors seek to protect their interests among the party's elected officials.

In this essay, we have attempted to describe the conditions under which the Republican National Committee was forced to operate in the 1964–66 period. In a broader sense, we have described the convolutions that take place in an out-party after it has suffered a major defeat. Close association with the actors in this drama has prevented us saying all that might be said. We have described the major occurrences in the Republican Party in the postelection period; these events have provided a basis for the development of generalizations concerning political parties at the national level in a time of party travail. It is possible that these generalizations may eventually lead to a more complete theory of the operation of political parties in the United States.

7

.

THE GOLDWATER IMPACT:
CYCLICAL VARIATION OR
SECULAR DECLINE?

.

BERNARD COSMAN AND ROBERT J. HUCKSHORN

In a two-party system, the minority party is no less important to
the functioning of the political system than is the majority party.
Indeed, the minority party occupies a special position of prominence in democracies and is essential to the working of a democratic regime; for "to the minority falls the role of criticism, of
opposition, and of preparation for the day when it may become
the government itself."[1]

In examining the Goldwater election and its aftermath, this
volume has been primarily concerned with the impact of the
Goldwater campaign upon various components of the minority
party system. Inevitably, such an analysis leads to questions extending beyond any one element of the minority party and em-
bracing the entire minority-party system. The preceding essays
have viewed the minority party from various vantage points and
in terms of various political actors and events, but the underlying
theme for all has been the rebuilding of a viable Republican

Party, able to fulfill its role as critic and loyal opposition when out of power, ready to govern when in. Ultimately, the test of this rebuilding is at the ballot box. Not surprisingly, then, the most important question that emerged in the wake of the 1964 election was "Can the Republican Party recover from an electoral disaster of such magnitude, or was 1964 set in the more general context of a long-term decline of the GOP as a viable second party?" In short, was the Goldwater defeat a cyclical variation or part of a secular decline?

This question is not unique to the 1964 electoral disaster. Robert Donovan noted that, "After Alfred E. Smith lost to Herbert Hoover in 1928, Silas Bent, a former publicity director of the Democratic National Committee, wrote a gloomy article for *Scribner's* called 'Will the Democrats Follow the Whigs?' And the Whigs were much on the Republican mind after Alfred M. Landon's defeat by Franklin D. Roosevelt in 1936."[2]

For a century, postelection speculation predicting the demise of the disadvantaged party has proved premature. Invariably, the minority party succeeded in rebounding—usually, but not always, at the next election. The off-year election of 1966 was no exception. The Republican Party made substantial gains, including a net of eight governorships. It won 23 of 35 gubernatorial races, thereby shifting the party balance from 35 Democratic and 17 Republican governors to an even split of the fifty states. Furthermore, the states captured by the Republicans included most of the large and populous ones. In the Senate, the GOP experienced a net gain of three seats, raising its over-all total to 37. The new Republican senators included the first Negro to be elected to that body in this century. In the House of Representatives, the GOP showed a net gain of 47 seats, thus altering the party balance from 295 Democratic and 140 Republican to 248 Democratic and 187 Republican. And, in state legislative contests, the GOP netted 153 senate seats and 387 house seats, a total of 540. The gains overcame the devastating loss of 500 state legislative seats in 1964. In all, the Republicans gained control of 40.9 per cent of state legislative seats, their best showing in four years.

The geographic spread of victory also indicates a resurgence of Republican voting. Republicans won governorships from Democrats in ten states: Alaska, Arizona, Arkansas, California, Florida, Maryland, Minnesota, Nebraska, Nevada, and New Mexico. Only two governorships were lost—in Kansas and Maine. Republican Senate seats were won in Illinois, Oregon, and Tennessee, and House seats in all regions of the country—seven in the East, nine in the South, twenty-one in the Midwest, and ten in the West. The GOP percentages of the total vote in these contests not only were well above those of 1964 but also exceeded those of 1962, as is shown in Table 1.

TABLE 1.

REPUBLICAN PERCENTAGES OF TOTAL VOTE, 1962–66

Year	For Governorships	For Senate	For House of Representatives
1962	49.3	48.9	47.5
1964	45.0	42.4	42.3
1966	51.1	50.7	48.2

Supporting this voting picture, the Gallup Poll of December 14, 1966, reported a restoration of "the normal vote pattern shattered in [the] 1964 GOP debacle." It was Gallup's view that "many of the college-trained persons in business and professional occupations, and persons in high income levels, who jumped the political fence in numbers to vote for Johnson in 1964, have returned to the GOP ranks." Most significant, perhaps, was Gallup's finding that the proportion of the electorate identifying with the GOP in 1966 returned to pre-1964 levels.

Since 1952, the Survey Research Center of the University of Michigan has been recording the underlying distribution of party identifiers within the electorate by asking respondents the following: "Generally speaking, do you usually think of yourself as a Republican, a Democrat, an Independent, or what? [If Republican or Democrat] Would you call yourself a strong (R) (D) or a not very strong (R) (D)? [If Independent] Do you think of yourself as closer to the Republican or Democratic party?"

Classifying American voters from 1952 to 1964 as either Strong, Weak, or Independent Democrats or Republicans, the Michigan group used party identification to construct an estimate of the normal vote—the vote that could be expected if short-term forces such as candidate appeal or issues did not disturb the basic distribution of party loyalties. According to the SRC, the normal Democratic Party vote for the period 1952–60 was approximately 54 per cent. Eisenhower won the presidency in 1952 and 1956 despite his party's deficit of identifiers because he was able to hold the bulk of the Republican voters and, at the same time, make heavy inroads into the ranks of Independents and Independent and Weak Democrats. The SRC classified the Eisenhower victories as "deviating" elections because the voting outcomes differed from the underlying distribution of party identifiers. The 1960 election, seen in terms of party identification, was labeled a "reinstating" election because the party with the majority of identifiers was returned to the White House, albeit by the narrowest of margins.

During the Eisenhower-Nixon epoch, short-term forces, primarily Eisenhower's personal appeal in the 1950's and the question of religion in 1960, favored the GOP. In 1964, the net impact of short-term forces shifted heavily to the Democratic side, except in the deepest reaches of the South. The SRC analysis in Chapter 2 of this book showed quite clearly the favorable impact of Goldwater's states'-rights strategy upon white Deep South electorates. Analysis of Deep South Republican leadership, in Chapter 3, revealed its attitude to be supportive of Senator Goldwater's states'-rights orientation and of his economic conservatism as well. The Deep South's enthusiasm for Goldwater set that subregion off from the rest of the nation. Elsewhere, Goldwater and the GOP were grievously disadvantaged by the pull of short-term forces. Indeed, after reviewing the data on party identification gathered by the SRC in 1964, Angus Campbell noted "a Democratic gain of several percentage points which goes beyond what might have been expected from . . . false reports or from errors associated with sampling."[3] Campbell raised the question of whether the United States was "entering a period of party realignment which will increase the prevailing Democratic advantage in the party balance."[4] He observed, "There are indications in our survey data of a movement of this kind. . . . If the events of the last four years have indeed set the stage for a movement toward a new

TABLE 2.

PARTY IDENTIFICATION AND THE VOTE, 1964 AND 1966

Party Identification	President (1964)			Congressman (1966)			Senator (1966)			Governor (1966)		
	No.	Dem.	Rep.	No.	Dem.	Rep.	No.	Dem.	Rep.	No.	Dem.	Rep.
Strong Dem.	186	98%	2%	144	92%	8%	63	92%	8%	170	88%	12%
Weak Dem.	253	86%	14%	169	82%	18%	82	68%	32%	131	65%	35%
Independent Dem.	83	88%	12%	52	62%	38%	29	59%	41%	43	53%	47%
Independent	81	59%	41%	49	53%	47%	21	48%	52%	34	44%	56%
Independent Rep.	61	41%	59%	46	33%	67%	25	16%	84%	37	30%	70%
Weak Rep.	143	40%	60%	110	22%	78%	44	9%	91%	89	12%	88%
Strong Rep.	109	10%	90%	95	13%	87%	45	7%	93%	72	4%	96%

Source: Survey Research Center, University of Michigan, May 25, 1967.

level of party balance, we may see profound changes in the nature of party competition in American politics."[5]

The SRC's 1966 nation-wide survey of the political attitudes and behavior of the American electorate provides at least a partial answer to Campbell's question. These data suggest that the underlying distribution of party identifiers continues to exhibit far more stability than change. Party identification and the vote confirmed the existence of a definite trend toward the GOP in gubernatorial and senatorial races. As is shown in Table 2, Strong Republicans and, especially, Weak and Independent Republicans returned to Republican ranks in 1966. Moreover, the party's candidates in gubernatorial and senatorial races gained the support of far larger proportions of Strong, Weak, and Independent Democrats than had Senator Goldwater in 1964. Of particular significance were Republican majorities among Independents. Republican resurgence was less evident in voting for the House of Representatives, although 1966 GOP candidates did better among all types of party identifiers except Strong Republicans than those on Goldwater's ticket had.

All of this is extraordinarily suggestive of the restoration of a more or less normal voting balance between the parties. In the light of these data, 1964 appears as a cyclical variation rather than part of a secular decline. If this is, in fact, the case, a second set of questions is raised. At the global level, the question is "What are the chances of the Republican Party's becoming the majority party?" The immediate answer at this point in time is that the chances are not good. Sudden partisan change is the exception, not the rule, in American politics. The reality is that partisan change of major proportions occurs infrequently, usually in response to major crises such as the Great Depression. The available evidence suggests that, even during that period, partisan change did not come all at once but developed through a series of elections, what the SRC describes as a "realigning era."

The stability of party loyalties is amply demonstrated by the distribution of party identifiers since 1952, which is shown in Table 3.

There is nothing in this pattern to suggest voter realignment on a grand scale. Neither is the pattern static. There has been a

TABLE 3.

PARTY IDENTIFIERS, 1952–66 (In Per Cents)

Year	Democrat		Independent			Republican		
	Strong	Weak	Demo-crat	Inde-pend-ent	Re-publi-can	Weak	Strong	Other
1952	22	25	10	5	7	14	13	4
1954	22	25	9	7	6	14	13	4
1956	21	23	7	9	8	14	15	3
1958	23	24	7	8	4	16	13	5
1960	21	25	8	8	7	13	14	4
1962	23	23	8	8	6	16	12	4
1964	26	25	9	8	6	13	11	2
1966	18	28	9	12	7	15	10	1

Source: Survey Research Center, University of Michigan, May 25, 1967.

dropoff in the proportion of the electorate identifying as Strong Democrats, but this has been accompanied by an increase in the proportions of Weak Democrats and Independents—nothing, in other words, to suggest a massive buildup of Republican identifiers. Moreover, voters seldom change their party self-identifications all at once. In particular, the strong party identifier usually does not abandon his established affiliation immediately to join the opposition. A more normal pattern is that of the strong party identifier who becomes a weak party identifier, then becomes an Independent, and, finally, identifies with the opposition party. Table 2 does not entirely rule out the possibility of a gradual shift in view of the change between 1964 and 1966.

If anything, the relative stability of party identification over time reinforces Charles O. Jones's point that "Historically, political parties in the United States have had to assume semi-permanent roles as majority and minority parties." In his analysis of the Republican Party, Jones identified many of the obstacles to a realignment favoring the GOP. In addition to the persistence of partisan attachment, these include

> . . . the low level of issue awareness of the part of voters, the tendency to reelect congressional and senatorial incumbents, the political advantages that accrue to the majority party from their control of the

machinery of government combined with the disadvantages suffered by the minority party in their not having research agencies available to develop policy alternatives, the greater attention given the majority party in the mass media, the likelihood that a minority party President will be hamstrung by having to work with a majority party Congress, and the lack of an effective, centralized party organization.[6]

Despite these and other obstacles, there is always the possibility that a great national crisis for which the majority party bears the blame might produce a noticeable realignment in the nation. The race issue has the potential of becoming a realigning issue. An international crisis of major proportions perceived by the electorate as a monumental administration blunder might well harbor that same potential. In the absence of such a crisis, the distribution of mass opinion gives no indication of realignment at this point in time. For the predictable future, a more reasonable question is that of whether or not the Republican Party can capture the White House in 1968.

Looking to the 1968 election, it is well to remember the vast uncertainties that abide in any presidential year. To see the need for maintaining a cautious attitude toward seemingly predictable political events, the reader need only recall the confident predictions of Republican victory in 1948, the narrowness of President Kennedy's plurality in 1960, or the GOP's break with tradition in nominating Senator Goldwater in 1964. It has not been our intention in this book to engage in prophecy or prescription. Rather, we have sought to displace prescription with description, and the reader may, if he wishes, draw from these descriptions of the Republican Party since 1964 certain "lessons" for 1968. These, together with certain of the known factors of American politics, provide the framework within which the presidential politics of 1968 will fit.

As the Republican Party enters the lists for 1968, it must face up to the fact that it is the minority party of this political era. The GOP exists in what is, essentially, a hostile environment—an environment in which only one-third of the electorate identify themselves, even casually, as Republicans. This fact more than any other compels the attention of party leaders, political strategists, and interested citizens. The response of Goldwater Republicans to the party's minority status was the theory of the "stay-at-home conservatives," those Republicans who could not bring themselves to vote for the "me-too" GOP candidates they felt their presidential party had foisted upon them since 1940. The 1964 election exposed this political myth. No less apparent was the general unpopularity of conservative policy positions outside the ranks of hard-core Republicans. The negative appeal of conservatism cannot be explained solely as a function of negative voter response to Goldwater. Obviously, the Senator was the minority candidate of the minority party and he did not enjoy a favorable image among the mass of voters. Even more unfavorable to his cause, however, was the conservative policy he articulated. The reality of 1964 was that neither a conservative candidate nor his policies received a favorable response.

This is not to deny some particular Republican gains from the Goldwater effort. The Republican organization was expanded, and it was successful in establishing a broader financial base, although much of this breakthrough occurred before 1964. Nor can one dismiss the highly touted southern strategy, which netted most of the electoral votes the Arizona Senator was to receive. The once-solid South has been breaking up since the early 1950's. Arkansas and Florida now have Republican governors; Texas and South Carolina have Republican senators; and twenty-three Republicans represent eight of the eleven southern states in the House of Representatives. In short, another of the realities of American presidential politics that Republicans need to contemplate in 1968 in that the South is now a prime target area for the GOP. However, the party needs to proceed with care before again hitching a ride with the race issue. The emerging Negro vote in the South and the need for major inroads into large-state electoral-vote blocs outside that region should impel the party to consider its future course in the South with care. In 1964, the possibility of a third-party candidacy of Governor George Wallace caused grave concern among the followers of Senator Goldwater. It was feared that Wallace would disrupt the implementation of their southern strategy—an expectation seemingly confirmed by a Gallup Poll of July, 1964. Gallup found that, in a three-way race with Wallace, Johnson lost 7 percentage points in the South and Goldwater lost

12. Wallace had 18 per cent of the southern vote. The anxieties of Goldwaterites about the efficacy of the southern strategy were relieved when, three days after the Republican National Convention, Governor Wallace withdrew as a presidential candidate.

Four years later, former-Governor Wallace has again emerged as a potential candidate. This time, there is less likelihood that he will withdraw. A Gallup Poll of April 23, 1967, provided an early measurement of the possible impact of his candidacy. Gallup asked, "Suppose the Presidential election were held today. If Lyndon Johnson were the Democratic candidate and George Romney were the Republican candidate, and Governor George Wallace were the candidate of a third party, which would you like to see win?"

In a three-way race, Wallace was preferred by 13 per cent of the national sample; Johnson, by 43 per cent; and Romney, by 35 per cent. In the South, Wallace had a plurality of 35 per cent, Johnson had 32 per cent, and Romney trailed with 26 per cent; without Wallace, Romney had 52 per cent to Johnson's 43 per cent. With Nixon substituted for Romney and without Wallace, the Republican candidate tied Johnson in the nation, each having 48 per cent; with Wallace in, Nixon dropped to 36 per cent, as opposed to Johnson's 46 per cent and Wallace's 12 per cent. Seven months later, in November, 1967, the Gallup Poll showed that Wallace continued to draw more support away from Nixon than Johnson. Without Wallace, the President led Nixon 47 to 45 per cent. With Wallace, Johnson's support dropped by 3 per cent, and Nixon's by 7 per cent. Wallace hurt Nixon most in the South, cutting Nixon's percentage in the region from 45 to 25.[7]

While only preliminary soundings of the potential Wallace impact, these polls are extraordinarily suggestive of the futility of repeating the southern strategy of 1964. A political party, especially a minority party, can ill afford to ignore a region with 128 electoral votes. Beyond this, there is the fact that the South will have roughly one-fourth of the total delegates at the 1968 Republican National Convention; this makes it a potentially powerful force in the selection of a candidate. Yet, a strategy that accommodates the traditional southern point of view costs far more than it gains in a national election.

What kind of candidate should the Republican National Convention nominate in 1968? What strategy should the GOP adopt? We offer no firm answers to these questions, beyond those that seem to be obvious. The Republican candidate in 1968 must cast his net broadly to retain the votes of the party faithful and to regain the independent and weak party identifiers who defected in 1964. Many of these voters returned to their party to vote for Republican candidates for governor, congressman, and senator in 1966. Nevertheless, the restoration of a more normal party balance in 1966 still leaves the GOP in a minority position. Thus, the Republican presidential candidate must win converts among "Independents" and "Weak Democrats" while, at the same time, holding almost all Republican identifiers. He must, in other words, avoid the extreme right and steer toward the center of the political spectrum. The center is dynamic, not static. Increasingly, it is composed of younger, urban-based, better-educated voters. Barring an international disaster or a domestic crisis that might throw the election to the Republicans while contributing nothing to long-range party strength, it is to these voters that the GOP must appeal.

A first-term incumbent Democratic president is generally assured of renomination, if he again chooses to run. On the other side, the list of potential Republican challengers is expanding to include both the obvious and the obscure. The various polling agencies have begun to take preliminary soundings within the mass of the electorate. The central question that remains is whether the Republican Party will heed the basic realities of American politics.

■

NOTES

■

CHAPTER 1

1. Cornelius P. Cotter and Bernard C. Hennessy, *Politics Without Power: The National Party Committees* (New York: Atherton Press, 1964).

2. "Report of Republican National Chairman, William E. Miller, before the Republican Conference, House of Representatives, Washington, D.C., February 5, 1964" (mimeo.), pp. 6, 10, 12.

3. Moley's view of American politics was expressed vigorously in his *The Republican Opportunity in 1964* (New York: Duell, Sloan & Pearce, 1964). In particular, see pp. 89 and 141.

4. The bulk of Moley's memorandum to Goldwater was published as an appendix to *The New Methodology: A Study of Political Strategy and Tactics* (Washington, D.C.: American Institute for Political Communication, 1967), pp. 191–93.

5. Nelson W. Polsby, "Strategic Considerations," in Milton C. Cummings (ed.), *The National Election of 1964* (Washington, D.C.: The Brookings Institution, 1966), pp. 100–101.

6. A similar example was the campaign film *Choice*. Feeling Goldwater had approved the film's purpose, its producers did not intend to show the candidate how they attempted to achieve that purpose. Premature press publicity forced their hand. The incident is discussed on page 38.

7. Because the handbills did not name a sponsoring organization, Claiborne was charged with violating the New Jersey election laws. The case was finally brought to trial in the spring of 1966. The prosecution could not establish willful duplicity, and Claiborne was acquitted.

CHAPTER 2

1. The most fertile elaboration of this classic script is contained in Anthony Downs, *An Economic Theory of Democracy* (New York: Harper, 1957).

2. *New York Times,* July 19, 1964.

3. This finding is not as absurd as it might appear if the reader has failed to grasp the import of the preceding text. That is, in 1952, it was the most intense and ideologically "pure" Republicans who tended to prefer Taft to Eisenhower, much as, twelve years later, their counterparts chose Goldwater over the other Republican alternatives. It was the less ideologically committed (either by persuasion or because of lack of ideological sensitivity) who were more satisfied with the Eisenhower candidacy. The erstwhile Taft supporters did not perversely turn out at higher rates because they were disappointed with the Convention's choice; they did so because their striking commitment to Republicanism compelled them to more ardent support of its candidate whatever his ideological position.

4. See "The Concept of a 'Normal Vote,'" Chapter 1 in A. Campbell, P. Converse, W. Miller, and D. Stokes, *Election and the Political Order* (New York: John Wiley & Sons, 1965).

5. In our estimation, some challengers with insufficient national exposure have been prematurely discouraged from competition by poll results that might well have changed radically with greater exposure.

6. Lodge's strong grass-roots popularity was one of the untold stories of the 1960 election, when he ran for vice-president. Well known for his televised confrontations with the Russian delegation to the United Nations, he was far and away the most widely recognized and warmly regarded first-time vice-presidential candidate in any election since 1952. Given the tarnish that seems to accompany second efforts at the presidency in American elections and that would, undoubtedly, have hurt Nixon, it may well be that Lodge, had he been acceptable to the Republican Party leadership, could have pushed Lyndon Johnson to a closer race than any other of the Republican hopefuls in 1964.

7. While these rates may sound mountainous, it should be remembered that the expected defection rates for most of these groups are rather low—in the vicinity of 10 per cent. Nonetheless, 40 per cent of the Rockefeller Republicans in our sample voted for Johnson.

8. We have mentioned this possibility in some seriousness simply because often, in the past, we have found public perceptions of party differences on major issues totally confused and muddy. Even on issues where the politically sophisticated see marked party differences, general public inattention and the ambiguities that politicians exploit to blur the edges of their positions combine to produce either lack of recognition of differences or very conflicting impressions of what those differences are at any given time. See Angus Campbell *et al., The American Voter* (New York: John Wiley & Sons, 1960), pp. 179 ff.

9. Philip E. Converse, "A Major Political Realignment in the South?" in Allan P. Sindler (ed.), *Change in the Contemporary South* (Durham, N.C.: Duke University Press, 1963).

10. These religious effects are described in Converse *et al.,* "Stability and Change in 1960: A Reinstating Election," *American Political Science Review,* LV (June, 1961), 269–80.

11. In our data, expressions of party loyalty from the South, which had been slowly losing Democratic strength throughout the 1950's, show a sudden rebound in 1964. However, all of the rebound can be traced to southern Negroes; the downward trend among southern whites continued at about the same pace.

12. Take, for example, the charge made by Democrats and some Republicans that Goldwater was "impulsive." This allegation reverberated in the public and came to make up one of our largest single categories of negative references to Goldwater. "Impulsiveness" is a personality trait that might have been less plausible for some other right-wing leader; yet, the charge took root and began to flourish with respect to a cluster of policies that Goldwater shared with other Republican leaders of similar persuasions. It seems quite arbitrary to decide that it is exclusively either the person or the policy that is "impulsive."

13. Undoubtedly, in such an observer's impressions as to how opinion stood, letters were not weighted equally: Some letters were more cogent than others, some were more distressed, and so on. But, as a rough first approximation, one can imagine that what registered as "public opinion" on a particular issue in the mind of such an observer was closely related to the mere frequency of letters pro and con.

14. See H. Alker and B. Russett, "On Measuring Inequality," *Behavioral Science*, IX, No. 3 (July, 1964), 207–18.

15. We wish to stress that it remains a crude approximation, in part because we do not know, letter by letter, what political opinions the respondent was expressing. Conceivably, in many cases, they lay outside the range of any of our items. But the exercise is worth completing, in part because it is likely that our hypothetical observer generalizes beyond the specific content of letters ("if ultraconservative opinion on issue x is running about 30 per cent, then it is likely that ultraconservative opinion on issue y would run at about the same level if something made that issue salient") and in part because the systematic lines of displacement of "letter opinion" from public opinion in the mass electoral sense are, undoubtedly, valid in their general direction, whatever the details.

16. The wordings of the issue items involved in Figs. 1c and d were as follows:

(For 1c) "Some people are afraid the government in Washington is getting too powerful for the good of the country and the individual person. Others feel that the government in Washington has not gotten too strong for the good of the country. What is your feeling?"

(For 1d) "Some people think our government should sit down and talk to the leaders of the Communist countries and try to settle our differences, while others think we should refuse to have anything to do with them. What do you think?"

Figure 1e is based on a set of questions that asked people to indicate their affective reactions toward a variety of groups, including "conservatives" and "liberals." The scores for the figure are based on the difference in reaction to the two stimuli.

17. It is likely that this contingent is roughly coterminous with the 40–50 per cent of the American electorate that we have described elsewhere as having no impression as to what such terms as *conservative* and *liberal* mean. See

Philip E. Converse, "The Nature of Belief Systems in Mass Publics," in
David E. Apter (ed.), *Ideology and Discontent* (New York: The Free Press of
Glencoe, 1964), pp. 206–61. The data presented there were gathered in 1960.
In the 1964 study, we collected the same data on recognition of ideological
terms, thinking that perhaps the nature of the Goldwater campaign might
render these terms and meanings more salient to a wider public. The data
show that it did not.

CHAPTER 3

1. V. O. Key, Jr., *Southern Politics* (New York: Alfred A. Knopf, 1950),
p. 292.

2. The impact of Eisenhower backers upon southern Republican organizations in 1952 is described in Paul T. David, Malcolm Moos, and Ralph M.
Goldman (eds.), *Presidential Nominating Politics in 1952: The South* (Baltimore: The Johns Hopkins University Press, 1954), Vol. III.

3. The most striking Republican surge came in 1962, in Alabama, where
Republican James Martin came within a single percentage point of unseating
incumbent Democratic Senator Lister Hill. The Martin-Hill contest is exam-
ined as a critical election in Walter Dean Burham, "The Alabama Senatorial
Election of 1962: Return of Inter-Party Competition," *Journal of Politics*,
XXVI (1964), 798–829.

4. See, especially, Robert D. Novak, *The Agony of the G.O.P. 1964* (New
York: Macmillan, 1965).

5. This overlap extended from the precincts upward through city, county,
and district organizations to the state level. The two organizations came together at the top as the state chairman in each Deep South state wore two
hats: one as party leader, the other as chairman of his state's Draft Goldwater
for President Committee.

6. The southern region's convention organization for Goldwater has been
described by the writer in "The Deep South at the Republican National Convention," an unpublished paper prepared when he was a National Convention
Fellow of the Eagleton Institute and the National Center for Education in
Politics, February, 1965.

7. Quoted in *Birmingham News,* July 16, 1964.

8. "Delegation" is used throughout this chapter to refer to both delegates
and alternates.

9. The proportion of replies from Deep South Republican delegations may
be compared with those of other studies of delegates and alternates that
also have relied upon the mail questionnaire. Working with national delegate
populations, Herbert McClosky, Paul J. Hoffman, and Rosemary O'Hara received responses from 44 per cent of the delegates and alternates to the
Republican and Democratic conventions of 1956 in their study "Issue Conflict
and Consensus Among Party Leaders and Followers," *American Political
Science Review,* LIV (1960), 406–27. The studies of delegates to the 1948 Republican and Democratic conventions by Charles L. Braucher and David W.
Tuttle reported in Paul T. David, Ralph M. Goldman, and Richard C. Bain,
The Politics of National Party Conventions (Washington, D.C.: The Brookings Institution, 1960), had response rates of 53 per cent and 44 per cent, respectively.

10. The numbers of respondents from each state delegation who were delegates and alternates were as follows: Alabama, 12 delegates and 12 alternates; Georgia, 17 delegates and 18 alternates; Louisiana, 10 delegates and 13 alternates; Mississippi, 13 delegates and 12 alternates; and South Carolina, 13 delegates and 11 alternates.

11. Washington, D.C.: The Brookings Institution, 1960. In addition to the work of David and his associates, there are a growing number of studies of particular types of party leaders, including state delegation chairmen. See, for example, Samuel J. Eldersveld and Dwaine Marvick, "National Convention Leadership: 1952 and 1956," *Western Political Quarterly*, XIV (1961), 176–94; Robert S. Hirschfield, Bert E. Swanson, and Blanche D. Blank, "A Profile of Political Activists in Manhattan," *Western Political Quarterly*, XV (1962), 489–506; Samuel C. Patterson, "Characteristics of Party Leaders," *Western Political Quarterly*, XVI (1963), 332–52; Thomas A. Flinn and Frederick M. Wirt, "Local Party Leaders: Groups of Like Minded Men," *Midwest Journal of Political Science*, IX (1965), 77–98.

12. The proportion of female delegates, 22 per cent, represented a substantial increase over 1952, when the ladies constituted only 7 per cent of the region's total delegate population. See David *et al.*, *The Politics of National Party Conventions*, p. 516.

13. *Ibid.*, p. 327. The youthfulness of southern Republican leaders has been apparent for some time. See, for example, Kenneth Vines, *Two Parties for Shreveport* (New York: Holt, Rinehart & Winston, 1959); Virginius Dabney, "What the GOP is Doing in the South," *Harper's Magazine*, CCXXVI (1963), 86–94; and Bernard Cosman, "The Republican Congressman from Dallas" (Master's thesis, University of Alabama, 1958).

14. Percentage bases exclude cases where there was no response.

15. Among the state delegations, Mississippi and South Carolina had the largest proportions of recent immigrants, 24 per cent and 17 per cent, respectively, and the smallest proportions of "lifers," 20 per cent and 34 per cent. Louisiana and Alabama had the largest proportions of "lifers," 48 per cent and 46 per cent, respectively. Alabama had no recent immigrants, and Georgia and Louisiana had only one each.

16. The occupational distribution of Deep South Republican delegates and alternates provides some interesting contrasts with that of delegates to the 1948 Republican National Convention, reported in David *et al.*, *op. cit.*, p. 338. In 1948, more than one-third of the Republican delegates were lawyers and judges, while one-fourth fitted into a business category, which included merchants, manufacturers, contractors, realtors, insurance agents, and bankers. Few more than 2 per cent of the delegates were engineers or physicians. In comparison with the Republican delegates of 1948, larger proportions of the Deep South Republican delegates and alternates of 1964 were engaged in business occupations and as physicians and engineers. A substantially smaller proportion from the Deep South were lawyers—a difference presumably explainable by the long-time Democratic dominance within the region.

17. Income distributions within the states exhibited some variations. Majorities of the Alabama (50 per cent) and Georgia (55 per cent) delegations and a plurality of the Mississippi delegation (41 per cent) reported annual incomes in excess of $20,000. In Louisiana and South Carolina, the modal income category was $10,000–$14,999, although, in both of these states, the

largest proportions of delegates and alternates had annual incomes greater than $15,000.

18. There were some differences in religious affiliation among the state delegations. Episcopalians predominated in Alabama (33 per cent), Louisiana (41 per cent), and South Carolina (41 per cent); Methodists, in Georgia (37 per cent); and Presbyterians, in Mississippi (28 per cent). There were no Catholics in the Georgia or South Carolina delegation and no Jews in the latter delegation or in that of Alabama or Mississippi. The highest percentage of Catholics appeared, as expected, in Louisiana, 27 per cent. Georgia had the largest percentage of Jews, 6 per cent.

19. See, for example, Donald S. Strong, *The 1952 Presidential Election in the South* (University of Alabama Bureau of Public Administration, 1955) and *Urban Republicanism in the South* (University of Alabama: Bureau of Public Administration, 1960), and Bernard Cosman, "Presidential Republicanism in the South," *The Journal of Politics,* XXIV (1962), 303–22.

20. Data for class identification of adult Americans was taken from Marian D. Irish and James Prothro, *The Politics of American Democracy,* 3d rev. ed. (Englewood Cliffs, N.J.: Prentice-Hall, 1965), p. 37.

21. See, for example, Herbert Hyman, *Political Socialization* (Glencoe, Ill.: The Free Press, 1959), and Robert E. Lane and David O. Sears, *Public Opinion* (Englewood Cliffs, N.J.: Prentice-Hall, 1964).

22. Quoted in *The New York Times,* January 4, 1964.

23. See, for example, Angus Campbell, Philip E. Converse, Warren E. Miller, and Donald E. Stokes, *The American Voter* (New York: John Wiley & Sons, 1960).

24. Angus Campbell, Gerald Gurin, and Warren E. Miller, *The Voter Decides* (Evanston, Ill.: Row, Peterson, 1954), p. 216.

25. *Conservative,* as used here, denotes negative attitudes toward governmental involvement in the economy, as well as resistance to governmental policies for promoting social welfare and equalitarianism.

26. V. O. Key, Jr., *Public Opinion and American Democracy* (New York: Alfred A. Knopf, 1961), p. 211.

27. *Ibid.,* p. 218. See also Lane and Sears, *op. cit.,* pp. 96–97.

28. Key, *Public Opinion and American Democracy,* pp. 229–32. Key found that those adult Americans who ranked high on the SRC participation scale tended to hold more intense opinions than those who ranked low, although the differences in intensity of opinion between high and low participators were not always spectacular, nor for that matter did they always exist. On the school-integration question, a larger proportion of intense opinion emerged among low participators than among high participators. See also the summary of research relating to participation as a function of attitude and attitude intensity in Lester B. Milbrath, *Political Participation* (Chicago: Rand McNally, 1965), pp. 50–64.

29. McClosky, Hoffman and O'Hara, *loc. cit.*

30. American Institute of Public Opinion release, January 3, 1965.

31. A Gallup Poll pointed to a major shift in the opinions of southern whites on at least one phrasing of the school-integration question: "Would you, yourself, have any objection to sending your children to a school where a few of the children are colored?" Of the southern white parents questioned, 62 per cent stated that they would not object; two years earlier, only 38 per cent had registered this opinion. See American Institute of Public Opinion release,

May 23, 1965. Herbert H. Hyman and Paul B. Sheatsley also reported increasing support for integration among whites in both the North and South over time. See their "Attitudes Toward Desegregation," *Scientific American*, CCXI (1964), 16–23.

32. Key, *Public Opinion and American Democracy*, p. 104.

33. *Ibid.*, p. 30.

34. Murray Clark Havens, "The Radical Right in the Southwest: Community Response to Shifting Socio-economic Patterns," paper read before annual meeting of American Political Science Association, Chicago, September 9–12, 1964.

35. *Ibid.*, p. 2.

36. The reader will, of course, want to know to what extent the membership of the nonparty groups of the far right overlapped that of the Deep South Republican delegations. It had been widely reported, both before and after that 1964 National Convention, that the far right had infiltrated the Republican Party at all levels. See, for example, the series of articles by political reporters of the *St. Louis Post Dispatch* published under the title "Ultra-conservatism in America." While the questionnaire used in our study did not elicit information about the nonpartisan group affiliations of Deep South Republicans, there was an opportunity, through interviews with the delegates and alternates at the Convention, to find out about their group affiliations. Before and during the convention week, the writer conducted at least one interview with each of more than sixty Deep South delegates and alternates. The generalization that emerged from these interviews was that no more than three or four members of any one state delegation also doubled as members of the John Birch Society. One delegate whom this writer interviewed and who was particularly frank in identifying John Birchers emphasized one of the stresses between members of this group and the party members: "One thing I don't like about the John Birchers, though, is that they use the party, but they'll retreat to their own small groups to further their own purposes." Havens observed, in his study, that "Although the lines between extremists and ordinary conservatives are often blurred, with both, for example, providing many enthusiastic supporters for the presidential candidacy of Senator Barry Goldwater, they may also be bitter enemies, especially in matters of local politics." *Ibid.*

37. The Republican proportion of the presidential vote in twenty-three nonwhite, Deep South precincts, identified by the National Broadcasting Company for use in its "Operation Ballot," amounted to a minuscule 1.6 per cent. In sharp contrast was the actual GOP share of the presidential vote in the Black Belt of the Deep South states, defined here as counties with nonwhite majorities. The Republican percentages ranged downward from 90.1 per cent in Mississippi to 76.1 per cent in Alabama, 68.5 per cent in Louisiana, 64.5 per cent in South Carolina, and 61.4 per cent in Georgia. Presumably, the bulk of this vote was cast by whites. See Bernard Cosman, "An Overview of Southern Republicanism," paper read before annual meeting of the Southern Political Science Association, Durham, N.C., November 9–11, 1964.

38. Quoted in the *Atlanta Constitution*, May 4, 1964.

39. The political neutralization of Negroes is the major theme of white southern politics. Less attention has been given to the low levels of political participation characteristic of lower-status whites. V. O. Key, Jr., for example, compared the participation rates of blue-collar workers in the North and

South. The contrast was particularly sharp at the lowest level of participation: 51 per cent in the North, 19 per cent in the South. Key opined that "if the blue-collar vote in the South should double, southern conservatives in Congress would probably become less numerous." *Public Opinion and American Democracy*, p. 105.

40. For that matter, many Negroes did not have favorable perceptions of the Republican Party before Goldwater. On this point, see Donald R. Matthews and James W. Prothro, "Southern Images of Political Parties: An Analysis of White and Negro Attitudes," *Journal of Politics*, XXVI (1964), 82–111.

41. *Ibid.* See also Campbell *et al., op. cit.*, p. 185.

42. Robert J. Donovan recommends this as the strategy for the GOP in the non-Deep South. See his *The Future of the Republican Party* (New York: Signet Books, 1964), pp. 79–87. For a similar but partisan view, see the report of the Ripon Society *Election '64* (Cambridge, Mass.: The Society, 1965). On the matter of strategy, it should be emphasized that developments within the Democratic Party will play a significant, indeed critical, role in determining the selection and outcome of GOP strategies, both in the immediate and the distant future. Although this chapter has not discussed the possibilities for the traditional party of the South, it is now apparent that students of political behavior will need to broaden their span of attention to include developments within both political parties, particularly since voting divisions heretofore visible only within the Democratic Party have now begun to emerge in interparty competition. On this critical indicator of the possible formation of durable party loyalties, see Walter Dean Burnham, *Journal of Politics*, XXVI (1964), 798–829.

CHAPTER 4

1. Joseph A. Loftus, "Democrats Form Negro Vote Unit," *New York Times*, January 20, 1965.

2. All data were compiled by the Citizens' Research Foundation. By agreement, the *Congressional Quarterly* published some data in "1964 Political Campaign Contributions and Expenditures," Special Report, Part 1, Weekly Report No. 3, January 21, 1966. However, the present study contains additional data not included in the *Congressional Quarterly* compilation, which accounts for differences from that compilation.

3. In this study, most data comparisons with other years are derived from Alexander Heard, *The Costs of Democracy* (Chapel Hill: University of North Carolina Press, 1960); Herbert E. Alexander, *Financing the 1960 Election* (Princeton, N.J.: Citizens' Research Foundation, 1962); and Gore Committee, *1956 General Election Campaigns*, Report to the Senate Committee on Rules and Administration, 85th Cong., 1st Sess. (1957).

4. Heard, *op. cit.*, p. 376.

5. Labor spending is combined with that of the Democrats, on the assumption that most organized-labor money goes to support them. Heard's ratio for 1956 has been revised to include deficits. See Heard, *op. cit.*, pp. 19–20; Alexander, *op. cit.*, pp. 9–11.

6. Percentages for 1948, 1952, and 1956 are derived from Heard, *op. cit.*, pp. 48, 51 (Tables 2 and 3). Data for 1960 come from Herbert E. Alexander, *op. cit.*, p. 57.

Republican and Democratic Contributions of $500 or
more to National-Level Committees

Year	1948	1952	1956	1960	1964
Democratic	69%	63%	44%	59%	69%
Republican	74%	68%	74%	58%	28%

7. Even more impressive—and a more accurate measure—is that, of the total Republican contributions from individuals, 72 per cent were received in sums of less than $500, compared with 30 per cent for the Democrats. For the only two major Democratic committees on which information is available —the National Committee and the Johnson-Humphrey Committee—a total of $1.25 million was received in sums of less than $100. This amounts to about 38 per cent of total individual contributions to these two committees.

8. Heard, *op. cit.*, p. 45.

9. The $7 million or more in small contributions were almost half of the $15 million presidential-campaign costs, though about $1 million of these small contributions had been raised for the Republican sustaining fund before Goldwater was nominated.

10. Robert G. Spivack, "Men Behind Goldwater," *Look*, November 3, 1964, p. 48.

11. One writer (*ibid.*) stated that there were three financial crises in this period, particularly after Goldwater's defeat in the New Hampshire primary. See also Robert D. Novak, *The Agony of the G.O.P. 1964* (New York: Macmillan, 1965), p. 287.

12. Novak, *op. cit.*, pp. 342–47. Perhaps the ultimate in enthusiastic support came from a Seattle physician who willed 5 per cent of his $250,000 estate to Senator Goldwater for his campaign for the promotion of conservative government and then died before the Republican Convention took place. *New York Times*, June 19, 1964.

13. Alexander, *op. cit.*, p. 18.

14. Where one headquarters alone contained 14,000 square feet of space.

15. The Rockefeller campaign received indirect assistance from a book publisher who admitted putting $40,000 into a campaign to sell the Governor's book *The Future of Federalism*. Robert C. Doty, "$40,000 To Be Spent Promoting Rockefeller Paperback Reprint," *New York Times*, October 1, 1963.

16. *New York Times*, March 5, 1964.

17. Figures are adjusted for lateral transfers of funds among committees. Not included in this total is an item of $1,519 reported as spent by the Oregon Scranton for President Committee. *Summary Report of Campaign Contributions and Expenditures: 1964 General Election* (Compiled and published by Tom McCall, Secretary of State of Oregon), 1965, p. 2.

18. One solicitation by telegram of 1,900 Republicans resulted in about $50,000 in contributions. This, and another solicitation by telegram, cost $8,000 to make.

19. The bank account of the Lodge campaign could not be situated in Massachusetts, Lodge's state, because Massachusetts law requires consent of a candidate before campaigning commences. Goldwater groups in Massachusetts had the same problem in the preannouncement period.

20. Rowland Evans and Robert Novak, "The Unmaking of a President," *Esquire*, November, 1964, p. 162.

21. Mary McGrory, "Lodge Campaign Rapture Fades," in the Washington, D.C., *Evening Star*, May 14, 1964.

22. Donald Janson, "Nixon Backers Jubilant over His 31% Share of Nebraska Vote," *New York Times,* May 14, 1964.

23. Heard, *op. cit.,* p. 335.

24. Alexander, *op. cit.,* pp. 16–18.

25. Harold Faber (ed.), *The Road to the White House* (New York: McGraw-Hill, 1965), p. 78.

26. Seymour Martin Lipset, "Beyond the Backlash," *Encounter,* November, 1964, p. 21.

27. Rowland Evans and Robert Novak, "Goldwater Spenders," *New York Herald Tribune,* September 20, 1964.

28. Including canceling a poll that, undoubtedly, would have brought more bad news. James McCartney, "Barry Given 'Results' Oct. 23, Then Tried To Curb Expenses," *Washington Post and Times Herald,* November 12, 1964.

29. For example, part of the 1960 campaign deficit consisted of unpaid air-travel bills charged for press seats on campaign flights. In 1964, the Republicans sought deposits before permitting reporters to accompany candidates.

30. For an extended discussion of political broadcasting, see Herbert E. Alexander, "Broadcasting and Politics," in M. Kent Jennings and L. Harmon Zeigler, *The Electoral Process* (Englewood Cliffs, N.J.: Prentice-Hall, 1966), pp. 81–104.

31. *Financing Presidential Campaigns* (Washington, D.C.: Government Printing Office, 1962), pp. 24–27. The American Political Science Association appointed a Commission on Presidential Campaign Debates, which made a report on the subject in 1964. See "Report of the Commission on Presidential Campaign Debates" (Washington, D.C.: The American Political Science Association, 1964).

32. From 1959 to 1964, basic rates increased 31 per cent in network television, 41 per cent in spot television, 9 per cent in network radio, and 21 per cent in spot radio. "The Decade of Incentive: Marketing Review and Forecast, '64–'65," based on studies prepared by Marplan, a market-research component of the Interpublic Group of Companies, Inc., January, 1965, p. 31.

33. See Earl Mazo's forthcoming book *Polling for Political Power* (New York: Doubleday, in press).

34. Thomas W. Benham, "Polling for a Presidential Candidate: Some Observations on the 1964 Campaign," *Public Opinion Quarterly,* XXIV, No. 2 (1965), p. 185.

35. This analysis reflects most national Republican Party and campaign income; state committee quota payments or contributions to support the national party amounted, in 1964, to about 15 per cent of their total income, which can be estimated at about $2.7 million.

36. Contributions of $500 or more were counted for 1964 if made to the following committees: Americans for Goldwater, Brothers for Goldwater, Campaign Committee for Goldwater-Miller, Citizens for Goldwater-Miller, National TV Committee, Republican Campaign Committee, Republican National Committee, Republican National Finance Operations Committee, Republican Television Committee, Solid South Speaks for Goldwater Committee, Women Voters for Goldwater-Miller. Contributions were counted for 1960 if made to Builders Committee for Nixon-Lodge, Committee for the Real Nixon, Independent Television Committee, National Nixon-Lodge Club, National Volunteers for Nixon-Lodge, Nixon-Lodge Unlimited, Republican Campaign Dinners, Republican National Committee, Television Committee, Vote Getters

for Nixon-Lodge. Not included were contributions to senatorial, congressional, or other nonpresidential committees. Contributions to the Republican National Committee over the whole year were included in both 1960 and 1964. Multiple contributions by one individual were counted as the number of contributions the individual made.

37. Richard Dougherty, *New York Herald Tribune,* January 31, 1965.

38. In early 1964, Republican National Chairman Miller said a survey showed state Republican organizations owed $2 million. *Congressional Quarterly,* March 27, 1964, p. 618.

39. One estimate puts Goldwater's fund-raising total at Republican functions from 1960 to 1963 at $6.3 million, mostly for party coffers in local areas. David Kraslow, "Goldwater's Debt to Rockefeller," Chicago *Sun-Times,* July 12, 1964.

40. See Special Report No. 17 of Group Research, Inc., "Barry Goldwater and the Organized Right Wing," October 12, 1964.

41. Joseph A. Loftus, "Goldwater Sees a Myth in Right-Wing 'Big Money,'" *New York Times,* October 28, 1963.

42. Special Report No. 16 of Group Research, Inc., "The Finances of the Right Wing," September 1, 1964.

43. One survey indicated that the "pure Goldwater vote lies between 2,500,000 and 3,000,000," compared with the 24,000,000 to 24,500,000 Republican votes he received. Louis H. Bean and Roscoe Drummond, "How Many Votes Does Goldwater Own?" *Look,* March 23, 1965, p. 75. Louis Harris, after analyzing the preferences on specific issues of samples of voters who were interviewed during the 1964 campaign, estimated the number of "hard-core, down-the-line Goldwater supporters" at 6,000,000. See the Harris Survey, *Washington Post and Times Herald,* January 11, 1965.

44. Evetts Haley, *A Texan Looks at Lyndon* (Canyon, Tex.: Palo Duro Press, 1964); Phyllis Schlafly and Chester Ward, *The Gravediggers* (Alton, Ill.: Père Marquette Press, 1964); Phyllis Schlafly, *A Choice Not an Echo* (Alton, Ill.: Père Marquette Press, 1964); John A. Stormer, *None Dare Call It Treason* (Florissant, Mo.: Liberty Bell Press, 1964).

45. "Fair Comment," Fair Campaign Practices Committee, Inc., 1965, p. 2.

46. In addition, the Citizens for Goldwater-Miller paid at least $5,000 to the Palo Duro Press, publisher of *A Texan Looks at Lyndon.*

47. In a nonscurrilous category was the latest book written by Barry Goldwater, *Where I Stand* (New York: McGraw-Hill, 1964), which was sold in large numbers. Scattered items indicating expenditures totaling $74,000 for this book were found in various Republican fund reports at the national level.

48. Arnold Forster and Benjamin R. Epstein, *Danger on the Right* (New York: Random House, 1964), pp. 272–80.

49. Donald Janson, "Rightists Buoyed by the Election; Open New Drives," *New York Times,* November 23, 1964.

50. Perhaps as a sop, the Goldwater leadership provided funds for the recount and related legal expenses in Nevada's senatorial contest between Democrat Howard W. Cannon and Republican Lieutenant Governor Paul Laxalt. The recount established Cannon as the winner.

51. Filed reports indicate Republican allocations to candidates for Congress were slightly higher than in 1960.

52. "Text of Dean Burch's Letter to GOP," *New York Herald Tribune,* January 3, 1965.

53. Walter R. Mears, "1964 GOP War Chest To Back Conservatives," *Washington Post and Times Herald*, December 23, 1965.

54. The $4.2 million figure includes Booster Club funds set aside for use in the congressional elections of 1966. For 1965 receipts and expenditures at the national level, see *Congressional Quarterly*, January 14, 1966, p. 41.

55. David S. Broder, "G.O.P. Study Finds Johnson and Party Slipping in North," *New York Times*, January 2, 1966.

56. William L. Warner, veteran director of the Republican National Committee, who had started the sustaining fund, in 1962, did not return after the election.

57. Washburn had been executive director of the Republican Congressional Boosters Club. Kovac left in a blaze of publicity, though he had been planning for months to resign. The Kelly-Kovac caper concerned parts of a list of large contributors, IBM plates, some master keys to desks at the national headquarters, and some prints of the film *Choice*—all supposedly missing, and all reportedly found by William C. Kelly, an assistant to Ray Bliss, in Kovac's office. Kovac charged that his desk drawer had been forced open and his "constitutional rights" affronted, whereupon Kelly was fired, and it was later revealed that a $3,000 contribution of his was returned. It was later alleged that certain RNFC mailing lists had been exchanged for lists belonging to other organizations and companies, with the implication that some lists may have been sold for private or party gain and some may have been made available to right-wing splinter groups. The truth has been obscured by charge and countercharge. See *Newsweek*, July 5, 1965, pp. 20–21.

58. See Herbert E. Alexander, *Financing the 1964 Election* (Princeton, N.J.: Citizens' Research Foundation, 1966), pp. 84–95.

59. Sterling F. Green, "Conservative Group Sets Up Headquarters, Reveals Aims," in the Washington, D.C., *Evening Star*, March 19, 1965.

60. John W. Fenton, "Birch Society Seeks $12 Million for '66 Campaign," *New York Times*, March 8, 1965.

61. John D. Morris, "G.O.P. Terms Splinter Groups a Drain on the Party's Income," *New York Times*, May 28, 1965.

CHAPTER 5

1. This case study, part of a broader study of House leadership, was made possible by a grant from the Social Science Research Council's Committee on Political Behavior. It is based on observation of events from early December, 1964, to January, 1965, and interviews with over forty Republican representatives and ten key staff members during and after the Ford-Halleck contest. I would like to acknowledge my indebtedness to these members and also to numerous readers of an earlier draft. While I have tried to avoid excessive footnoting, I have made extensive use of newspaper accounts from the *Washington Post*, *The New York Times*, and *The Wall Street Journal*. I have not attributed quotations directly in order to protect the anonymity of the members and staff.

2. Halleck was given his choice of several high-ranking positions on committees on which he had previously served, including Rules, Government Operations, and House Administration. He selected Public Works in order to continue his fight for a deep-water harbor near the Burns Waterway site, in

his district, a project that has come into conflict with the Indiana Dunes National Lakeshore Park bill.

3. Charles O. Jones, *Party and Policy-Making: The House Republican Policy Committee* (New Brunswick, N.J.: Rutgers University Press, 1964), pp. 32–38; Joe Martin, *My First Fifty Years in Politics* (as told to Robert J. Donovan) (New York: McGraw-Hill, 1960), pp. 3–19.

4. "Ford Election Sparks Shifts in GOP House Strategy," *Congressional Quarterly Weekly Report*, XXI (February 8, 1963), 149–56. From Ford's point of view, his candidacy was not a planned step on the road to the minority leadership. As he recalled these events in 1965: "There was no design, no specific plan to go after the minority leadership, at least in my mind, when we made that campaign. But it enabled me to establish a rapport with this group—these young fellows like Charlie Goodell and Bob Griffin. It showed us what could be done if you were organized and were able to carry through your plans. Of course, then, we didn't have as much time. It was kind of a spontaneous candidacy. But we got our feet wet, and we learned how and what we had to do in order to be successful."

5. For descriptions of the usefulness of this device for interparty cooperation and of a similar operation, referred to as Halleck's "clinic," see Neil MacNeil, *Forge of Democracy: The House of Representatives* (New York: McKay, 1963), pp. 81–84.

6. Mimeographed press release, December 21, 1964, p. 1.

7. Halleck's choice of George Goodling of Pennsylvania over Silvio Conte of Massachusetts for a minority vacancy on the Migratory Bird Conservation Commission, as well as his appointment of Jack Westland of Washington instead of John Saylor of Pennsylvania for a vacancy on the National Forest Reservation Commission, illustrates the problem. Both Westland and Goodling were among the Republican incumbents defeated in 1964. Conte and Saylor were early and active Ford supporters. Victory brings its reward, however. Late in January, 1965, Ford appointed Conte to the Migratory Bird Conservation Commission and Saylor to the National Forest Reservation Commission, *Congressional Record* (daily ed.) *Digest*, February 1, 1965, p. D57.

8. A full-page advertisement in *The New York Times* listing the sixty-two House members who endorsed Goldwater prior to the Convention concluded, "We are convinced that the nomination of Senator Barry Goldwater by the Republican Party will result in substantial increases in Republican membership in both Houses of Congress." *New York Times*, July 7, 1964.

9. Marshall McNeil, "Halleck Meets Opposition," *Washington Daily News*, October 28, 1964.

10. Ronald Sharp, "Michigan Congressman Praises Halleck as U.S. Minority Leader," *Warsaw* (Indiana) *Time-Union*, October 29, 1964.

11. For the origins of the Wednesday Club, its subsequent enlargement, and the role its members played in the Ford-Halleck contest and its aftermath, see Paul Duke and Stanley Meisler, "Republicans After the Debacle: 1. The Frustrated Moderates," *The Reporter*, February 11, 1965, pp. 26–28.

12. Excerpts from the Curtis letter are reprinted in *Congressional Quarterly Weekly Report*, XXII (December 4, 1964), 2766, 2789. The quotations are taken from a copy of the original letter.

13. Rowland Evans and Robert Novak. "Inside Report: The December Caucus," *Washington Post*, November 30, 1964.

14. On January 14, 1965, just prior to the vote that re-elected Arends as

Republican whip, the Republican Conference adopted an amended version of this proposal. Ford, as minority leader, had already given up his position on Appropriations; Byrnes had indicated his intention to resign as Policy Committee chairman; and Arends had decided to step down to second-ranking minority member on Armed Services. If a party leader resigns or is deposed in the future, he will reassume the position on his committee to which his previous seniority entitled him.

15. A possible candidate for higher office before 1964, Byrnes had all but been eliminated from consideration, because of unfavorable publicity arising from his relations with the Mortgage Guaranty Insurance Corporation of Milwaukee, a company that had also figured in the Bobby Baker hearings. For background, and Mr. Brynes's subsequent denial of any "wrongdoing or intention of wrongdoing," see *The Wall Street Journal*, November 22, 1963; *Congressional Record*, CIX, 22634–42.

16. Another Republican House member compared Ford's decision to run with Eisenhower's acceptance of a draft, in 1952—a response to a call to public duty: "My impressions of Ford are that he is not personally ambitious, but rather desirous of filling whatever role that he could and should fulfill. He was not a guy dying to become Minority Leader." Several of Ford's colleague's, however, pointed out that he began his political career by defeating an incumbent Republican congressman, Bartel J. Jonkman, in 1948; that he did not discourage discussion of his possible candidacy for the vice-presidential nomination, in 1960 and 1964; and that he has not abandoned consideration of higher national office.

17. "The inside strategy is likely to define situations as 'family matters,' and to feature face-to-face interaction among members. The outside strategy is likely to evoke a more ideological, issue-oriented definition of the situation. Interaction among members is more likely to take place through third persons, lobbyists, and the press." Nelson W. Polsby, "Two Strategies of Influence: Choosing a Majority Leader, 1962," in Peabody and Polsby (eds.), *New Perspectives on the House of Representatives*, p. 268.

18. Robert K. Walsh, "Two House Factions Ask Open Caucus Voting," *Washington Star*, December 31, 1964; "Halleck, Ford Both Claim Leadership Victory," *Washington Post*, January 1, 1965. The Ford forces went so far as to allow the wire services' representatives to examine the lists they had compiled in order to authenticate the latter's counts.

19. Halleck, as Republican Congressional Campaign Committee chairman, rode the crest of a net gain of fifty-six House seats in the 1946 election. A fellow Rules Committee member, Clarence J. Brown of Ohio, was one of several major contenders. Another was the present Senate Minority Leader, then Representative Everett Dirksen of Illinois, *New York Times*, January 3, 1947.

20. White's first column of this nature, "Unrest in Congress: Knives Drawn in Both Parties," *Washington Post*, December 9, 1964, illustrates the hazards of premature prediction: "But that the varicolored rebellions in the House—whether against the Halleck Republican orthodoxy or the Williams-Watson Democratic heterodoxy—will come to nothing whatever is a sure bet already." Events subsequently proved him wrong on both counts. White's later columns were more cautious but as strongly pro-Halleck: "Verdict on Halleck: Purge of GOP Leader Opposed," *Washington Post*, December 23, 1964; "New Congress: Senseless Bloodletting Abounds," *Washington Post*, December 30, 1964. For examples of other columns sympathetic to Halleck, see Arthur Krock, "In

the Nation: Ancient Ritual Impending in the G.O.P.," *New York Times,* December 22, 1964; Richard Wilson, "Halleck Has Impressive Record for Action on Major Legislation," *Minneapolis Tribune,* December 24, 1964; and Raymond Moley, "Halleck vs. Ford," *New York Herald-Tribune,* January 3, 1965. Several of these columns were clipped, photocopied, and sent to House Republicans by a member of the Indiana delegation.

21. "Laird Seeks to Head House GOP Conference," *Washington Post,* December 30, 1964. The strategic advantages enjoyed by Laird are summarized in a column by Rowland Evans and Robert Novak, "Laird Is Sitting Pretty: Wisconsin Congressman Will Win Whether Halleck or Ford Gets GOP Leadership," *Washington Post,* December 27, 1964.

22. Cramer and Poff were subsequently elected to the positions of vice-chairman and secretary of the Conference for the Eighty-ninth Congress. In early January, both positions were accorded higher status, as part of the formal leadership, as a result of Quie Committee recommendations and conference approval.

23. One of the more enjoyable stories that circulated through the corridors of Capitol Hill after the vote attributed to Senate Minority Leader Dirksen the following comment, allegedly made in a Senate minority caucus, Monday morning, before the House Conference results were known: "Charlie is in good shape—that New York fellow made a deal with Halleck and he will win by thirty votes." This apparently true story helps to illustrate the vast informational gulf that separates the two sides of the Capitol.

24. Nelson W. Polsby, "Two Strategies of Influence . . . ," in Peabody and Polsby, *op. cit.,* p. 243.

CHAPTER 6

1. Nelson W. Polsby, "Strategic Considerations," in Milton Cummings (ed.), *The National Election of 1964* (Washington, D.C.: The Brookings Institution, 1966), p. 107.

2. See also Robert L. Peabody, "Party Leadership Change in the United States House of Representatives," *American Political Science Review,* LXI (September, 1967), 675-93.

3. Cornelius P. Cotter and Bernard C. Hennessy, *Politics Without Power: The National Party Committees* (New York: Atherton Press, 1964).

4. The Republican National Committee is larger than the Democratic National Committee because Republican state chairmen automatically become members if (1) the state voted for the Republican presidential nominee in the last election, (2) the majority of the state's congressional delegation are Republicans, or (3) the state has a Republican governor. *Rules Adopted by the Republican National Convention* (San Francisco, July 13, 1964), Rule No. 26.

5. For example, during the Eighty-ninth Congress, freshman Democratic congressmen swept in by the Johnson landslide held weekly meetings with representatives of various executive agencies, using only the physical facilities of the Democratic National Committee. These agency representatives described programs of potential benefit to the congressmen and told them how to secure the benefits of government programs for their constituents. *Wall Street Journal,* September 8, 1965.

6. See, for example, Senator Goldwater's letter criticizing Governor George Romney for his failure to support actively the national ticket in 1964, *Los Angeles Times*, May 15, 1966.

7. A severe critique of the Goldwater campaign is contained in the Ripon Society's *From Disaster to Distinction: A Republican Rebirth* (New York: Pocket Books, 1966).

8. Stephen Shadegg, *What Happened to Goldwater?* (New York: Holt, Rinehart & Winston, 1965).

9. As quoted in an article by Frank N. Jones, "GOP Heading for a Policy 'Shoot Out,' " *Washington Post*, August 12, 1965.

10. For a state-by-state breakdown of Republican state legislative losses, see Republican National Committee, *The 1964 Election* (Washington, D.C.: Republican National Committee, 1965), pp. 74–75.

11. For a discussion of GOP financial affairs in the post-1964 period, see Walter Pincus, "The Fight over Money," *The Atlantic*, CCXVII (April, 1966), 71–75; George Lardiner, Jr., "Goldwater Fund Surplus Now Aids GOP in South," *Washington Post*, September 24, 1966; Walter R. Mears, "1964 GOP War Chest To Back Conservatives," *Washington Post*, December 23, 1965; and Herbert E. Alexander, "Money and Votes: Party Finance, 1964," Chapter 4 of this book.

12. For a summary of the Bliss election, see Earl Mazo, "Burch's Resignation Split the Goldwater Bloc," *New York Times*, January 14, 1966.

13. On Senator Goldwater's decision not to oppose Bliss's election, see the Mazo account cited above.

14. Ray C. Bliss, "The Role of the State Chairman," in James M. Cannon (ed.), *Politics U.S.A.: A Practical Guide to the Winning of Public Office* (Garden City, N.Y.: Doubleday, 1960), pp. 160–61.

15. The Bliss approach to political organization is well summarized in a pamphlet released by the National Committee in 1966 entitled *The Elements of Victory*.

16. Bliss receives an annual salary of $30,000.

17. Ripon Society, *From Disaster to Distinction: A Republican Rebirth* (New York: Pocket Books, 1966), pp. 90–115.

18. Another significant GOP policy advisory committee was the Republican Committee on Program and Progress, popularly known as the "Percy Committee." For a discussion of its activities, see Cotter and Hennessy, *op. cit.*, pp. 195–204. On out-party policy committees, in general, see Republican Coordinating Committee, *The Development of National Party Policy Between Conventions* (Washington, D.C.: Republican National Committee, 1967).

19. Cotter and Hennessy, *op. cit.*, p. 208—for a full discussion of party policy committees, see chaps. 10 and 11; see also Charles O. Jones, *Party and Policy: The House Republican Policy Committee* (New Brunswick, N.J.: Rutgers University Press, 1964). For an official description of the Republican Policy Committee, see *The Republican Conference and Committees of the Conference in the United States House of Representatives—90th Congress* (Washington, D.C.: House Republican Conference, 1967).

20. Republican Governors' Association, *The Declaration of Denver* (Denver: Republican Governors' Association, 1964), pp. 2–3.

21. Republican Coordinating Committee, *Brief Position Papers and Other Documents Relating to the Republican Coordinating Committee* (Washington, D.C.: Republican National Committee, 1967), p. 1.

22. *Ibid.*, p. 2.

23. Later in 1965, the Republican State Legislators' Association petitioned the Coordinating Committee for representation. The Committee acceded to the legislators' request, and F. F. ("Monte") Montgomery, speaker of the Oregon House of Representatives and president of the Republican State Legislators' Association, was named a committee member.

24. Members of the Republican Coordinating Committee, 1965–66:

Presiding Officer—Ray C. Bliss, Chairman, Republican National Committee

Former President
Dwight D. Eisenhower

Former Presidential Nominees

Barry Goldwater (1964)
Richard M. Nixon (1960)

Thomas E. Dewey (1944 and 1948)
Alfred M. Landon (1936)

Senate Leadership

Everett M. Dirksen
  Minority Leader
Thomas H. Kuchel
  Minority Whip
Bourke B. Hickenlooper
  Chairman, Republican Policy
  Committee

Leverett Saltonstall
  Chairman, Republican Conference
Thruston B. Morton
  Chairman, National Republican
  Senatorial Committee

House Leadership

Gerald R. Ford
  Minority Leader
Leslie C. Arends
  Minority Whip
Melvin R. Laird
  Chairman, Republican Conference
John J. Rhodes
  Chairman, Republican Policy
  Committee

H. Allen Smith
  Ranking Member, Rules Committee
Bob Wilson
  Chairman, National Republican
  Congressional Committee
Charles E. Goodell
  Chairman, Planning and Research
  Committee

Representatives of the Republican Governors' Association

John A. Love (Colorado)
Robert E. Smylie (Idaho)
George W. Romney (Michigan)

Nelson A. Rockefeller (New York)
William W. Scranton (Pennsylvania)

Republican National Committee

Ray C. Bliss
  Chairman
Mrs. C. Wayland Brooks
  Assistant Chairman
Mrs. Collis P. Moore
  Vice-Chairman

Donald R. Ross
  Vice-Chairman
Mrs. J. Willard Marriott
  Vice-Chairman
J. Drake Edens, Jr.
  Vice-Chairman

Representative of the Republican State Legislators' Association
F. F. Montgomery, Speaker, Oregon House of Representatives

Staff Coordinator
Robert L. L. McCormick

After the 1966 elections, the Coordinating Committee was expanded to include three additional governors and two additional representatives each from the House and the Senate. Four original members—Governors Robert E. Smylie of Idaho, and William A. Scranton, of Pennsylvania and Senators Thruston Morton of Kentucky, and Leverett Saltonstall of Massachusetts—were replaced either as a result of the elections or as a result of changes in party offices. The new representatives of the Governors' Association were Governors John A. Volpe (Massachusetts), Raymond P. Shafer (Pennsylvania), John H. Chaffee (Rhode Island), Nils A. Boe (South Dakota), and Daniel J. Evans (Washington). Additional representatives of the House Leadership were Richard H. Poff, Secretary of the Republican Conference, and William C. Cramer, Vice-Chairman of the Republican Conference. The new members from the Senate leadership were Milton R. Young, Secretary of the Republican Conference, Margaret Chase Smith, Chairman of the Republican Conference, George Murphy, Chairman of the Republican National Senatorial Committee, and Hugh Scott, Vice-Chairman of the National Republican Senatorial Committee.

25. Republican Coordinating Committee, *Brief Position Papers and Other Documents Relating to the Republican Coordinating Committee* (Washington, D.C.: Republican National Committee, 1967), p. 3.

26. These task forces were on "The Functions of Federal, State, and Local Governments," "Human Rights and Responsibilities," "The Conduct of Foreign Relations," "Job Opportunities," "Federal Fiscal and Monetary Policies," and "Problems of the Aging."

27. See Republican Coordinating Committee, *Latin America-United States: Progress or Failure?* (Washington, D.C.: Republican National Committee, 1966).

28. See Alexander Heard, *The Costs of Democracy* (Garden City, N.Y.: Anchor Books, 1962), chap. 11.

29. Herbert E. Alexander, *Financing the 1964 Election* (Princeton, N.J.: Citizens' Research Foundation, 1966), p. 110.

30. See the account by Paul Hope, "Union of Conservatives Is Reported Foundering," in the Washington, D.C. *Evening Star,* April 11, 1966.

31. Republican National Committee, *Report by the Chairman to the Republican National Committee,* New Orleans, January 23–24, 1967, p. 5.

32. *Report of the Committee on Big City Politics* (Washington, D.C.: Republican National Committee, 1962).

33. *Ibid.*

34. On the big-city program, see John F. Bibby, *The Republicans and the Metropolis: The Role of National Party Leadership,* Research Monograph No. 8 (Chicago: Center for Research in Urban Government, Loyola University, 1967).

35. Republican National Committee, *Report by the Chairman to the Republican National Committee,* New Orleans, January 23–24, 1967, p. 11.

36. David S. Broder, "Political Parade: Bliss Proves a Good GOP Caretaker," *Washington Post,* November 15, 1966.

CHAPTER 7

1. V. O. Key, Jr., *Politics, Parties, and Pressure Groups,* 5th ed. (New York: Thomas Y. Crowell, 1964), p. 206.

2. Robert T. Donovan, *The Future of the Republican Party* (New York: Signet Books, 1964), p. 3.

3. Angus Campbell, "Interpreting the Presidential Victory," in Milton C. Cummings, Jr. (ed.), *The National Election of 1964* (Washington, D.C.: The Brookings Institution, 1966), pp. 278–79.

4. *Ibid.*, p. 281.

5. *Idem.*

6. Charles O. Jones, *The Republican Party in American Politics* (New York: Macmillan, 1965), p. 140.

7. Reported in *The New York Times*, December 4, 1967.

CONTRIBUTORS

HERBERT E. ALEXANDER is Director of the Citizens' Research Foundation and Visiting Lecturer at the University of Pennsylvania. Dr. Alexander, who was Associate Director of the Money and Politics Project of the Institute of Research and Social Science at the University of North Carolina, has also taught in the Department of Politics at Princeton University. During 1961–62, he was Executive Director of the President's Commission on Campaign Costs and, between 1962–64, he served as a consultant to the President. He is presently a consultant to the Department of the Treasury and to the House Administration Committee. Among his other works, Dr. Alexander is the author of *Money, Politics and Public Reporting; Financing the 1960 Election; Responsibility in Party Finance;* and *Financing the 1964 Election.*

JOHN F. BIBBY, Assistant Professor of Political Science at the University of Wisconsin-Milwaukee, has had extensive firsthand experience of Republican Party operations. He has served as Director of the Arts and Sciences Division of the Republican National Committee, as Administrative Aide to Republican National Committee Chairman Bliss, and as Director of Research for the House Republican Conference. Dr. Bibby, National Committee Fellow of the American Political Science Association, Fellow in Government of the Brookings Institution, and, in 1964, National Convention Fellow of the National Center for Education in Politics and the Eagleton Institute of Politics, is the author of *The Republicans and the Metropolis: The Role of National Party Leadership,* the co-author of *On Capitol Hill: Studies in the Legislative Process,* and a contributor to the forthcoming *The Republican Papers.*

265

AAGE R. CLAUSEN, former Assistant Study Director of the Survey Research Center of the University of Michigan, is Assistant Professor of Political Science at the University of Wisconsin. A Ford Foundation Fellow, Dr. Clausen is also the co-author of numerous monographs, which have appeared in scholarly journals devoted to the social sciences.

PHILIP E. CONVERSE of the Survey Research Center is Associate Director of the Inter-University Consortium for Political Research and Professor of Political Science and Sociology at the University of Michigan. He received a Fulbright Fellowship for research in political behavior in France in 1959–60. Dr. Converse is a joint author of *The Voter Decides, The American Voter,* and *Elections and the Political Order,* and a frequent contributor to scholarly journals.

BERNARD COSMAN is Associate Professor of Political Science at the University of Alabama and a Research Associate of the university's Bureau of Public Administration; from 1965–67, he also served as Special Assistant to the Vice-President for Academic Affairs. In 1964, Dr. Cosman observed the Republican Convention as a National Convention Fellow of the National Center for Education in Politics and the Eagleton Institute of Politics. A contributor to scholarly journals and a co-author of several studies, Dr. Cosman is the author of a highly praised analysis of southern presidential politics, *Five States for Goldwater: Continuity and Change in Southern Presidential Voting Patterns.* In 1964, he was Associate Director of "Operation Ballot" for the NBC Southern Regional Center and, in 1966, he was Director of the statewide NBC Election Unit in Alabama. He continues to serve as an analyst and consultant to NBC and to the Public Broadcast Laboratory (ETV).

ROBERT J. HUCKSHORN is Professor of Political Science at Florida Atlantic University. A recipient of fellowships from the Hayes Foundation and the Social Science Research Council, Dr. Huckshorn is the author of a number of monographs on aspects of state and local government and politics. A contributor to *Inside Politics: The National Convention, 1960* and the *American Government Annual, 1964–65,* he also serves as a consultant to Public Broadcast Laboratory (ETV). In 1960, Dr. Huckshorn was a National Convention Fellow of the National Center for Education in Politics (NCEP) and the Eagleton Institute of Politics; in 1962–63, he was an NCEP Republican National Committee Faculty Fellow. He was Associate Director of NCEP in 1963–64. His firsthand Republican Party experience also includes serving as an aide to the chairman of the Minority Subcommittee on Committee Staffing of the House Republican Conference; Staff Director and member of the Republican Coordinating Committee Task Force on National, State, and Local Government Affairs; and Chairman of the Policy Advisory Committee of the Republican Governors' Association.

KARL ALLEN LAMB, Fellow of Cowell College, Associate Professor of Government, and Assistant Dean of the Graduate Division of the University of California at Santa Cruz, is the co-author of *Congress: Politics and Practice* and *Apportionment and Representative Institutions: The Michigan Experience*. A Rhodes Scholar, Dr. Lamb has also had active political experience. In 1960, he was Executive Secretary of the Subcommittee on Civil Rights of the Republican National Convention and, in 1964, he was an NCEP Faculty Fellow with the Republican National Committee. A research aide in the 1962 Michigan gubernatorial campaign of George Romney, Dr. Lamb is, at present, an associate member of the California Republican State Central Committee.

WARREN E. MILLER, Professor of Political Science at the University of Michigan, has also taught at Syracuse University and the University of California at Berkeley. He received a Social Science Research Council grant for research on Congressional campaigns in 1957. Since 1959, Dr. Miller has been Program Director of the Survey Research Center and he is, presently, Executive Director of the Inter-University Consortium for Political Research. He is widely known for his contributions to scholarly journals and as a co-author of *The Voter Decides, The American Voter,* and *Elections and the Political Order*.

ROBERT LEE PEABODY is Associate Professor of Political Science at The Johns Hopkins University and has held fellowships from the Social Science Research Council, the Brookings Institution, the Ford Foundation, the American Political Science Association, and the Carnegie Corporation. He is the author of numerous scholarly monographs, the co-editor of, and contributor to, *New Perspectives on the House of Representatives,* and the author of *Organizational Authority: Superior-Subordinate Relationships in Three Public Service Organizations*. Dr. Peabody, who has also served as a Governmental Research Assistant with the Bureau of Governmental Research and Services of the University of Washington, was Assistant Director of The New York Times–Simulmatics Corporation Election Coverage Project in 1962 and Assistant Director of the American Political Science Association Study of Congress project in 1965–66.

INDEX